GRAHAM SUTHERLAND
INSPIRATIONS

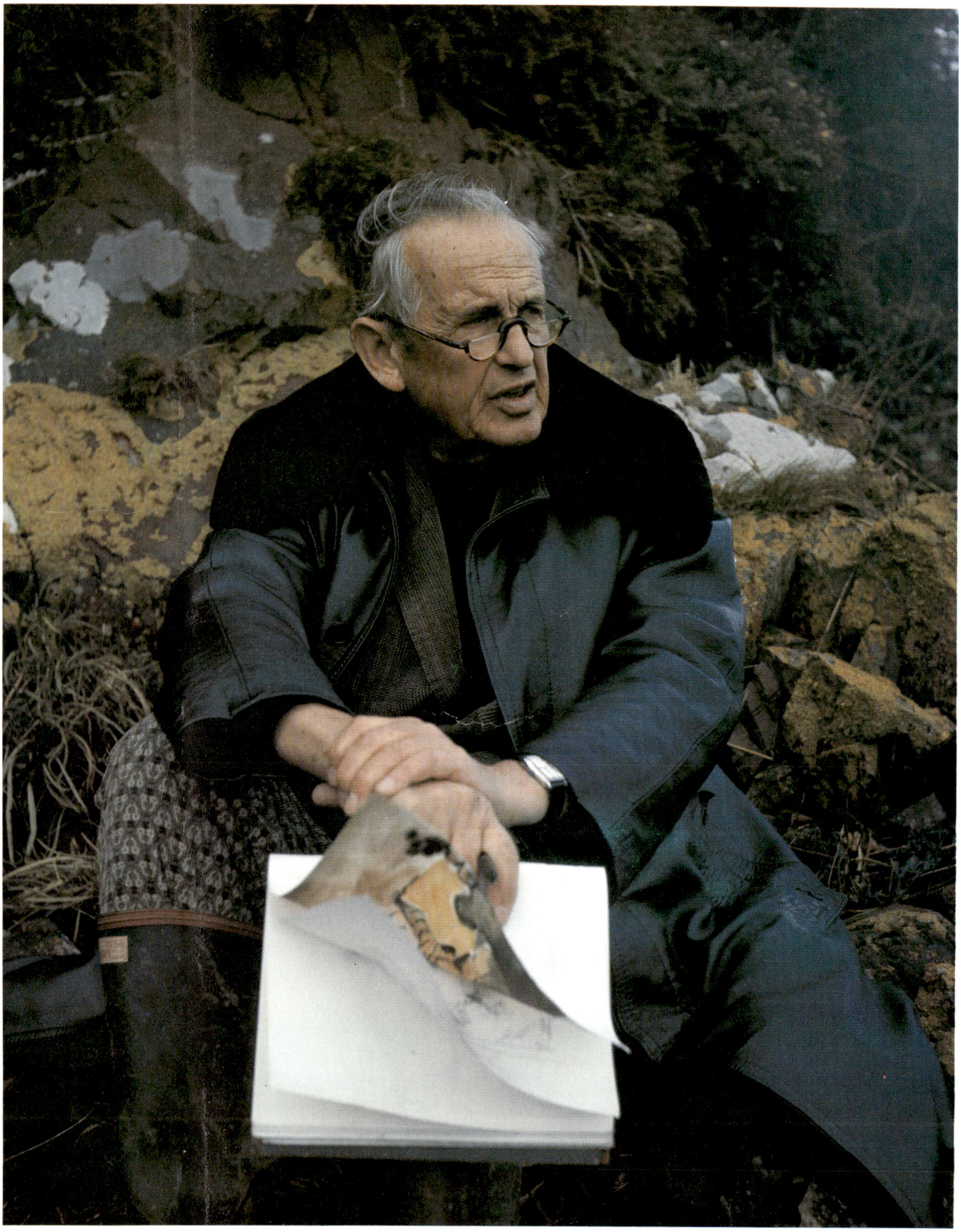

GRAHAM SUTHERLAND
INSPIRATIONS

Rosalind Thuillier

LUTTERWORTH PRESS
Guildford Surrey England

'All Nature is but art'
Essay on Man, Epistle I
Alexander Pope

First published 1982

Produced for Lutterworth Press by
Gulliver Publishing Co Ltd

Designed by Zena Flax Associates

ISBN 0 7188 2544 6

Printed and bound by
South China Printing Co, Hong Kong

Contents

List of Illustrations

Acknowledgements

First and above all I owe the inspiration of this book to the late Graham Sutherland OM and to his wife Kathleen and I am profoundly grateful for their courtesy, kindness and interest during time spent in their company. To my husband Gilbert Adams FRPS must go the remainder of the credit, for without his continued enthusiasm and support this book would not have been started, written or finished. I am deeply indebted to him especially for providing all the related illustrations of Graham Sutherland and the places which inspired him.

I should like to thank all the numerous people who gave so much of their time. These have included Mr Gordon Bennett whose co-operation has at all times been invaluable; Mr Gilbert Lloyd and Mr Longstaff of Marlborough Fine Art (London) Ltd; Messrs Christie, Manson and Woods; Barbara Putt and Rita Small of the British Council who allowed me so generously to use their offices on numerous occasions for purposes of research; Mr Milner Gray; Mrs Elizabeth Scott-Moore; Sir John Rothenstein; Mrs Lilian Somerville; Mr Robin Tanner; Signor G. Tinto; Dr Cannon-Brookes; Robin Garton; Mr Geoffrey Roberson Park; Mrs Sulivan; Mrs White, and so many others.

I am especially grateful to Doris Rhodes and Mary Chilton who bravely typed my manuscript; to Jenny Overton of Lutterworth Press and Joanna Jellinek who coped miraculously with its editing; to Jim Reynolds of Gulliver Publishing Company Ltd for his patient and invaluable co-operation throughout and to Zena Flax for her sympathetic handling of the pictures.

Together with my publishers, I should also like to thank all who have granted permission for the inclusion of copyright material in this work, or who helped in the obtaining of that permission, and in particular the following: Lord Clark for permission to quote from his excellent catalogue to the British pavilion, Venice Biennale 1952; Dr John Hayes, Director of the National Portrait Gallery, for permission to quote from *Portraits of Graham Sutherland*, 1977; Lady Hendy on behalf of her late husband; Anthony Sheil Associates, for permission to quote from *Conversations with Painters* by Noel Barber published by William Collins, Sons & Co Ltd, copyright © 1964 by Noel Barber; Dr Noble Frankland, Director of the Imperial War Museum, for permission to quote from the Imperial War Museum catalogue; Ediciones Poligrafa/SA and Thames & Hudson, for permission to quote from *Graham Sutherland: Complete Graphic Works* by Roberto Tassi; the Herbert Art Gallery and Museum, City of Coventry, for excerpts from their leaflet 'Christ in Glory in the Tetramorph'; the Pallas Gallery Ltd, for quotations from *Christ in Glory in the Tetramorph*, edited by Andrew Révai, published by them in 1964 (distributed by A. Zwemmer Ltd); the Trustees of the Graham and Kathleen Sutherland Foundation, Picton Castle Trust, for excerpts from the Foundation catalogue; and ADAGP, Paris. Graham Sutherland's 'Thoughts on Painting' appeared in *The Listener*, 1951.

For permission to reproduce works by Graham Sutherland and for providing photographs and permissions I am gratefully indebted to the Trustees of the Graham and Kathleen Sutherland Foundation, Picton Castle Trust; Signor G. Tinto; the Trustees of the Tate Gallery, London; Messrs Christie, Manson and Woods; The British Council; the Vicar of St Matthew's Church, Northampton; the Provost and Council, Coventry Cathedral; Konrad Adenauer Stiftung; Lord Goodman; Mr Hiram Winterbotham; the Arts Council of Great Britain; Birmingham Museums & Art Gallery; the Trustees of the Imperial War Museum, London; National Portrait Gallery, London; The Art Gallery of Toronto; Robin Garton Ltd; Southampton Art Gallery and Museums; City Art Gallery, Leeds; The National Museum of Wales; Crane Kalman Gallery; Very Rev. Walter Hussey. For other illustrations: A.C. Cooper, Rodney Todd-White, Lt Col. Ferguson, Stephen Meakins, Mrs Elizabeth Scott-Moore and Studio Jon.

Graham Sutherland often gave similar titles to works produced at different times. The reader will therefore discover that in the case of certain works a painting referred to in the text does not always bear the same date as the one that has been illustrated, although the title may be the same for both.

The illustrations selected for this book are those which best reflect the continuing source of Sutherland's inspiration and thereby convey the importance of Pembrokeshire in the artist's life.

Frontispiece Graham Sutherland
Photograph Gilbert Adams FRPS

Chapter I
INTRODUCTION

The structure of the natural world was vital to Graham Sutherland's art.

In 1977 he wrote to me, saying, 'Really Pembrokeshire or any other place for me is a "point de départ". That is to say, it is a vocabulary of forms. These forms, by their rhythmic relationship to each other and by their internal rhythms and character, appeal to me at the point where they are free more or less from their environment and then ready to lead a new life in pictorial form.' Although certain places may have provided the source of his inspiration, he never intended that any painting should specifically represent an exact place at a particular time.

He was inspired quintessentially by the natural origins of living matter, but was also intellectually concerned with how his individual discoveries and way of interpreting certain organic constructions could be adapted and made acceptable to a European art-buying public. When Sutherland began to paint seriously in the thirties he carefully prepared his artistic career by considering the type of contemporary painting then selling in

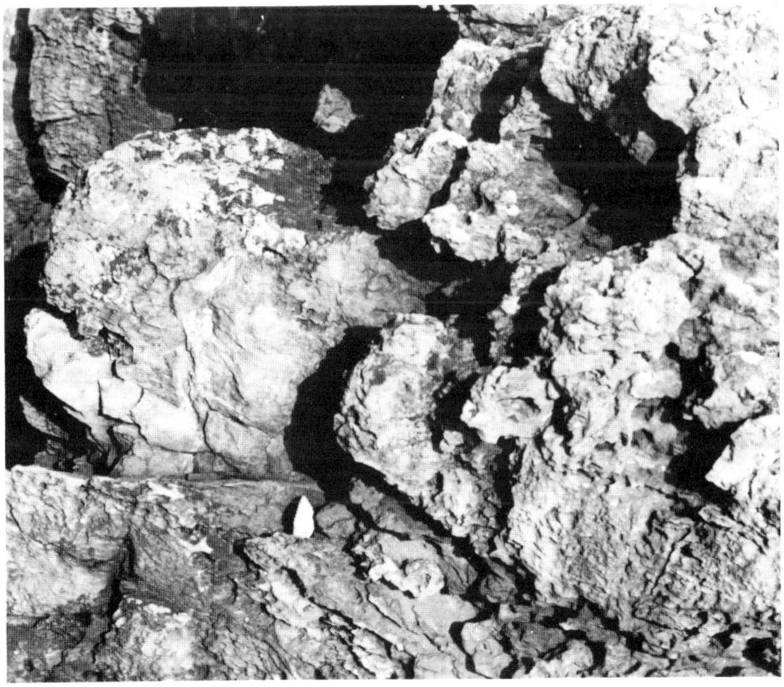

1 Sea-eroded forms
Photograph Gilbert Adams FRPS

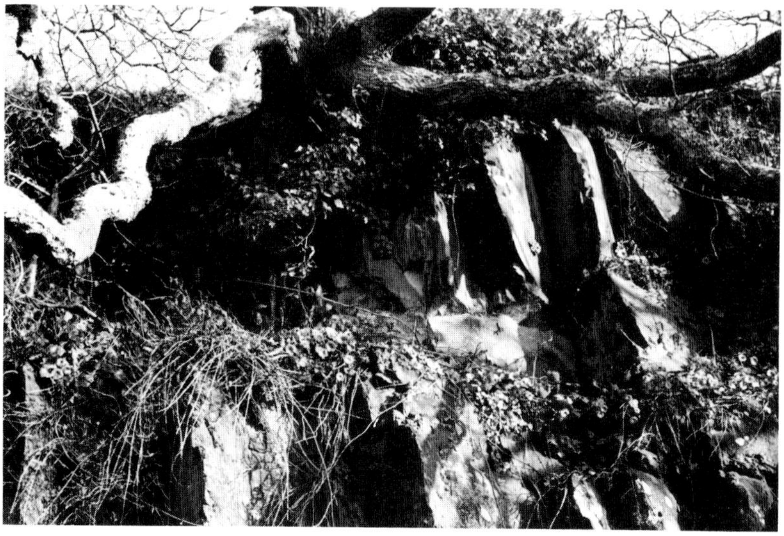

2 Oak branches hanging over Picton shore
Photograph Gilbert Adams FRPS

Opposite
3 The intricate structure of nature provided the source of much of Graham Sutherland's work
Photograph Gilbert Adams FRPS

Europe. Certain patterns which inspired him were, he felt, parallel to ideas being formed by the modern romantics there.

After his foundation at Picton Castle, Pembrokeshire, was opened in 1976, he said, 'I think paintings are best seen in the places where they were inspired.' The landscape images, especially those of sea and wind erosion around Welsh shores, were never factual representations, but were an amalgam of natural objects derived from a variety of sources, allowed to filter through his mind, and re-created in the new context of a composition. At the same time however, they remained closely related to their actual sources. 'The painting', he wrote to me in 1978, 'has to reveal itself gradually or immediately by itself and on its own merit – but of course it is interesting to see the source [of inspiration] as in Van Gogh or Cezanne.'

So strong was the influence of Pembrokeshire that it permeated all his work. Even in the giant hieratic tapestry of Coventry Cathedral one can feel a communication with South Wales. With the eye of a scientist, Sutherland unravelled the complex structure of nature; then re-created it using varying perspective, scale and colour. He constructed his images, not in a flash, but by quiet sustained study.

The minutiae of an area rather than the grand landscape excited Sutherland's imagination, although often he would observe in Pembrokeshire natural forms, such as sea-eroded rocks, 'precisely reproducing in miniature the forms of the inland hills'. Sometimes it was only on his return to a place, 'when the light had thrown up some unexpected form,' that a subject would reveal itself and he felt impelled to notate it; as many as twenty drawings might result from a single encounter. These drawings were then paraphrased and translated into their pictorial reincarnation without losing the structure and feeling of the original object. The use of unusual unexpected colour to convey tone, gave the final image a romantic and fluent language. It was important for him that in the final analysis of a painting the 'first *frisson* of an encounter' should be experienced or felt. He was guided and inspired largely by a philosophy

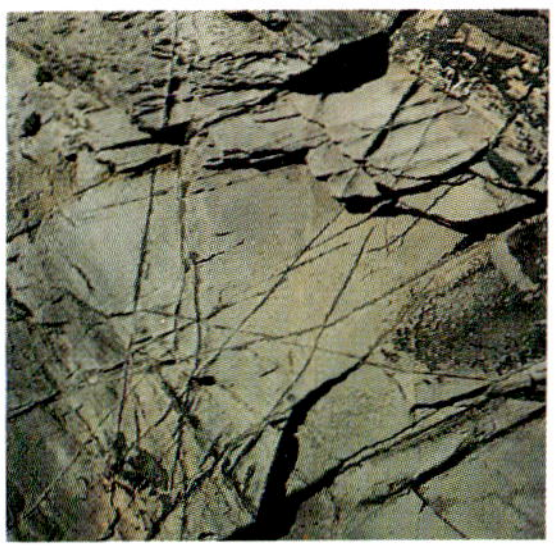
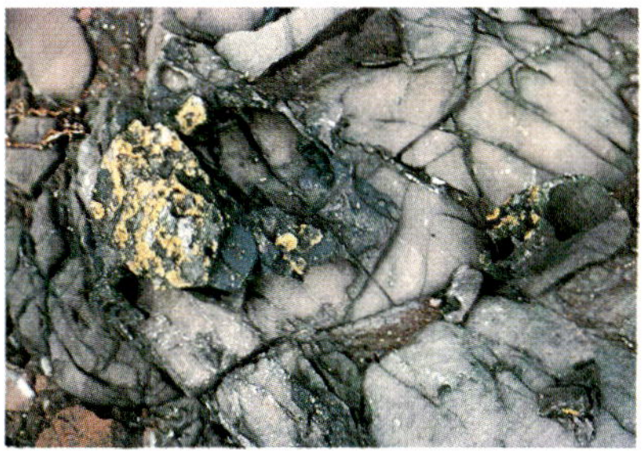
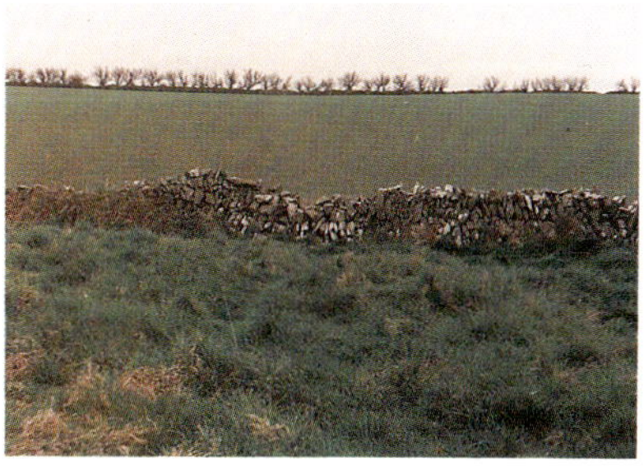
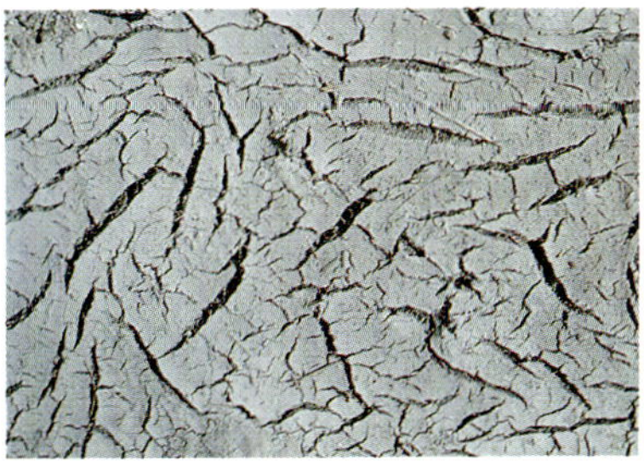
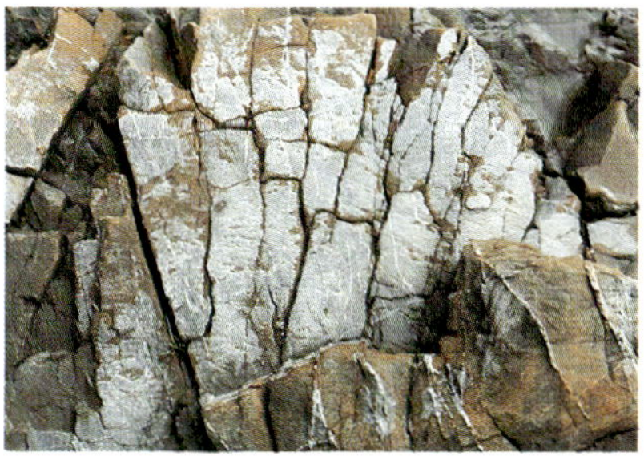
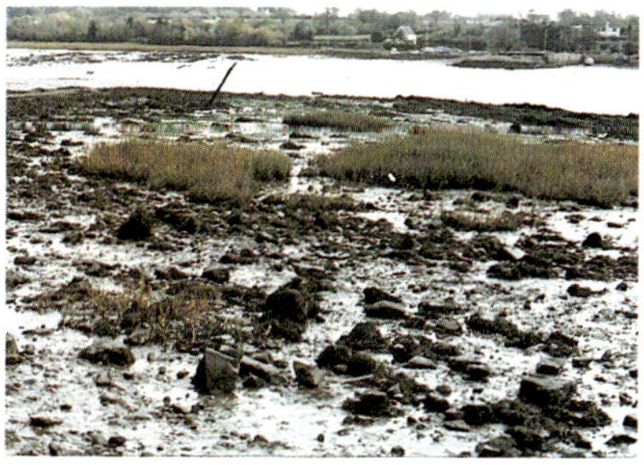
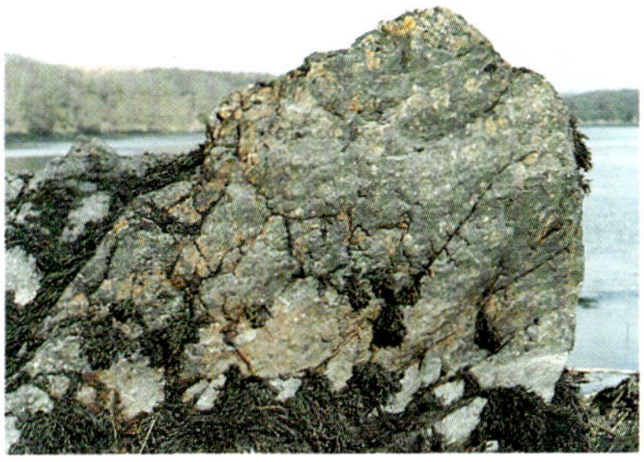
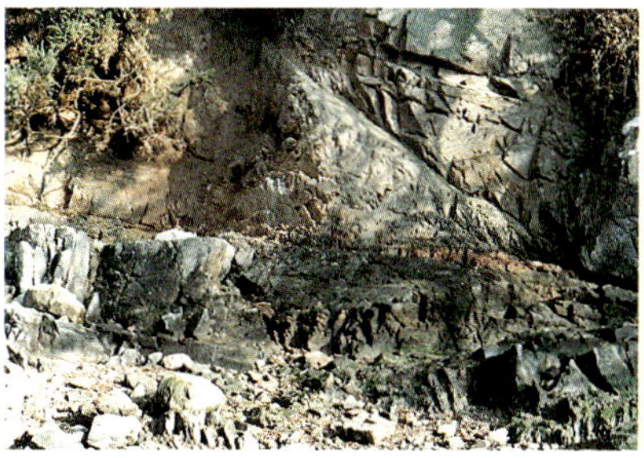
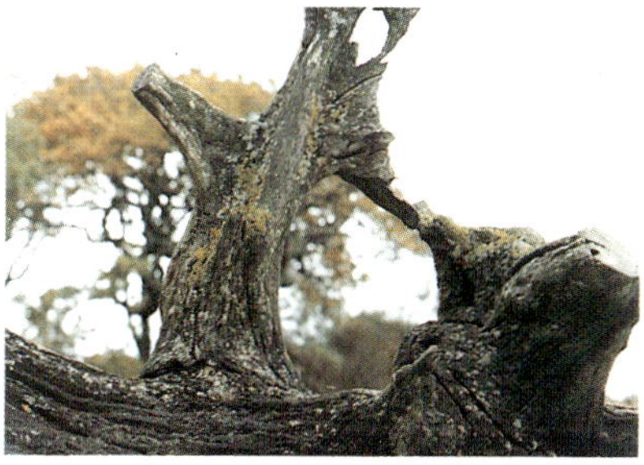
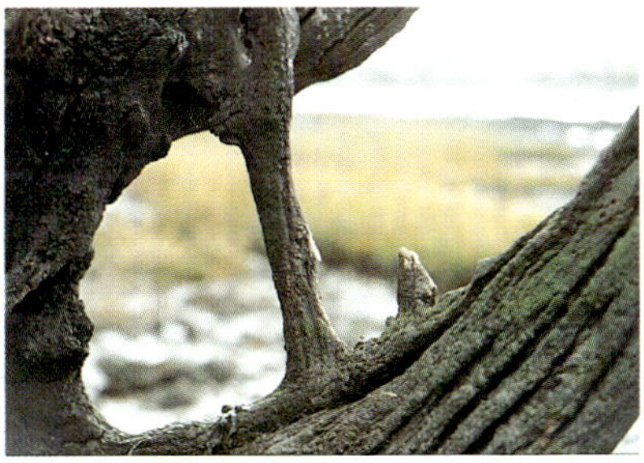
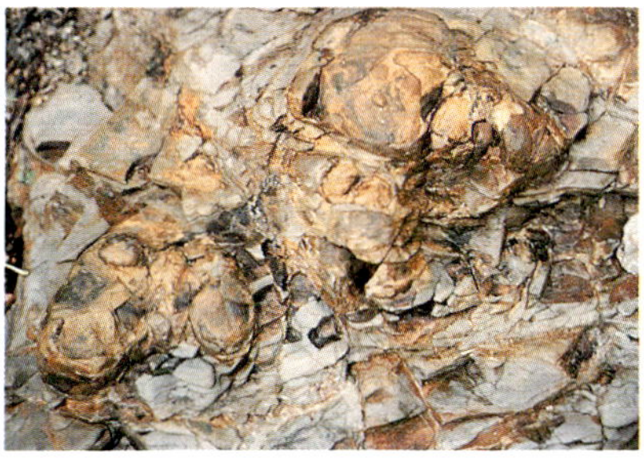
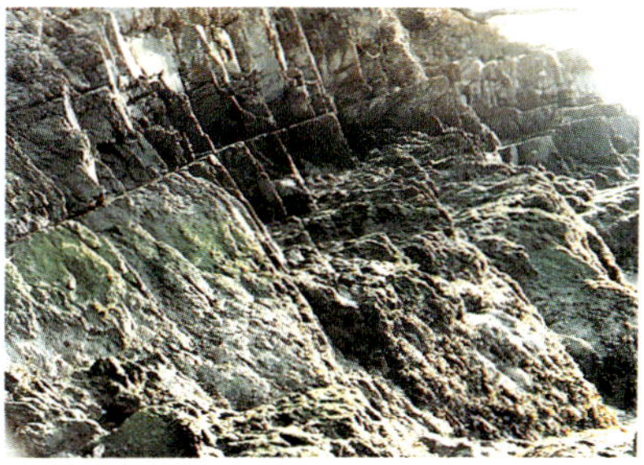
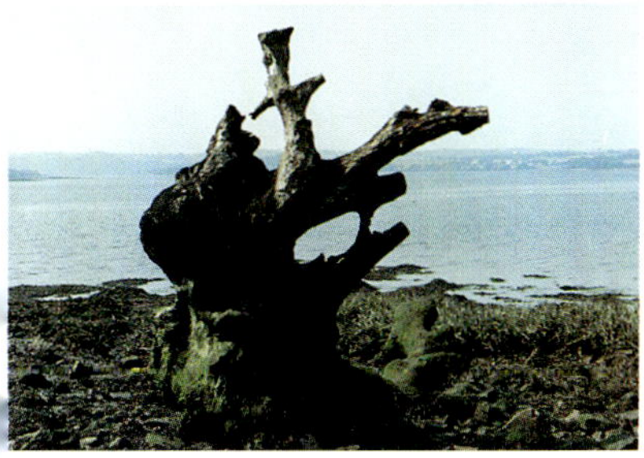
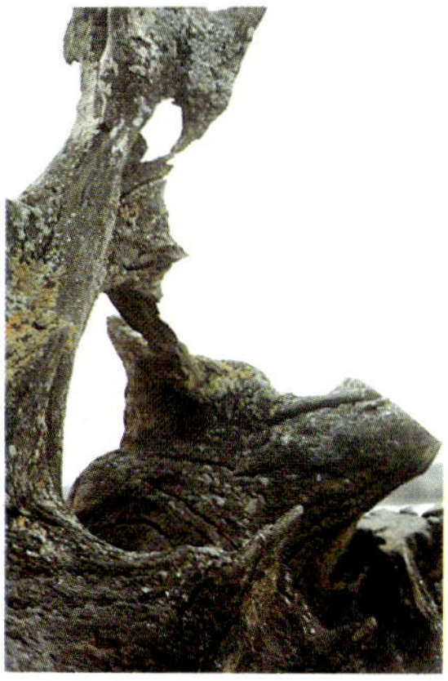

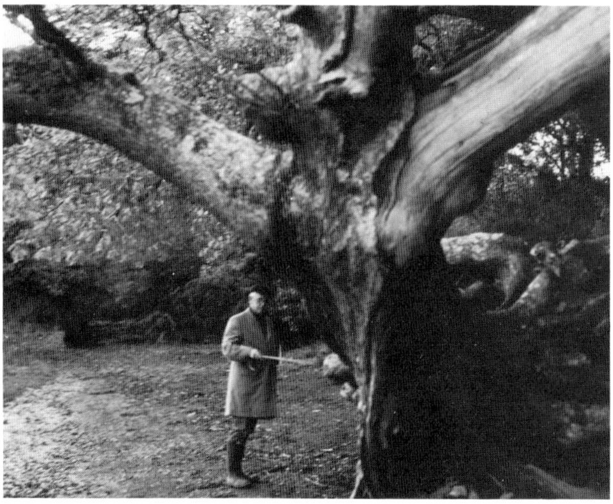

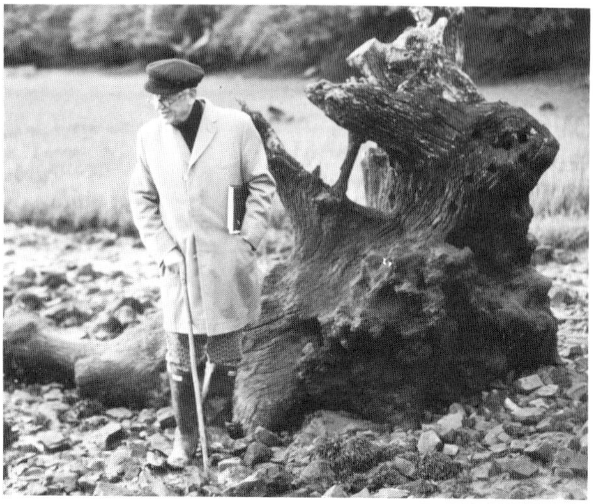

Above
4 Graham Sutherland studying the gnarled shapes of an oak bole on Picton shore
Photograph Gilbert Adams FRPS

Above right
5 Graham Sutherland walking on Picton shore
Photograph Gilbert Adams FRPS

of his own, rooted in nature, although contemporary influences are also quite evident. A painting for him was 'a separate entity, related to its source, yet self existing'.

From the beginning of his career he was totally committed to the professional and commercial aspect of his work, while never losing the integrity of the individual artistic process. His life became a series of paradoxes of thought and outlook, which in turn, I am sure, created the energy to work. He is admired principally for his vision, talent and inventiveness. Having once established a theme, he would pursue it with many variations which, on gaining acceptance, eventually won him

6 Rock forms
Photograph Gilbert Adams FRPS

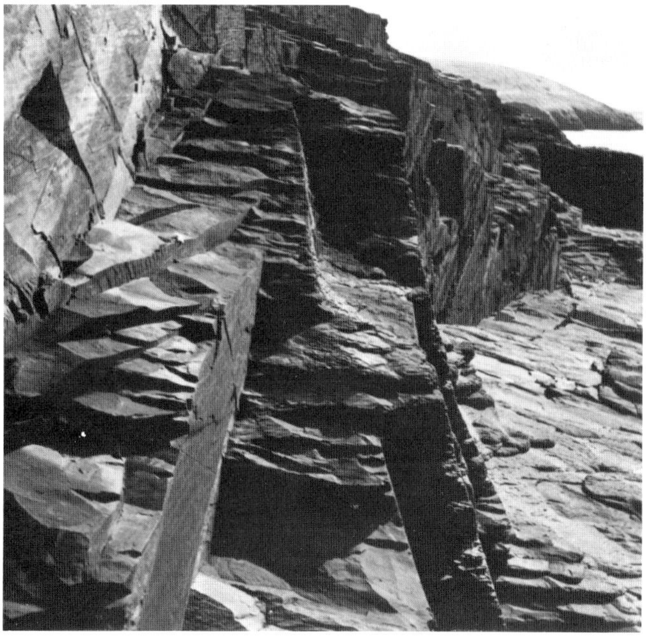

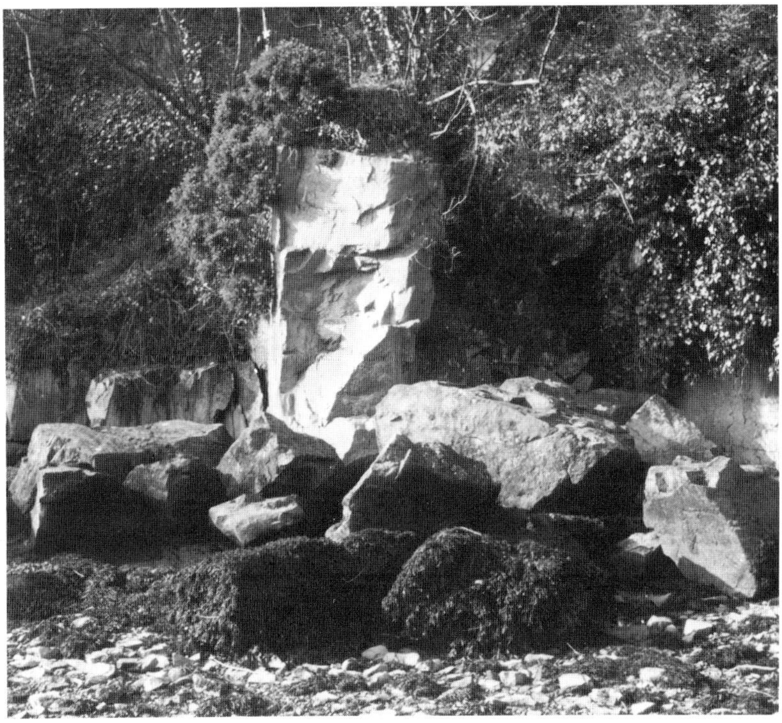

7 Rock tower
Photograph Gilbert Adams FRPS

recognition throughout the world. 'Remember Titian,' he once said to me, 'he was a late starter and so was I.'

In daily life he maintained a routine. During the latter years of his life, he spent some three months each year in Pembrokeshire, and there the regime was strictly followed. He did not like the wind, rain and damp, but found such weather conditions more compatible with his working schedule in England than were similar conditions in France. This he attributed to the extraordinary quality of light found in Pembrokeshire.

It was difficult to imagine that the figure who stumped through estuaries and over scrub near St Bride's Bay was a painter. Immaculately dressed in his decorative trousers, Jermyn Street shirts, covert coat, fur-lined mackintosh, mariner's cap and large wellingtons, he looked far more like the archetypal city businessman on holiday than an artist scrutinizing the anatomy of rock formations. When I asked him why he wore the mariner's cap, he replied, 'Well, I'm really a frustrated mariner. Have you ever seen Leonardo's *Waves*?' I hadn't, but I was convinced, knowing of the many hours he would spend walking through estuaries and over scrub, observing the pattern of bird flight and rest.

Sutherland became an international figure and his principal collectors were Italians. He was European by virtue of his life style, but he believed that 'no one can get out of their genealogical tree. Something comes out of the country where you are born, you cannot avoid it.' In a letter to me on this subject he added the words of Cocteau, 'The more a painter sings in his genealogical tree the more his singing is in tune.'

Chapter II
EARLY YEARS

Sutherland was brought up as a lover of the countryside and the partnership with nature remained throughout his life. He was born in August 1903, in London. His father, George H.V. Sutherland, a civil servant and lawyer, and his mother Elsie were both amateur painters and at the age of seven he instinctively took to formal drawing. Graham's grandfather was a keen walker, as was his father, and walking was a recognized pastime for the young Sutherlands. During Graham's boyhood the family lived first at Merton Park (making frequent outings to the home where Nelson had installed Lady Hamilton) and later at Sutton, in Surrey. After the First World War his father built a new home in the Sussex village of Rustington.

The gaps of five years between Graham and his younger brother and of ten between himself and his younger sister meant that he spent a great deal of time on his own. During the rather lonely years between ten and thirteen he went butterfly hunting and collected anything else too that his young eyes might seize upon. Later, recalling these days, he said, 'When I was young I became involved with things beyond what I saw – for instance I noticed the light falling on the interior wall of a disused shed, it created a strange mystery.'

At home, many evenings were spent listening to his parents and their friends playing string quartets or reading Shakespeare together. Amongst his parents' intellectual friends were a number of Germans who shared their love of, and interest in, music.

Graham was nine when he began school at Sutton in 1912, and in 1914 he went on to Epsom College as a day boy. The college had about three hundred boys, many of them sons of doctors. This being the period of the First World War, casualty lists from France would often contain the names of prefects and other boys who had left only a few months earlier. In spite of the happy atmosphere of the school, teaching did suffer through the absence at war of some of the masters.

Sutherland spent the school holidays drawing, painting and walking. Soon his father became concerned about how his son was to earn a living. Graham's uncle, who was then chief engineer at the Midland Railway works in Derby, was approached regarding the possibility of taking on the young school-leaver as an apprentice. The boy's classical education at Epsom College was not immediately beneficial, though over the years it did provide a sound basis for his approach to his own painting and encouraged his wide appreciation of the classical writers. In 1919 Sutherland went up to Derby to serve his apprenticeship. Anxious to do well, he did not admit that he found the work unsuitable. The year at Derby, however, was in no way wasted; he was involved principally with workshop production, from the flat sheet to the finished locomotive, and during his time there he became fascinated by machinery. After a year or so, he was called into the chief mechanical engineer's office and asked if he was happy, to which he replied, 'Well – yes and no.' The engineer then said, 'Well, you'll never make an engineer as you have no grasp of mathematics. I propose to write to your father and suggest that you take up art.'

Sutherland's father was not overtly enthusiastic about his son's pursuing an art training – more probably he was concerned at the possibility of his son's adopting a non-remunerative life style – but his mother considerably influenced her husband to allow their elder son to enrol at Goldsmiths' College School of Art in South London in 1921. Having agreed, Sutherland's father encouraged his son to study book illustration which he hoped might be a more commercial and eventually profitable course. Goldsmiths' College in the twenties produced a number of highly talented and well-respected printmakers whose success was not only due to personal vision and talent but was also the result of excellent and inspired teaching.

Frederick Marriott, the Head of Goldsmiths' School of Art, whose watchword was 'produce', was himself a leading engraver, and greatly encouraged the learning of engraving techniques; Sutherland remembered

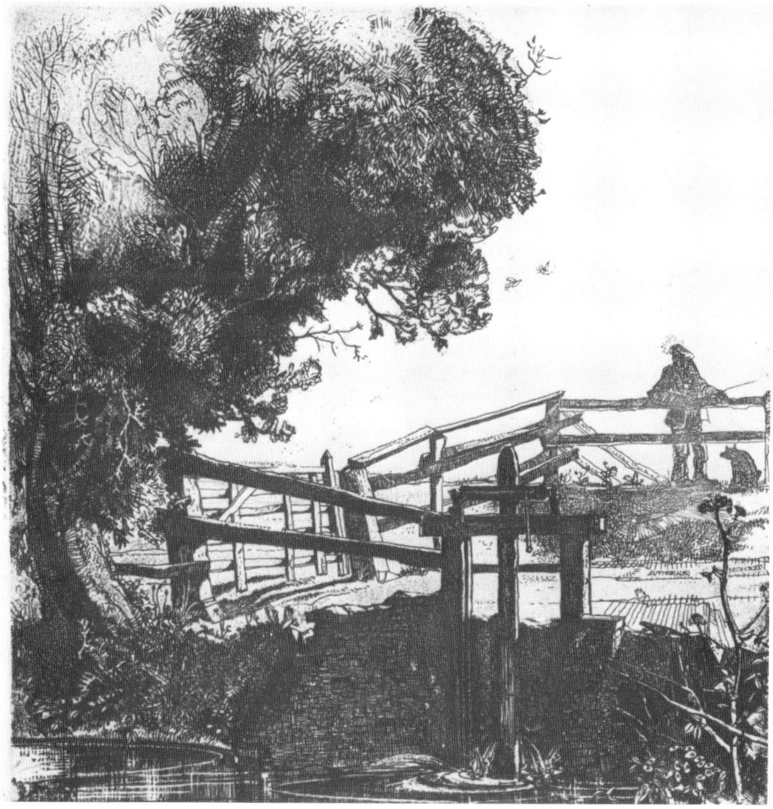

8 *The Sluice Gate*, etching, 1924
Photograph Robin Garton Ltd

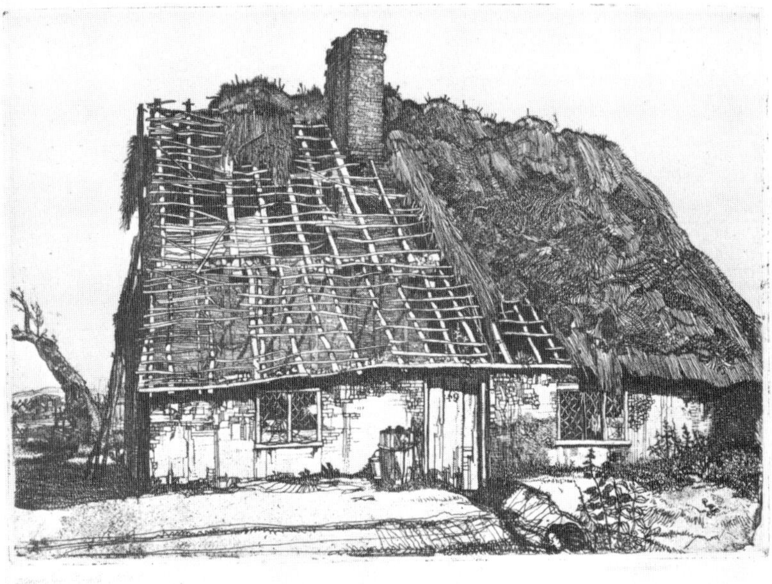

9 *Number Forty-Nine*, etching, 1924
Photograph Robin Garton Ltd

the bias being very much in this direction. Art school proved as much of a discipline as any other professional training and since Sutherland was a diligent and dedicated student he was to benefit enormously from the marvellous teaching of men such as Edmund Sullivan, the well-known illustrator and watercolourist. Sutherland was particularly impressed by his outstanding personality, elegant Irish looks, and his clothes – brown velvet trousers and jacket – as well, of course, as by his work.

Engraving was taught first by Malcolm Osborne and then by the very exacting teacher Stanley Anderson. The master etcher of Chipping Campden, Frederick Landseer Maur Griggs, greatly assisted and inspired Sutherland and, together with his friend and colleague Paul Drury, Sutherland was a frequent visitor to Griggs's home, Dovers House, Chipping Campden. To Griggs's particular pleasure, Sutherland became enthusiastic about the work of Samuel Palmer and the Shoreham circle. Later, when Sutherland's engraving days were over, the Palmer influence became less important – once Sutherland had seen the work of the French school, the impressionists, cubists, surrealists and others, and once he had begun to paint, a different romance entered his work, that of an inventor and constructor of images – but for the present, it was considerable, and of significance to his development.

Other teachers included the painter and illustrator Clive Gardiner, remembered by students as a very liberal man, who taught illustration and was to succeed Freddy Marriott as Head. He was a brilliant technician and could paint a complete portrait while students were watching. Harold Speed and Percival Buckman taught portraiture and Edward Jack figure drawing, the least successful of the subjects that Sutherland pursued.

Amongst Sutherland's contemporaries at Goldsmiths' was Paul Drury, who shared a bench with him when they were etching in the pastoral vein.

He became a life-long friend, even lending considerable encouragement to Sutherland when he returned to printmaking in the late fifties and sixties. There was also Rowland Hilder, himself a good etcher; Elizabeth Scott-Moore who found him not very talkative but a fastidious worker; and there was Bouverie Hoyton, the very fine etcher, Milner Gray – another of Sutherland's life-long friends – and Willy Larkins whom Sutherland considered 'a remarkable and inspired etcher making exceptional prints and drawings packed with insight' and one who 'managed to combine a highly complex technique with an air of simplicity'. Although it is generally accepted that Griggs inspired in others an admiration for the work of William Blake and Samuel Palmer, Sutherland himself said, 'I think it is true that he [Willy Larkins] was the first person to alert us [in about 1924-5] to the excellence of the etchings of Samuel Palmer.' Robin Tanner, who is still today, along with Paul Drury, a master etcher in the pastoral style, was a fellow student and admirer of Sutherland's. It was Tanner who said, 'Sutherland was a born etcher, especially in the pastoral vein.' Here it is appropriate to add that when he came to etching and engraving at art school, the linear exactitude he had learnt at the Midland Railway works enabled him to make rapid progress within the limited and rigorous processes which were required of him, and when faced later with the problems of line and composition in painting, he seems to have sought systematically to subdue the strength of line in deference to colour though he held ultimately that the structure of drawing was very important.

As well as being greatly admired, Sutherland was popular and would be remembered for his handsome looks and fastidious clothes. He recollected that students were rebellious in many respects, the men wearing black cloaks in what he described as the Palmeresque tradition and the girls being dressed very much in the fashion of Augustus John's wife Dorelia. Yet they had a dedication to work and often arrived some hours before the tutors in the morning – Willy Larkins, for instance, would be there at 6.30 am and Sutherland at 7 am.

Goldsmiths' inspired fundamentally an understanding of the great painters such as Rembrandt, Dürer, Goya, Millet, Seymour Haden and Whistler, Constable and J.M.W. Turner, together with, of course, William Blake and Samuel Palmer. More recent painters to whom the students were encouraged to look included Augustus John and Sickert, but at the time there seemed little influence from the French school. It was only much later that Sutherland became aware of the post-impressionists, and most especially of the work of Cézanne. In 1924 Sutherland, with Larkins and Drury, worked for Clive Gardiner, squaring up paper for and painting under his supervision the mural decorations of a pavilion at the British Empire Exhibition, Wembley, and it was Gardiner who introduced him to the post-impressionists.

In 1923 Graham Sutherland's first dry-point, *Barn Interior,* was shown at the Royal Academy. In 1925 his etching *Cain and Abel* was entered for the Prix de Rome for which he was a finalist runner-up. He was elected to the Royal Society of Painter-Etchers and Engravers, from which he was to resign in 1933 after the magnification of a rose tree in his etching *The Garden* shocked the conventional, causing the Society to refuse to show his work. It became apparent very early in Sutherland's career that the detail he could render was quite remarkable, given the limitations of the dry-point process. He was especially fortunate in benefiting from the fine tutors who developed his natural ability. Considering that his forte was not immediately recognized in the life-drawing class – though at that period it was an essential part of every art student's training to pursue almost the same anatomical study and discovery of the human frame as the student doctor – it is immediately interesting to study his portrayals of the lissom young girl in *Adam and Eve (The Expulsion from Eden)* (1924) and the Rembrandtesque heads of the two figures in *The Philosophers* (1924). Already in the twenties there is little doubt of his ability to portray in a landscape, powerful yet calm figures of immense sensitivity. Later we see these dissolve, become less important to his work, until they are almost entirely abandoned except in the studies of tin miners and the portraits, re-emerging at last in the great *Conspirators* series (Plates 122-124) of the late seventies.

When one considers the etchings of the Goldsmiths' days, it seems paradoxical that he should have said, much later, that people should be unidentifiable in landscape. In *The Village* (1925: Plate 10) the girl is working and the countryside shows evidence of all kinds of local agrarian occupations. Human endeavour is also captured in *Study of Houses (New Cross Backs)* (1922. Plate 11), where the washing is hanging out. The first engravings with editions of any size were exhibited at the Twenty-One Gallery in London, in 1925 and 1928, and included *The Black Rabbit* (Plate 13); *Cudham, Kent; The Sluice Gate* (Plate 8); *The Village* (Plate 10); *Cray Fields; May Green; Michaelmas;* and *The Meadow Chapel.* Sutherland actually told me that their moderate success was due to the fact that anyone could sell prints at that time. In fact the etching boom was enjoyed by both his friends Willy Larkins and Paul Drury. The work was to become the last

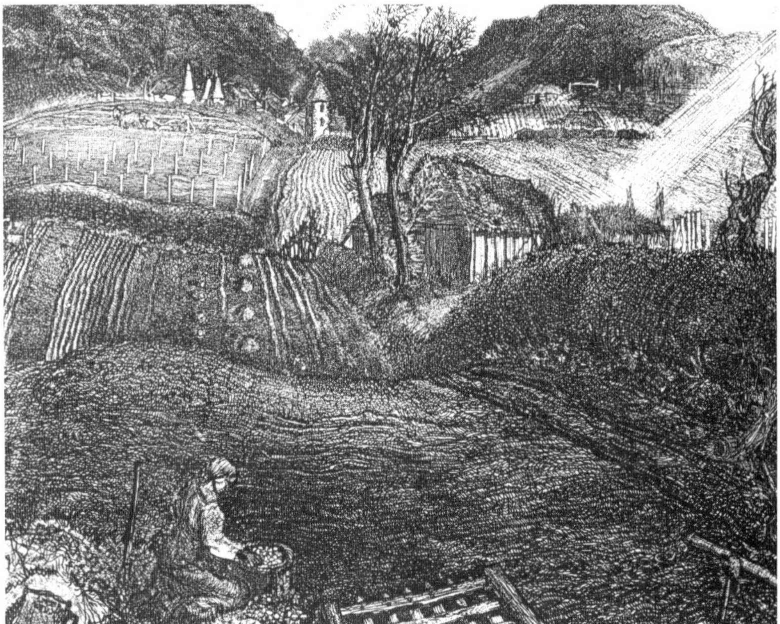

10 *The Village*, etching, 1925
Photograph Robin Garton Ltd

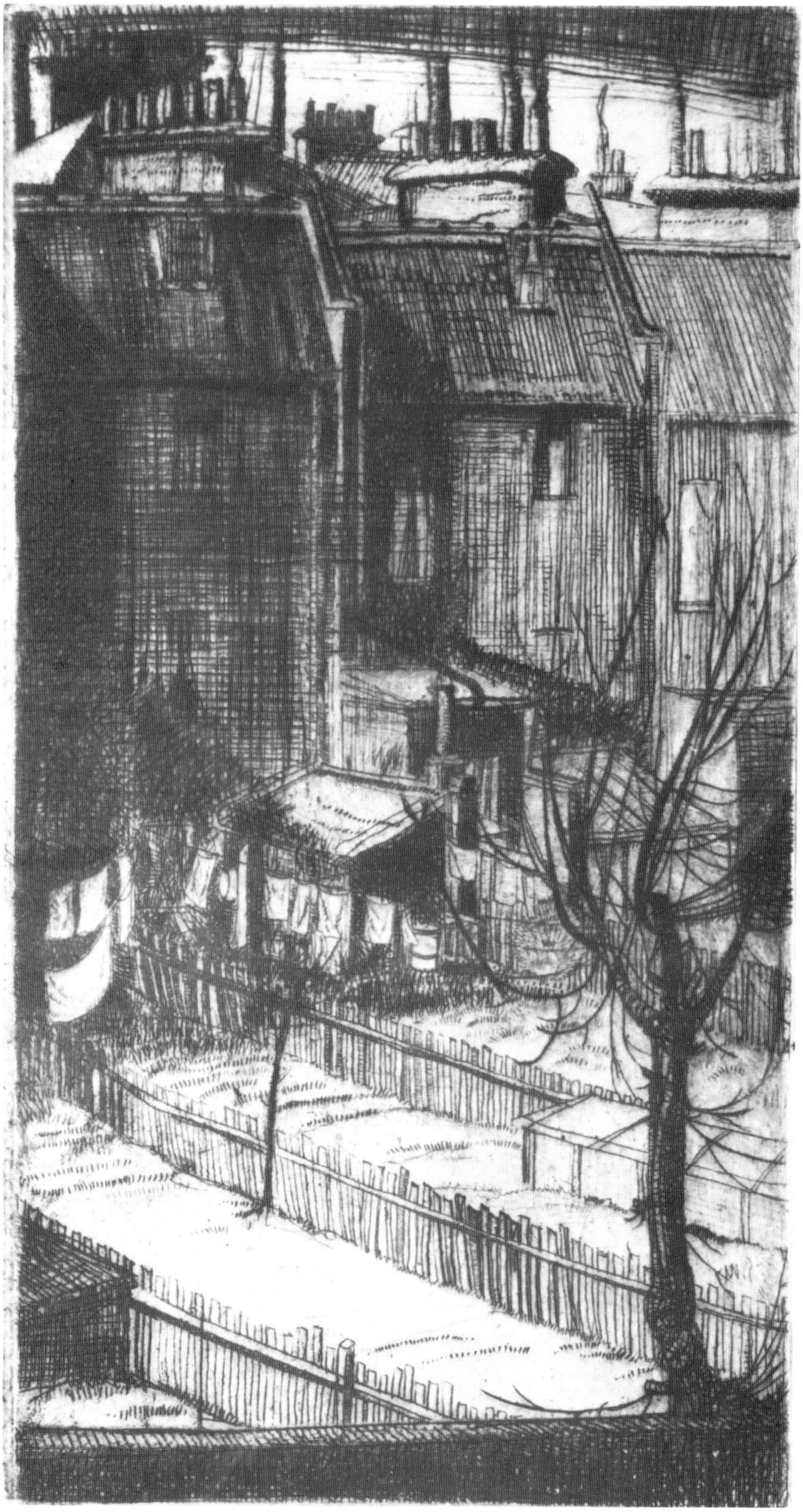

11 *Study of Houses (New Cross Backs)*, etching, 1922
Photograph
Robin Garton Ltd

flowering of the British school of etching. Sutherland's etchings by 1933 totalled thirty-five; thirteen of these demonstrate quite clearly the influence of Palmer, *Pecken Wood, St Mary Hatch* (Plate 12) and *Lammas* being typical. However, the breakthrough occurred in 1930 when Sutherland's own personal vision became apparent in *Pastoral*. The tree form began to speak that language which arose when it was, as he said, 'a question of starting with the concrete and recreating something more concrete'.

During his student days at Goldsmiths', Sutherland had lodged with his friend Milner Gray in an old Georgian house in Blackheath, keeping his etching press in the living-room. The friendship and working partnership were to last many years. They spent many weekends and holidays in the Kent countryside and Sutherland made many pencil sketches of the Darent Valley where they often walked. Frequent visits to Kent and Sussex, Arundel and the river Arun in particular, as well as the enthusiasm of his tutors, fostered Sutherland's ever-increasing admiration of William Blake and Samuel Palmer.

On his first day at Goldsmiths', Sutherland met the girl who was to become his wife and whose support he came to rely on for the next sixty years. She was a Roman Catholic and in 1926 Sutherland was converted to Catholicism. In that same year he left Goldsmiths' and was earning enough money from the sale of his prints to think of settling down; on 29 December 1927 he married the beautiful Kathleen Barry. Their first home was in Farningham, Kent; later, when they moved to Willow Cottage, Eynsford, not far away, they were joined by Sutherland's friend and erstwhile landlord, Milner Gray, who was to spend many years as the Sutherlands' lodger. In 1934 they moved a few miles down the Darent Valley to Sutton-at-Hone, and two years later settled at The White House, Trottiscliffe, which remained their Kent home. Sutherland had appreciated the inspiration of a 'good surround' of students at Goldsmiths', and now

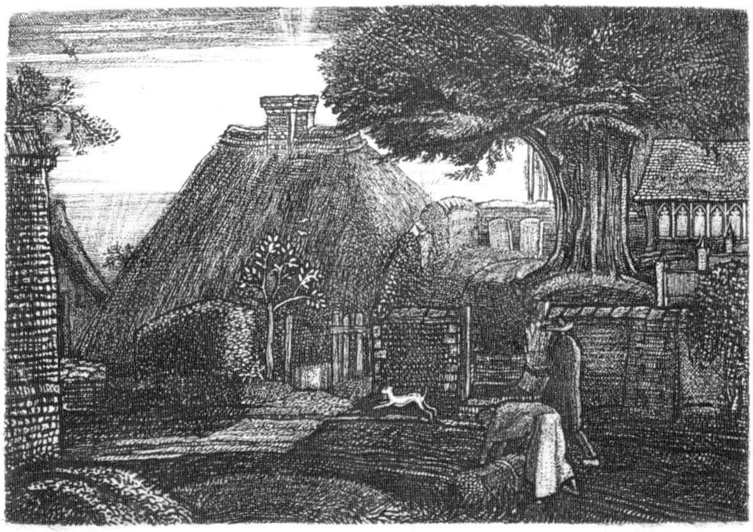

12 *St Mary Hatch*, etching, 1926
Photograph Robin Garton Ltd

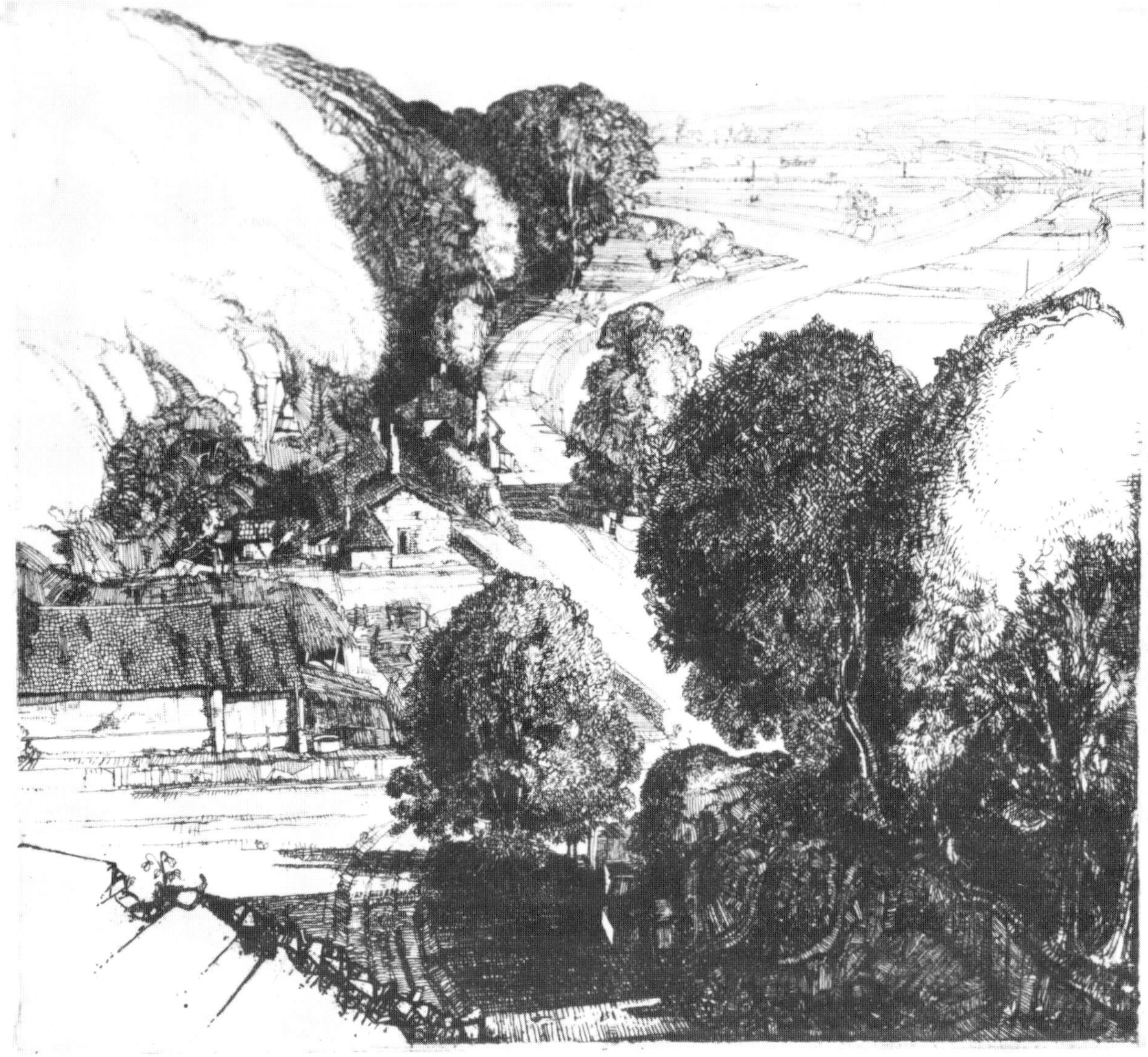

13 *The Black Rabbit*, etching, 1923
Photograph Robin Garton Ltd

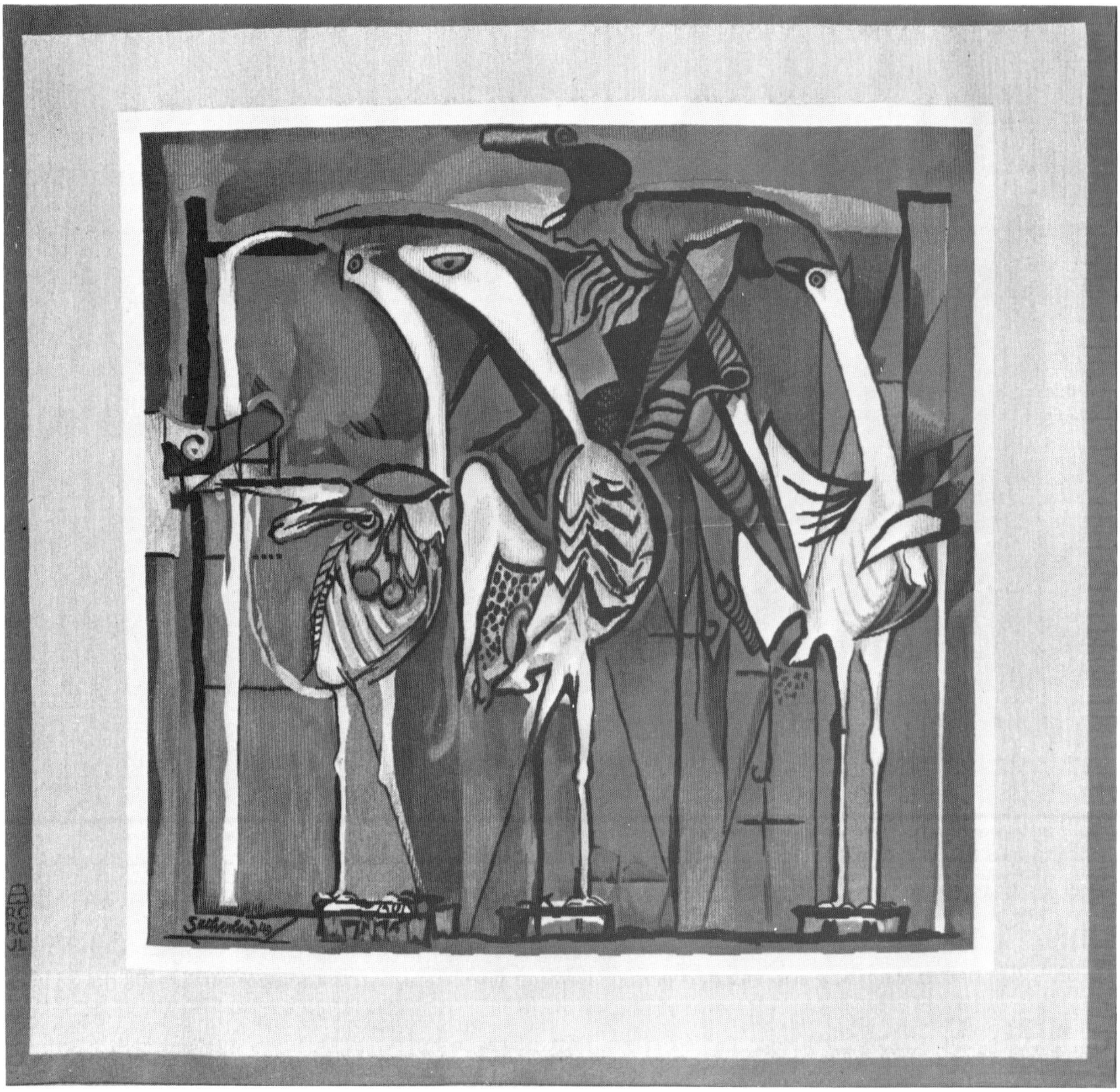

14 Tapestry woven by Edinburgh Tapestry Co Ltd to the design of Graham Sutherland, 1949
Edinburgh Tapestry Co Ltd

many of them were to join him at weekends in the country and remained an 'important circle of friends' all his life.

In 1930 the Americans, who had been the principal purchasers of Sutherland's prints, were on the brink of financial disaster and his print market vanished overnight. His wife, who had been a student of fashion and design at Goldsmiths', was able to use her talents and return to work to keep them both for a year. Then in 1932, after part-time teaching at Kingston Art School (evening classes) and Chelsea College of Art (engraving), Sutherland was appointed on a full-time basis to teach book illustration and composition at Chelsea. He remained in the post for the next seven years. He found the long day – 9 am to 9.30 pm – exhausting,

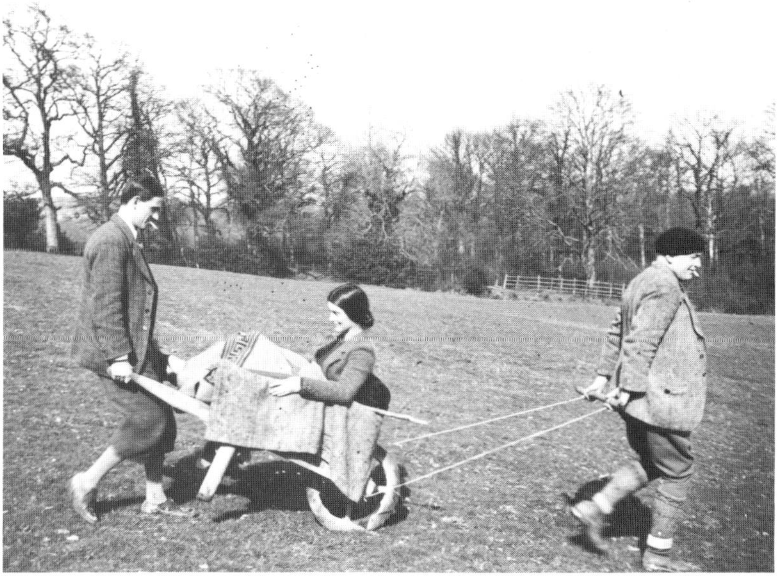

Left
15 Kathleen Sutherland being pushed in a wheelbarrow by Graham Sutherland
Photograph Mrs Scott-Moore

Below
16 Graham Sutherland and John Scott-Moore
Photograph Mrs Scott-Moore

but students remember him as a most helpful, humble and gracious teacher with beautiful hands and a remarkable presence. Two of his friends there were Henry Moore, teaching sculpture in place of Frank Dobson, and Milner Gray, who taught commercial art.

Milner Gray had started in 1924 the firm of designers, Bassett Gray, which Misha Black joined in 1932 and which in 1935 became Industrial Design Partnership. Amongst the associates of the company were a number of freelance artists, Paul Nash and Duncan Grant being two of those who were greatly encouraged. Sutherland himself was involved with illustrative work for the firm and helped considerably in the early days by demonstrating the merits of good design in industry. He, together with Clive Gardiner, then Head of Goldsmiths', and Edmund Sullivan, did a considerable amount of work for the practice. It was through his attachment to Bassett Gray that Sutherland was introduced to the executives of London Transport, Shell-Mex and other organizations, and invited to design posters. At the exhibition of Shell-Mex posters in 1935 Kenneth Clark (now Lord Clark) wished to be introduced to Sutherland and found him to be self-possessed and highly intelligent.

Through a series of pen and ink drawings, designs for cigarette packets, advertisements for Bassett Gray, designs for glass, ceramics, tapestry and posters, Sutherland progressed towards his own painting. During the busy years at Chelsea, Sutherland's holidays were habitually spent in Kent, Devon, Dorset and Sussex, where he painted straight representational landscapes. Very few of these paintings survive. It was away from the relative gentleness of those landscapes, however, that he was about to experience one of the most dramatic events of his life. In the spring of 1934 he went off to explore the primitive parts of Pembrokeshire. It was only then, he considered, that he first really learnt to paint. He was still very English both in character and in his approach to painting, but a far-reaching change was soon to develop.

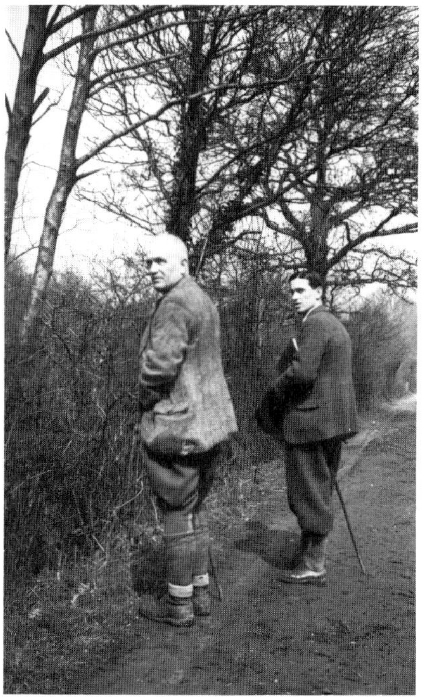

Chapter III
PEMBROKESHIRE

For Graham Sutherland the dramatic event of spring 1934 was seeing for the first time primitive forms and shapes assembled within a relatively small area of land. His reaction, as he began to wander around the terrain of St Bride's Bay, was immediate. Here was a total revelation, an 'ecstatic experience', a vital and intimate emotional encounter, reinforcing ideas that had been forming in his mind. He did not explain to me what those ideas were, but it can be concluded from his conversation with Noel Barber published in 1964 that he was aware already that his visual response to nature extended beyond the superficial; he was ready to look into the hidden parts of landscape. 'As a child I went out into the country a great deal . . . I got into the habit of looking at things closely – observing, analysing and drawing everything in the countryside.'[1]

When talking to Barber he said, 'Since 1936, through the pages of *Cahiers d'Art* and other French magazines, we in the British Isles were becoming more conscious of what was going on on the continent.'[2] He felt the pulse and rhythm of harmonious shapes and forms, and began to appreciate that they could be translated into a painting, irrespective often of dimension and perspective. The shapes that he suddenly saw brought about a deep awareness of a land bathed in primeval atmosphere. Pembrokeshire had for Sutherland a mysterious sinister pull, an all-dominating physical attraction which outweighed any subsequent relationship with a place or location for the rest of his life.

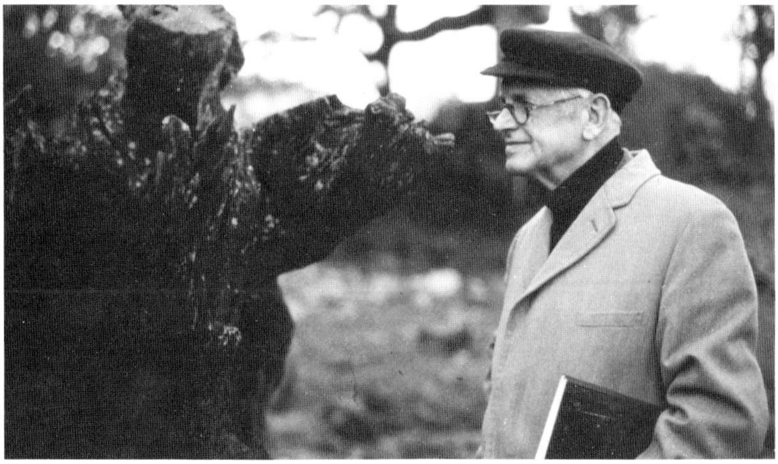

17 Graham Sutherland studying rotted tree trunk
Photograph Gilbert Adams FRPS

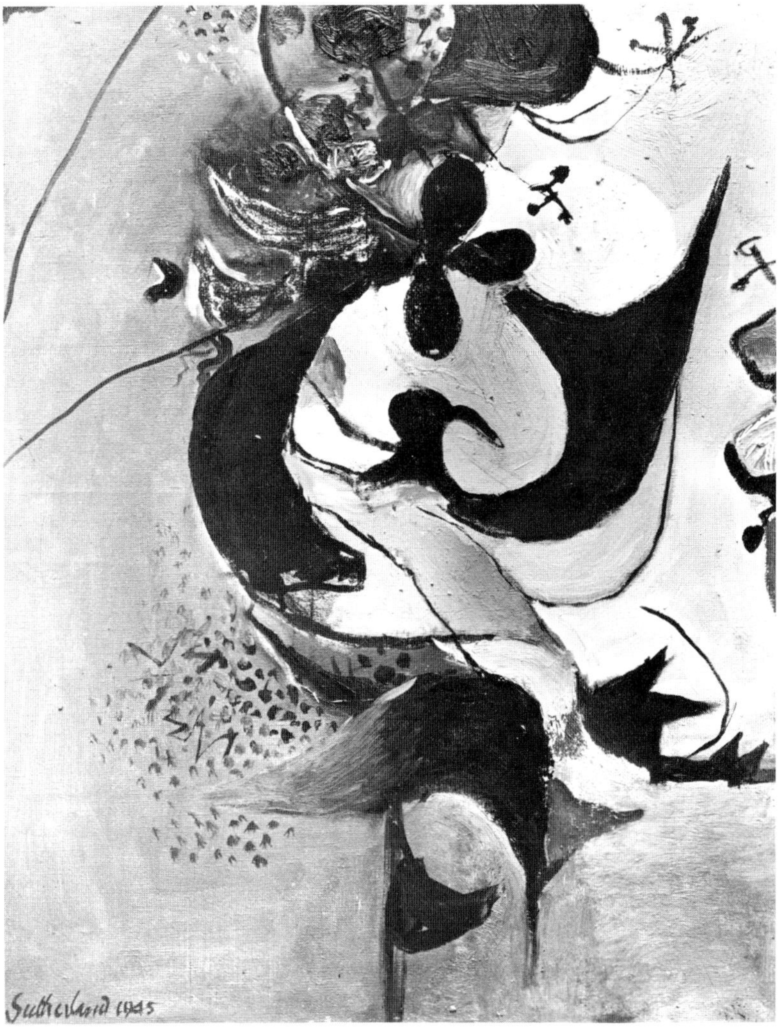

Left
18 *Lane Opening*, 1945
Southampton Art Gallery & Museums

This is one of the subjects Sutherland tried to re-create with the same initial excitement he had experienced in *Entrance to Lane*, 1939 (Plate 25)

Below
19 Graham Sutherland with author walking down to Sandy Haven estuary
Photograph Gilbert Adams FRPS

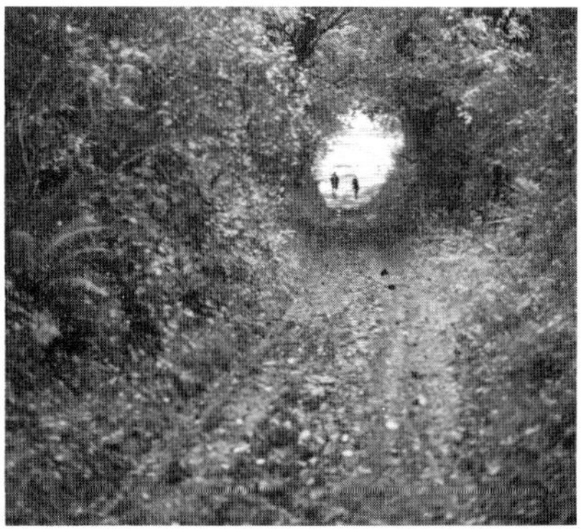

The country roads of Pembrokeshire in those days were only roughly surfaced, had no white lines and were crudely edged with boulders on either side. There were no signposts to indicate where one was; one could identify towns and villages only by reading the signs over shops or at railway stations, or by tracking them down on a map. Of this countryside Sutherland wrote to his friend Colin Anderson in 1942:

> At the risk of talking like a guide book, I must tell you of the area to the South, I shall never forget my first visit. We approached by a flat winding road and had slipped into one of the little valleys such as I have attempted to describe.
>
> To the left this opened out to reveal what appeared to be a watery inlet narrowing to its upper end. As the road progressed we caught further glimpses of this and curiosity was roused. We had intended making for a village called Dale, marked on the map as lying to the north side of the mouth of Milford Haven. Fortunately we missed the road and found ourselves descending a green lane buried in

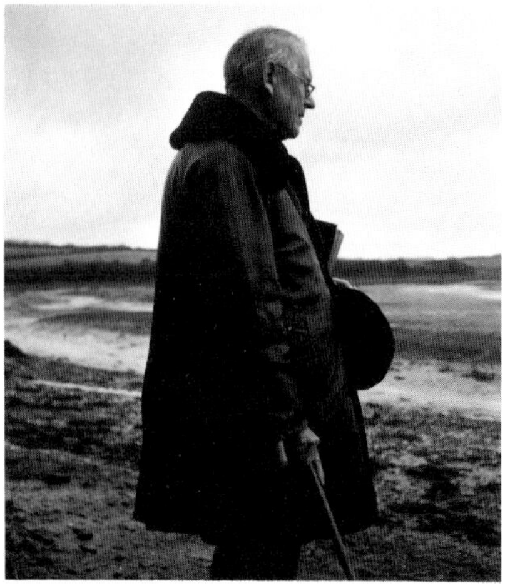

20 Graham Sutherland on Sandy Haven beach
Photograph Gilbert Adams FRPS

trees, which quite unexpectedly led to a little cove and beach by the banks of a narrow estuary.

Here is a hamlet – three cottages and an inn crouch under the low cliffs. A man is burning brushwood cut from a tree, bleached and washed by the sea. The flame looks incandescent in the evening light. The tide in the estuary (or pill as such inlets are called here) is out, and we walk across the sandy bed of the opening and look down at its winding length to the place where it narrows to the upper end.

I wish I could give you some idea of the exultant strangeness of this place, for strange it certainly is. Many people whom I know hate it, and I cannot but admit that it possesses an element of disquiet. The left bank as we see it is all dark – an impenetrable damp green gloom of woods which run down to the edge of low brackish moss-covered cliffs – it is all dark, save where the mossy lanes (two each side) which dive down to the opening, admit the sun, hinged, as it were, to the top of the trees, from where its rays, precipitating new colours, turn the red cliffs of the right hand bank to tones of fire. Do you remember the rocks in Blake's 'Newton' drawing? The form and scale of the rocks here, and the minutiae on them, is very similar. The whole setting is one of exuberance – darkness and light – of decay and life. Rarely have I been so conscious of the contrasting of these elements in so small a compass.

The right bank has fields above the cliff, some covered with ripe corn, others with rough gorse-clad pasture. The life-giving sound of the mechanical reaper is heard. Cattle crouch among the dark gorse. The mind wanders from contemplation of the living cattle to their ghosts. It is no uncommon sight to see a horse's skull or horns of cattle lying bleached on the sand. Neither do we feel that the black green ribs of half buried wrecks and the phantom tree roots, bleached and washed by the waves, exist, but to emphasise the extraordinary completeness of the scene. Complete too is the life of the few inhabitants – almost biblical in its sober dignity.

The people in this part appear quite incurious of the activities of a foreigner. The immense, soft-voiced innkeeper and his wife, small as he is big, sit, when they are not working, bolt upright forms on a hard bench in the cool gloom of the parlour which forms the only 'bar' of the inn, or they sit – for he is a ferryman and fisherman, as well as innkeeper – gazing across the ferry.

The quality here is magical and transforming – as indeed it is in all this country. Watching from the gloom as the sun's rays strike the further bank, one has the sensation of the after-tranquillity of an *explosion* of light; or as if one had looked into the sun and had turned away suddenly.

After a good deal of wandering about, I came upon two very remarkable passages of country situated in the arms of land which embrace the great area of St Bride's Bay. The arm towards the North is like an isosceles triangle on its side, the narrowest angle forming St David's Head to the West. One approaches across a wide plain from the North, its emptiness relieved by the interlocking of tightly packed strips of field and their bounding walls of turf-covered rocks. One soon notices an irregularity of contour on the horizon which resolves itself into what appears to be two mountains. As one approaches still

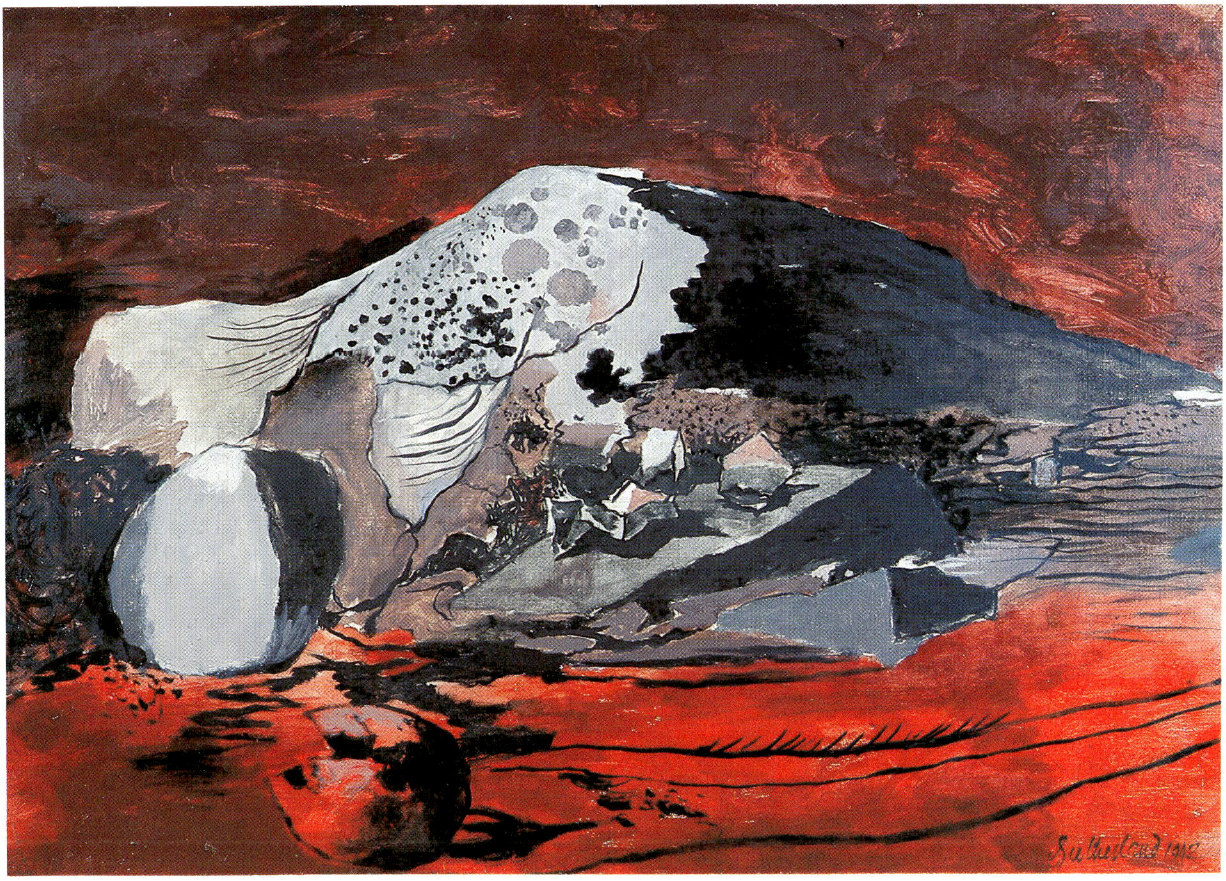

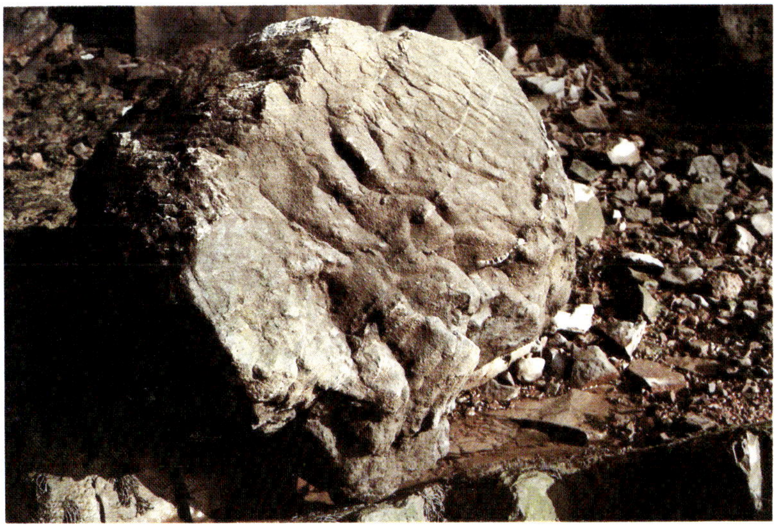

Above
21 *Red Landscape*, 1942
Southampton Art Gallery & Museums

Left
22 Rock shapes provided Sutherland with a wealth of inspiration
Photograph Gilbert Adams FRPS

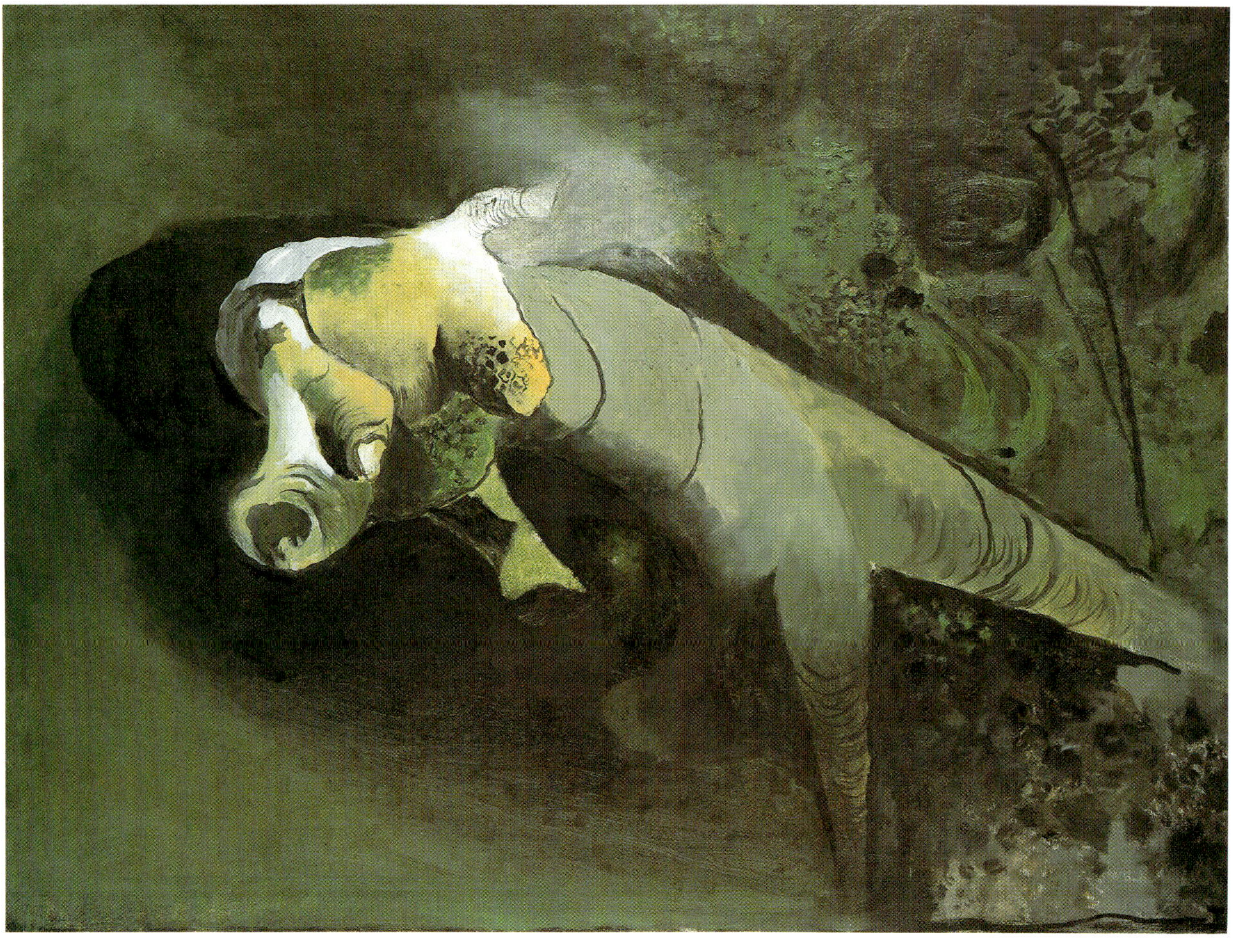

23 *Green Tree Form: Interior of Woods*, 1940
The Tate Gallery, London

closer one sees that these masses of rock scarcely attain a height of more than seven hundred feet. But so classically perfect is their form, and so majestic is their command of the smoothly rising ground below, that the mind comfortably corrects the measurement of the eye, and holds their essential mountainous significance. A rocky path leads round the slopes of the nearer mountain, where to the West, the escarpment precipitates itself to a rock-strewn strip of marsh, marked out with the crazy calligraphy of the foundations of primitive hut dwellings; from here the ground rises to a vast congregation of rocks, fallen cromlechs and goats' caves, which continue their undulating and bewildering disorder, until they plunge, in the terraces of St. David's Head, into the table of the sea. The Southern slopes yield to the plain again, but here the land gradually sloping to the sea is studded with rocky cairns of every size. Between these are fields, each with a spear of rock at its centre. It is as if the solid rock foundation of the earth had thrown up these spears to transfix and hold the scanty earth of the fields upon it. Farms and cottages – glistening white, pink and blue-grey, give scale and quicken by their implications our apprehension of the scene.

In this direction, nearer the sea, the earth is comparatively flat, but this flatness is deceiving and makes the discovery of little steep valleys more surprising. These valleys possess a bud-like intricacy of form and contain streams, often of indescribable beauty, which run to the sea. The astonishing fertility of [these] valleys and the complexity of the roads running through them is a delight to the eye. The roads form strong and mysterious arabesques as they rise in terraces, in sight, hidden, turning and splitting as they finally disappear into the sky. To see a solitary human figure descending such a road at the solemn moment of sunset is to realise the enveloping quality of the earth which can create, as it does here, a mysterious space limit, a womb-like enclosure – which gives the human form an extraordinary focus and significance.

It was in this country that I began to learn painting. It seemed impossible here for me to sit down and make finished paintings 'from nature'. Indeed, there were no 'ready made' subjects to paint. The spaces and concentrations of this clearly constructed land were stuff for storing in the mind. Their essence was intellectual and emotional, if I may say so. I found that I could express what I felt only by paraphrasing what I saw. Moreover, such country did not seem to make man appear little as does some country of the grander sort. I felt just as much part of the earth as my features were part of me. I did not feel that my imagination was in conflict with the real, but that reality was a dispersed and disintegrated form of imagination.

At first, I attempted to make pictures on the spot. But soon I gave this up. It became my habit to walk through, and soak myself in the country. At times I would make small sketches of ideas on the backs of envelopes and in a small sketch book, or I would make drawings from nature of forms which interested me and which I might otherwise forget. The latter practice helped to nourish my ideas and to keep me on good terms with nature. Sometimes, through sheer laziness, I would lie down on the warm shore until my eye, becoming riveted to some sea-eroded rocks, would notice that they were precisely reproducing in miniature the forms of the inland hills. At all events, I never forced myself here, or consciously looked for subjects. I found it better to visit the country because I liked it – and ideas seemed to come gradually and naturally. [3]

One particular place which made a deep visual and creative impact on him was a comparatively insignificant opening to a small copse; an archway of brambles draped with entwined bryony, by an overgrown trickling brook which flows down to Sandy Haven Pill. Here was the source of inspiration for *Entrance to Lane* (1939: Plate 25). Sutherland considered this painting to have the essential qualities of a landscape, yet there are no tree trunks; there is no visible evidence of normal natural forms. It was a question of translating the forms which he was using as subjects into an artistic process which would still remain closely related to nature. In *Entrance to Lane* dense arrangement of entangled form is only *suggested*.

The subject gives us an early glimpse of Sutherland's departure into romantic invention; it also contains clues to his abandoning of conventional perspective and to his virtuosity in handling colour. Wide areas

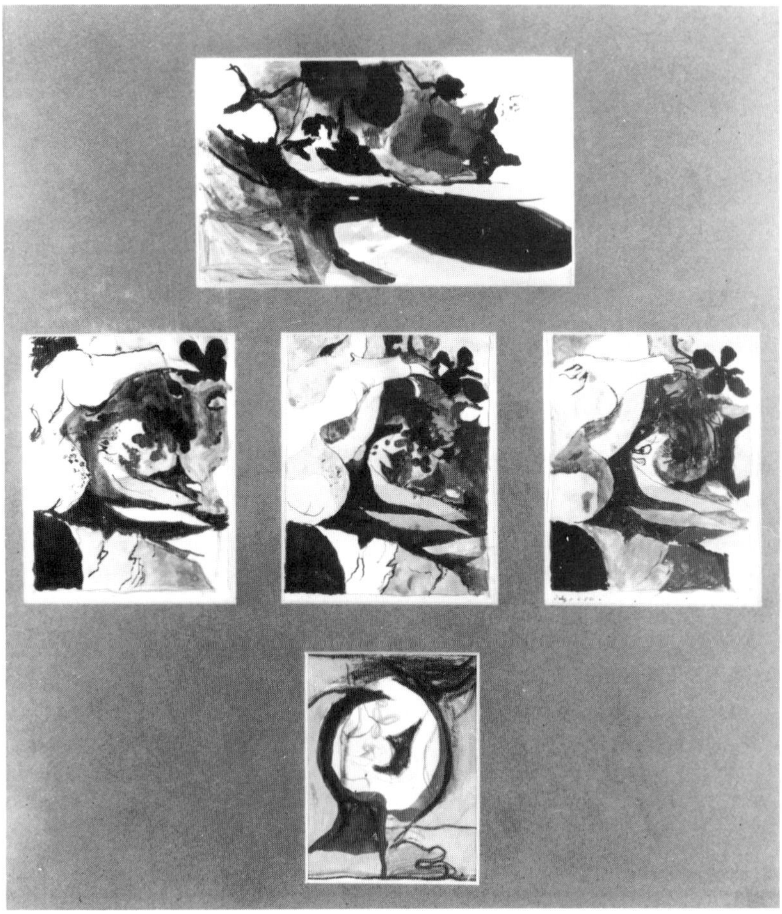

24 Five progressive studies for *Entrance to Lane*, 1939. Very Rev. Walter Hussey

Opposite
25 *Entrance to Lane,* 1939
The Tate Gallery, London

The subject of this painting inspired Sutherland to try some six years later to produce further works in the same lyrical manner but, he explained to the author, they never quite worked out so well. The titles referred to are *Green Lane, Entrance to Lane* and *Entrance to Lane with Interlacing Foliage,* all dated 1945.

of black give the main features of the composition added prominence. In eliminating detail from the archway of trees and its complex foliage, he was able to enhance the design of the natural structure and to convey, with a careful balance of colour, the rather sinister atmosphere of the place. He accepted, in this case, the ingredients provided by nature, sometimes adding, sometimes eliminating, but always balancing the design of areas. Shadows were as important as shapes, enriching the sense of the visual harmony. Curiously, shadows were most often used as shapes and patterns without any significant source of light to cause a shadow to be thrown. Light seemed always to play a dominant part in his mental processes but, strangely, his work seldom emphasizes it, though its effects are used to convey mood and atmosphere. Sutherland had, however, a great love of music and poetry, and his painting was informed by an innate sense of rhythmic cadence.

About the estuary at Sandy Haven Sutherland said, 'I am obsessed by those shapes in the mud.' It was here that he first became aware of the complexity of organic forms, the contours of land, the relationship between roots, rocks, and stones, the identity and juxtaposition of patterns, the relationship which one object fashioned by nature formed with another. Further into the estuary, behind the gulls wheeling over the

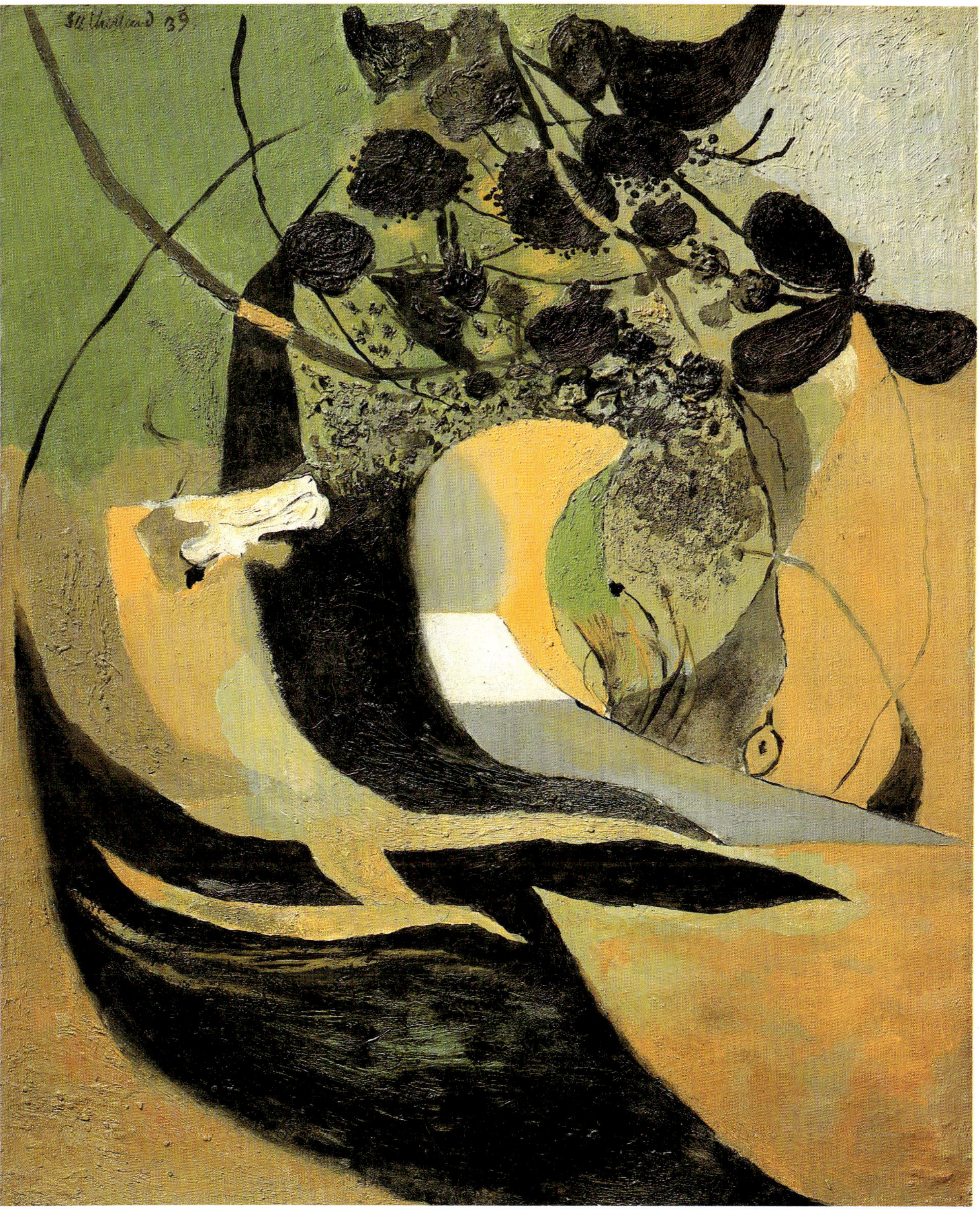

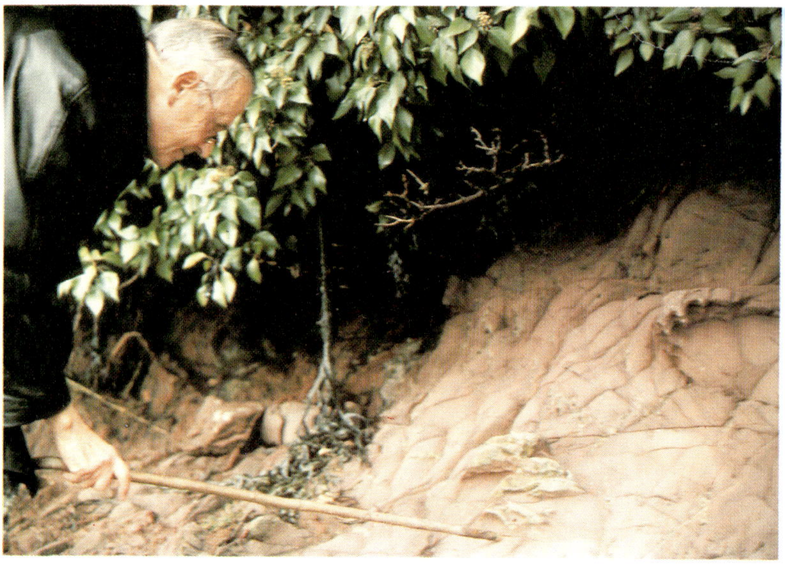

26 Graham Sutherland discovering the variety of patterns in rock
Photograph Gilbert Adams FRPS

mud flats, rests an almost circular solid-looking boulder which has the appearance of three discs welded together by nature. Its lichen-covered body is supported on a pedestal of rampant oak roots. This shape inspired Sutherland's earliest interest in round forms which later became significant in acting as a balance for his vertical and horizontal designs.

An amphitheatre of pink rocks, whose weathered shapes recall the stone forms constructed by man at Petra and Luxor, rises above the mud, overhung by umbrellas of lichen-covered oak. Along these strange tracts of land Sutherland would stump, continually in search of hidden organic minutiae. It was only then when, as he said, 'the beams of light [threw] rhythmic shapes upon the object' that he knew the time was ripe for him to start work. When he sketched, he did so rapidly, repeatedly and with anxious anticipation. He himself wrote, many years later:

> Since 1934, I have used sketchbooks. The reasons for doing this are twofold. Firstly, as a means of planning several versions in miniature of the ideas for the layout of a projected painting. Secondly to make drawings – almost it would seem at random, of something which I encountered: and in examining the sequence of structure before my eyes – with no apparent purpose in sight, except to follow the relationships between one form and another of the things which struck me. Such work can unlock, quite suddenly, the door to an idea which *might* become a painting.
>
> But the activity of drawing direct from nature has its pitfalls. I often put down too many facts – some drawings turn out to be quite useless to me. Others have to be redrawn several times in order to simplify and to clarify. I have had sometimes to return to the place specially because I have been too perfunctory in understanding the structure – what one has drawn seems lacking in equilibrium.
>
> Yet the overall activity of making these notes – (sometimes being led to make far more complex experiments) is enchanting to me and

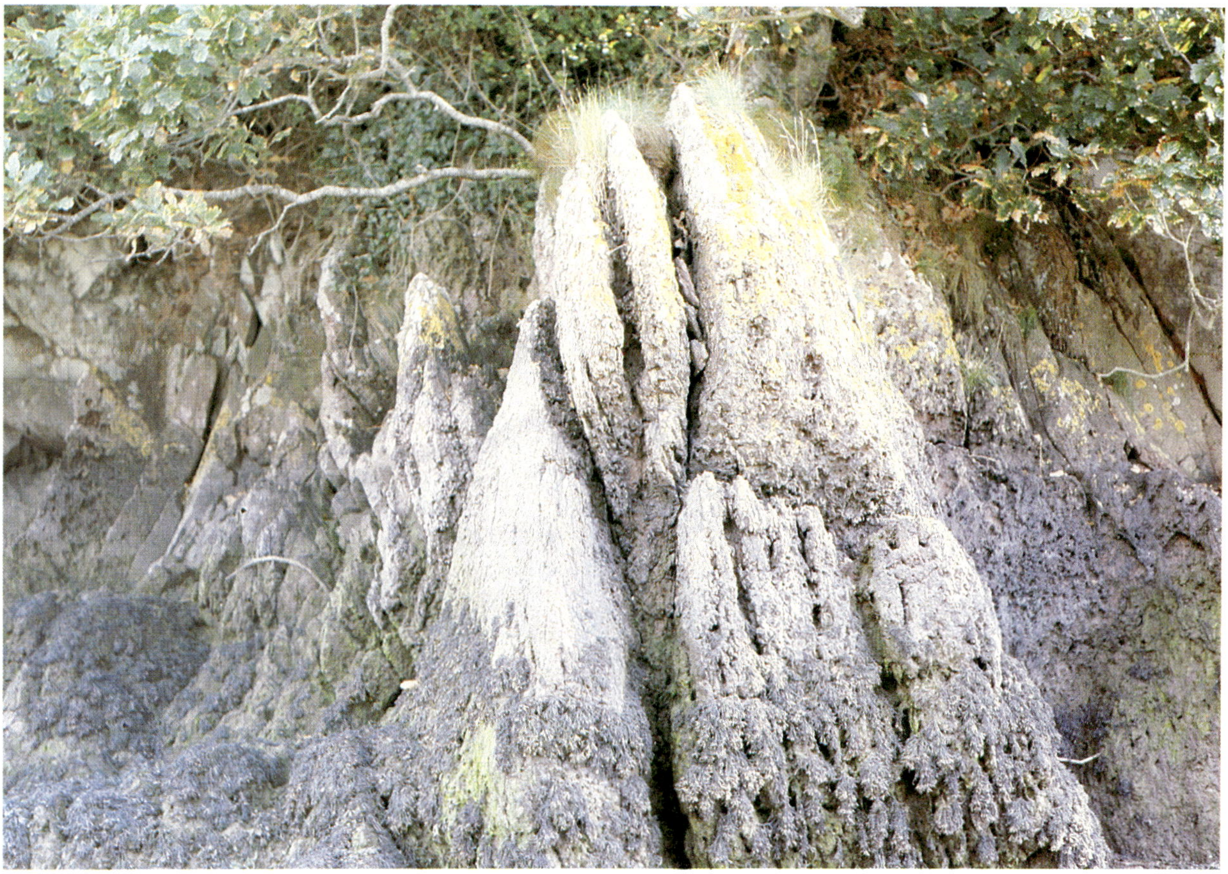

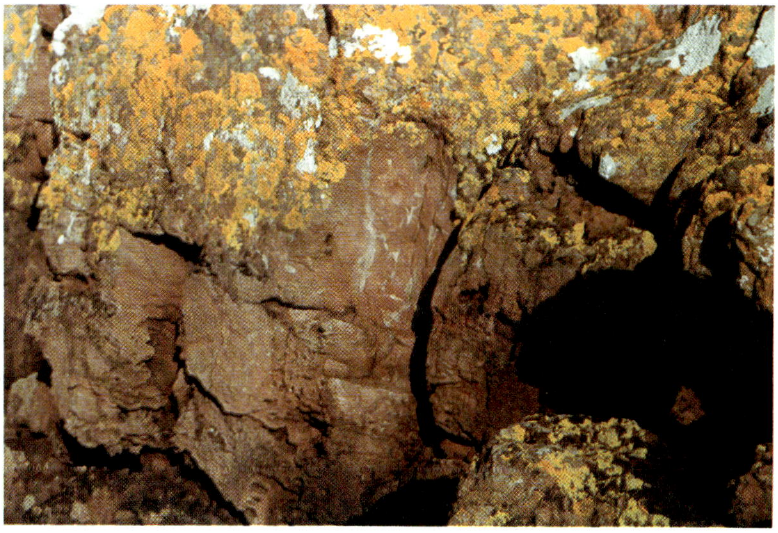

Above
27 Three discs
Photograph Gilbert Adams FRPS

Left
28 Lichen-covered rocks
Photograph Gilbert Adams FRPS

exciting. One feels one has no responsibility (as one has in painting) – or if one has, only to these so-called inanimate objects; they do not press me. There is simply the fascination of things seen, and trying to understand the principles of what one sees.

I do not pretend that the works in these pages are all particularly well done. Rain, *time*, fatigue, awkward and uncomfortable positions alter one's mood and make for variations in quality. Often one sees something fascinating which in reality is flat on the ground and one is moved in one's mind to raise it as an image.

All in all, I look on the hidden places where I work as a marvellous playground – my estuaries as great 'salons' where I am alone with the 'personages' I find. [4]

At the sketchbook stage he eliminated little; certainly he paraphrased; he ferreted for movement, associations of shapes, colours, patterns – the stone, the rock, the root, the mud. The spontaneity with which he produced his sketches was all-important. If he were to go on beyond the

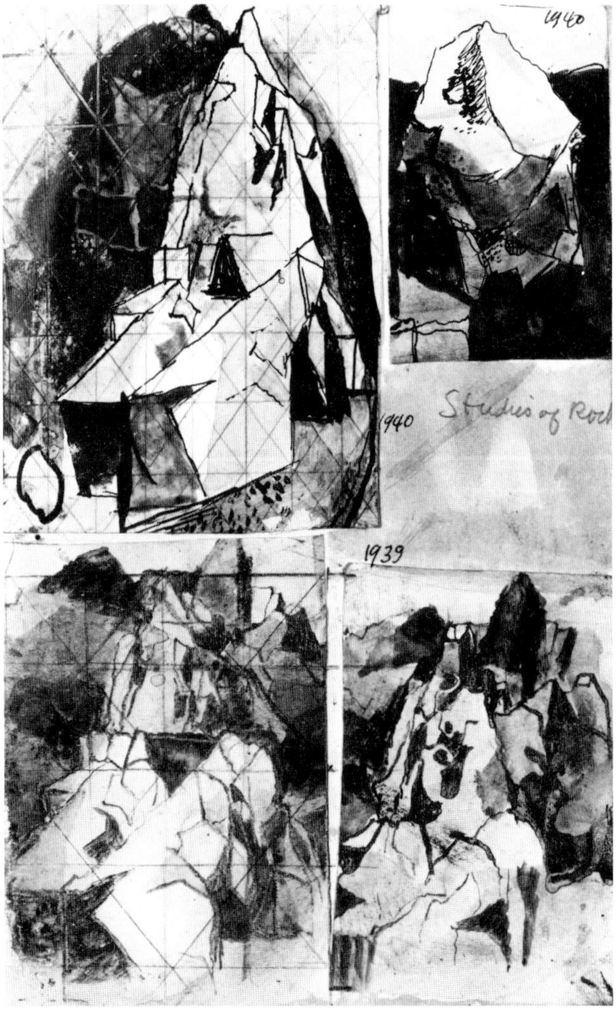

29 Four *Studies of Rock*, 1939-40
Graham and Kathleen Sutherland Foundation, Picton Castle Trust

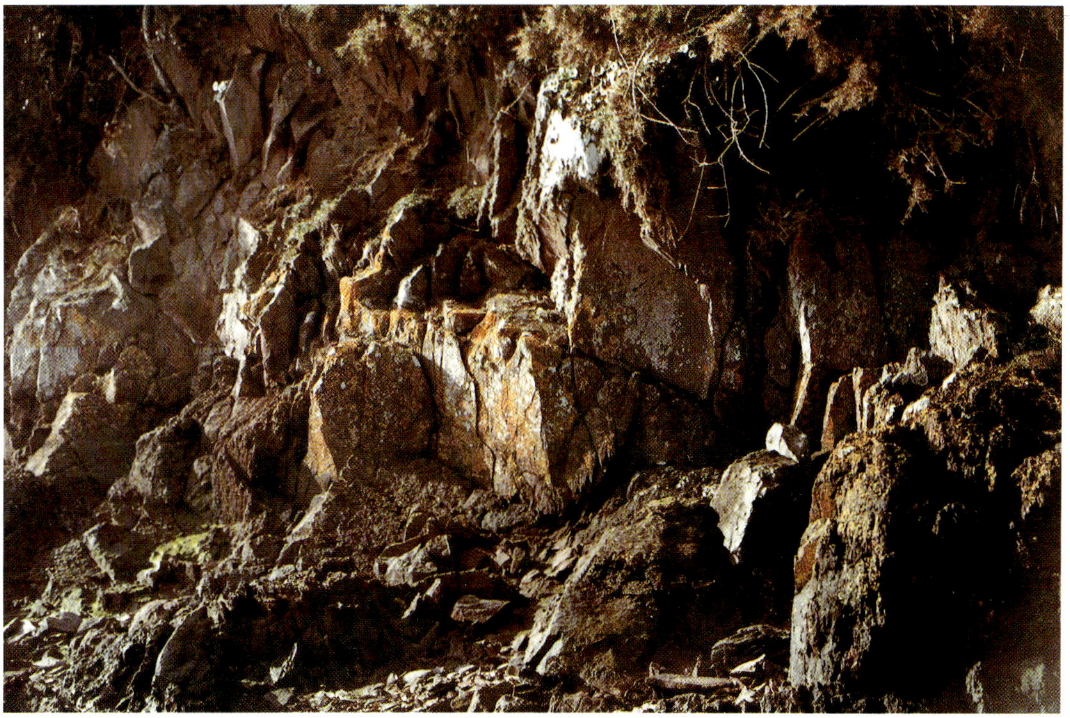

30 Rock study with shadow
Photograph Gilbert Adams FRPS

spontaneous statement, he would be likely to spoil the message that he wished to convey. The sketches were complete in themselves and required no further explanation. Inspired and exciting, these early Pembrokeshire landscapes were self-sufficient.

The rocks of Pembrokeshire, mostly grey, take on, with certain angles of the sun and rain, a curious ambivalence of colour so that at times they can appear mauve, at times pink, occasionally yellow. Dark, impenetrable corners of the estuary suddenly become lit with an incisive light, changing the greys to yellows, the red to purple. Sutherland responded to the richness of what he saw and the variety of topography which surrounded him and arranged his palette accordingly.

Painting, until this time, was a medium with which Sutherland had been barely acquainted. By 1934 his engraving and etching days were over. He was teaching composition and book illustration at Chelsea School of Art, and was ready to seek a new medium through which to earn his living and to gain recognition. His few earlier attempts at painting had been abandoned and the work thrown out. 'My early works were so inept,' he once said to me, 'I felt I had to discard them.' Until the beginning of the thirties Sutherland had been concerned with the broad landscape, the depiction of scenery. This was particularly well conveyed in *The Black Rabbit* (1923: Plate 13), an etching of a view in Sussex – a subject whose scenic qualities availed to him extensive compositional possibilities. It seems Sutherland's most successful expression of the general scene. He presented the elements with grandiose effect, in spite of the somewhat limited medium he was then using. For some years he portrayed the rural scenes of Dorset and Kent in a conventional landscape manner. Then, however, he began to seek new ways of representing what he saw, not by merely imitating but by producing something more personal and complementary to visible reality. He sought also ways in which his subjects could be accepted by a more European-inspired art public. Although he retained certain English qualities, his work became more exciting. The dual role of invention and professionalism began to emerge.

It was about this time that he began to take note of the type of work being exhibited in Europe and, in particular, of what was selling. He hoped to find commercial possibilities for his own painting. He had seen the inventive surrealistic style of Paul Nash's landscapes, but although he admired Nash's approach to landscape, he was not convinced that it was appropriate to his own vision. There are certain parallels at this time between the mystical shapes with which Nash was concerned and Sutherland's own discoveries of nature; these similarities are best seen in Sutherland's *Stones in an Enclosure* (1936: Plate 31), in his *Mên an Tol* (1933) and in Nash's *Event on the Downs* (1934). The parallel continued until the late thirties when Sutherland's portrayal of roots and boulders, became more personal, forceful, close-up, inventive and individual.

The acquaintance with Nash's landscape work gave Sutherland additional reassurance, convincing him that it would be possible to convey, not in Nash's surrealistic terms, but in his own language, his discoveries of the relationship of shapes in landscape. He was concerned to adapt his own awareness, his particular language, to the commercially accepted European modern art movement. That he wished to break with certain English traditions in painting is also clear. He was determined not

31 *Stones in an Enclosure*, 1936
Graham and Kathleen Sutherland Foundation Picton Castle Trust

The composition of this work can be said to have foreshadowed much of Sutherland's subsequent painting. Although Sutherland could not quite remember the location, he thought it was near Clegyr Boir; this elliptical stone is on the westward slope of the hill overlooking White Sands Bay.

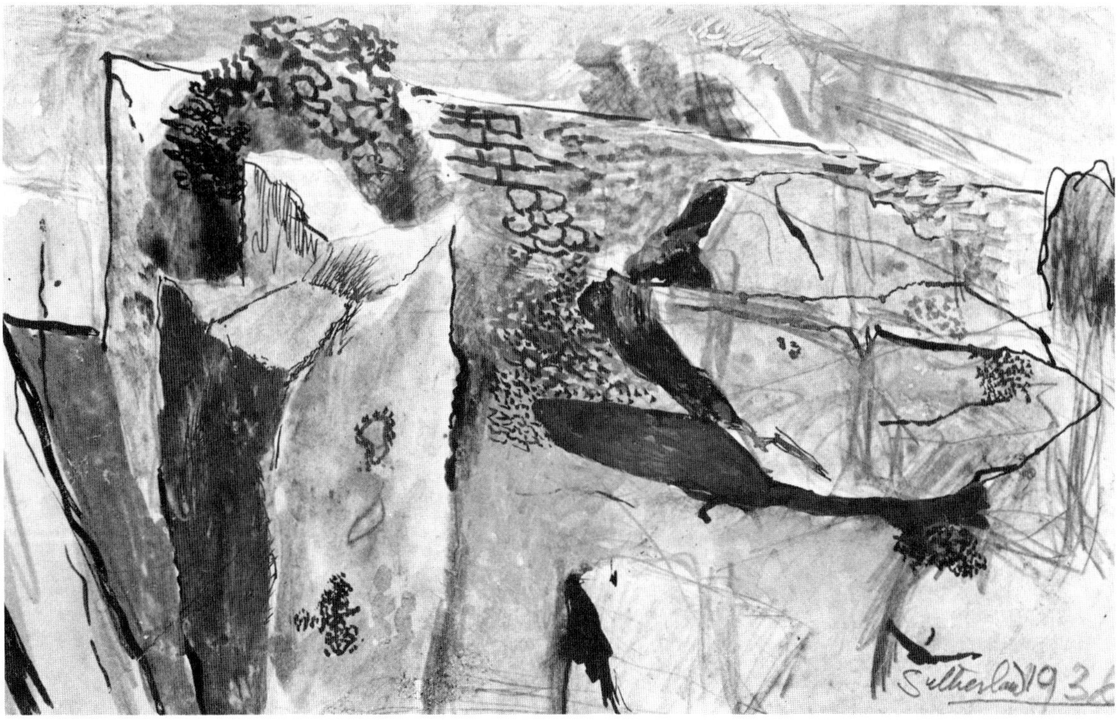

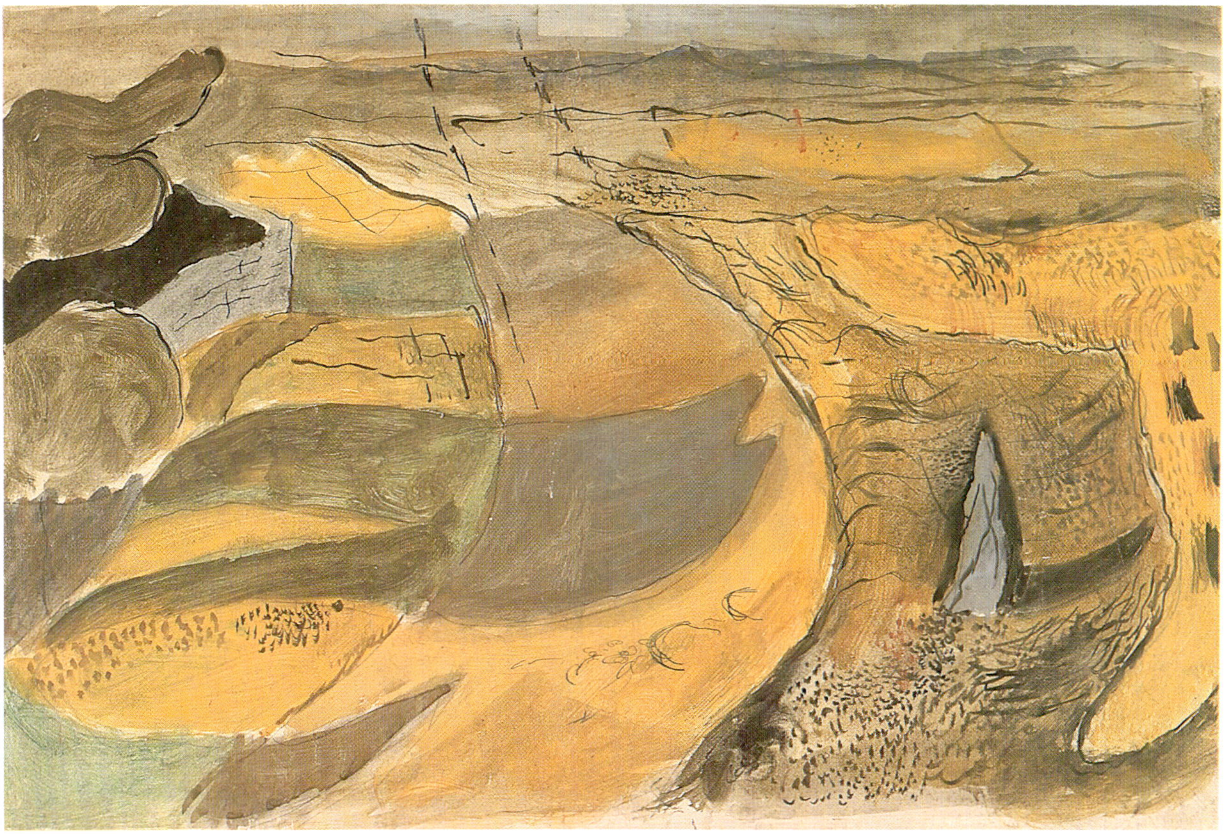

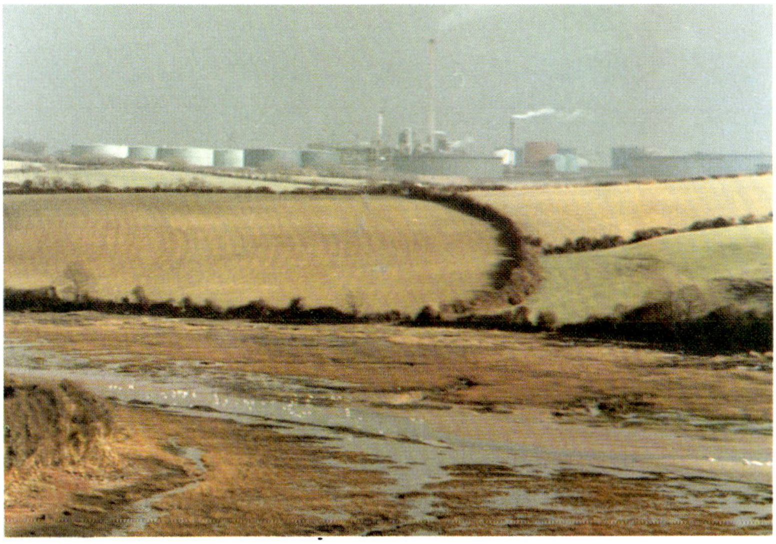

Above
32 *Pembrokeshire Landscape*, 1936
National Museum of Wales, Cardiff

Left
33 Pembrokeshire landscape, the horizon now peppered with oil refineries
Photograph Gilbert Adams FRPS

to become party to any of the schools which were then emerging in England. Through tenacity of spirit he invented his own style, slowly became recognized, and survived. He was, he told me, conditioned by what was happening on the continent to see in the forms that were captivating his attention in Pembrokeshire, certain reflections of compositional structure he had seen in European painting at that time. In so far as was possible for a yet untravelled painter, he had looked at paintings and reproductions of the work of many European artists, including Picasso, Kandinski, Miró and de Chirico, but at that time there was no direct connection between Sutherland and any of these painters. One does, however, observe a closer relationship of style much later, after the war, when the influence of the French painters in particular had a direct bearing on Sutherland's vision.

With this European dimension in mind, Sutherland tried to communicate the mystical quality of the Pembrokeshire landscape by breaking down the scenic element and concentrating, as Douglas Cooper says, 'on a few features which he found vitally expressive'. The twist in a cliff lane became the inspiration for a composition: the sort of undulating, curving, serpent-like roads which follow the sun, whose permeating rays strengthen the profile of the distant hills between Littlehaven and Newgale. These wriggling, uphill, branching routes proved to be an increasingly resonant and successful theme throughout Sutherland's work. *Welsh Landscape with Roads* (1936), *Solva and Valley above Porthclais* (1935), *Gower Landscape* (1941), *Landscape with Road* (1976), *Pembrokeshire Landscape* (1936: Plate 32) and *Porthclais with Setting Sun* (1979: Plate 111) are all works that convey an obsession with the way in which excavation has cut through the natural landscape. When he became inspired by a series of shapes he returned to it often, producing paintings which were more or less 'variations on a theme'. Characteristic places which provided ever-increasing inspiration were Benton, Porthclais and Sandy Haven. It is up to the reader to decide whether the first or final work in a series is the more expressive.

Many painters endeavour to present a scenic view, especially those who have worked in Pembrokeshire. This was not the aim of Sutherland; he wished to dig deeper, to isolate the objects he saw, to paraphrase, and to bring about a rebirth. This he frequently did by eliminating much that was purely representational. He had a strong sense of obligation to communicate what he saw by using his own particular romantic poetry and, although wishing us to have an idea of the source of a painting and requiring that we should understand his language, he preferred to retain a certain sense of mystery. Although he maintained that areas and objects should not be exactly identifiable, he did, in a sense, interpret a scene or object hoping that the viewer would recognize it – that there would be a measure of rapport between viewer and painting.

About *Gorse on Sea Wall* (1939), one of the paintings which established his reputation and place amongst the then popular neo-romantics, he wrote in 1942 to a friend:

> The twisted gorse on the cliff edge, such as suggested the picture – twigs, like snakes, lying on the path, the bare rock, worn, and showing through the path, heath fires, gorse burnt and blackened

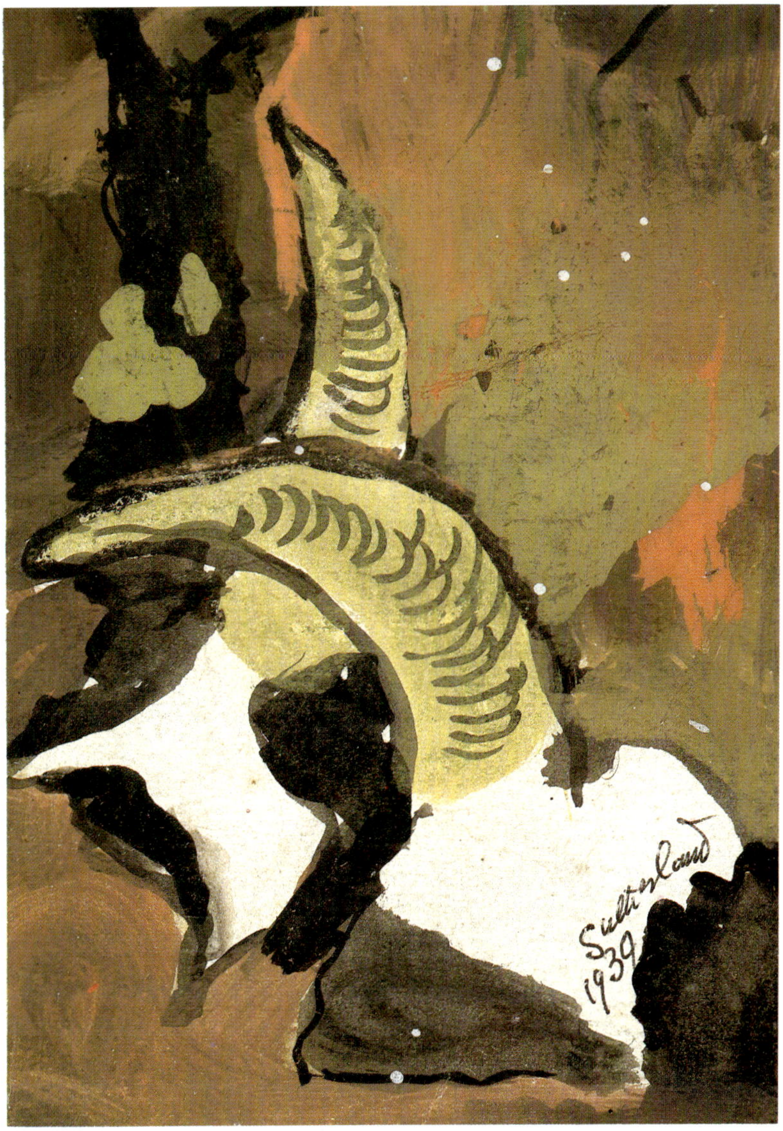

34 *Cow's Horns*, 1939
Crane Kalman Gallery, London

The shapes Sutherland found in these objects became later, in 1944, the subject of a series titled *Horned Forms* and later, in a modified form, the *Thorn* series.

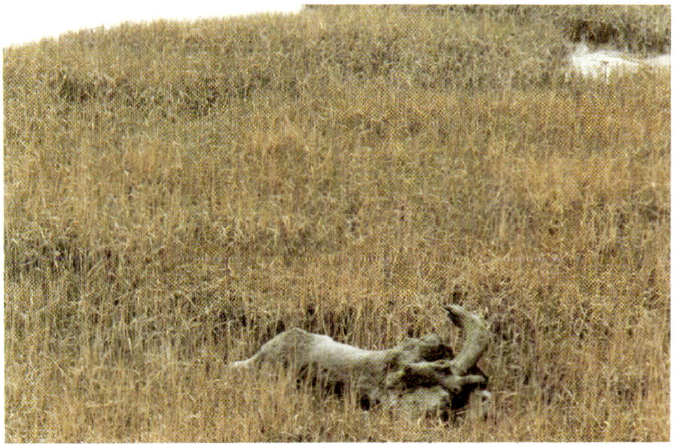

35 Dendritic shapes left rotting on the foreshore
Photograph Gilbert Adams FRPS

> after fire, a tin school in an exuberant landscape, the high, overhanging hedges by the steep roads which pinch the setting sun, mantling clouds against a black sky and the thunder, the flowers and damp hollows, the farmer galloping on his horse down the estuary, the deep green valleys and the rounded hills and the white structure, simple and complex. [5]

In the painting he took a dramatic yet simple vision and re-created the personal exciting essence which revealed itself at the time. 'It is necessary', he said, 'to work parallel with nature. We are deceived if we work contrary to our inclinations or to nature.'

Much later, writing about his mature work, he said:

> The mysteries of the boundaries of objects: an object lying on the grass in the sunlight, casting its shadow. The eye becomes a shuttle and drives the woof of the one between the weft of the other. If I feel I must paraphrase what I see, it is because to do so gives me a shock of surprise, a new valuation of things, as if I had never seen them before. I want to give the *look* of things to my emotionally modified forms.
>
> I believe that a painter's vision must grow out of reality – and that the mysteriously intangible must be made immediate and tangible. My forms are based on the principles of organic growth. With these I have been pre-occupied always. So too in painting, by a substitution – by personification, by a paraphrase or a special way of putting things we can shed a succinct light on the nature of things and emotions – enabling us to know more about their essence and causing them to hold more than their original meaning. [6]

Another place that particularly appealed to Sutherland was St Ishmael's, where he conceived the idea of *La Primavera* (1975: Plate 110) and *St Ishmael's* (1974-5: Plate 126). I have stood where the road branches out from St Ishmael's to Soldiers' Rocks, with the wind approaching from the east, bringing a snow shower swirling horizontally northward, inwards to land. The watch tower provides a dismal shelter from which to gaze on particles of mist in Milford Sound. These areas, to which Sutherland returned year after year, when the hawthorn was in full blossom, when the air was biting, seem full of ominous portent. And round that protrusion of land towards St David's, walking down to Porthclais in the setting sun, conscious of former stone dwellings around a minuscule inlet enclaved by dark hills, listening to the light dribble of water, is an ecstatic experience; a mystical attraction invites return, and certainly Sutherland felt the significance of this inlet. These little corners in a big land provided the inspiration for his early works and for his later Pembrokeshire landscapes.

Kenneth Clark described Sutherland's intimacy with nature in the following terms:

> Some object which he has passed dozens of times before, suddenly emerges from obscurity and becomes intensely real. For some mysterious reason it has provided the satisfactory visual equivalent of ideas and feeling which were at the time occupying his mind. It is usually a humble and unremarkable subject – not, as his imitators

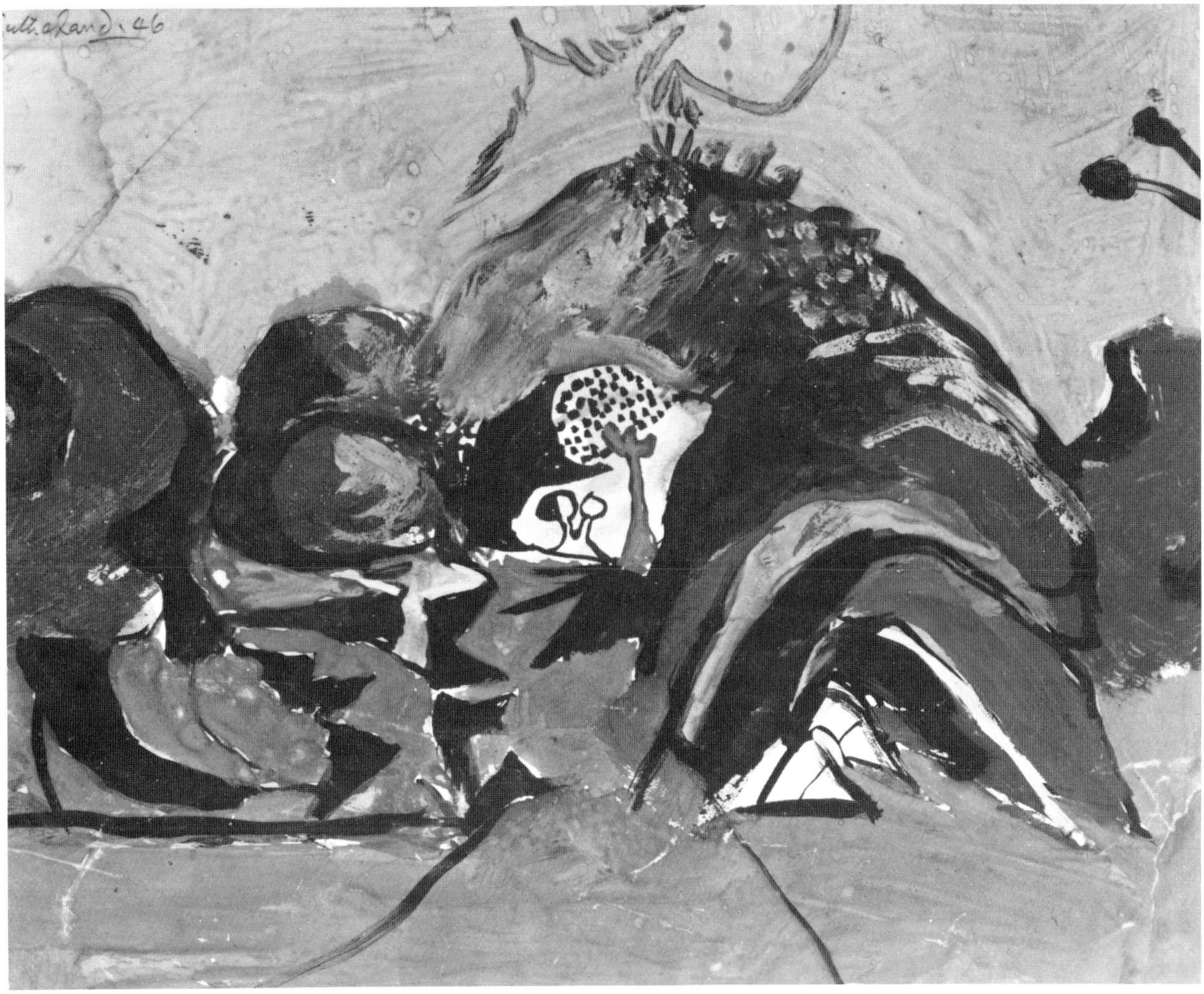

> suppose, a shape curious in itself; true, some of his tree roots were, from the start, rather alarming; but most of his *objets trouvés*, gorse, thorns, cow parsley, palm branches, are familiar spectacles which no one thought of finding strange till he recognized them. The object, then, announces itself, and is noted in a small, accurate drawing, and there begins a process of adaptation and pictorial discipline. It is brought more into conformity with the inner idea of which it was the rough equivalent. To some extent this is the process of all artistic creation, but with Sutherland it often produces a curious result; the objects found end by becoming new things, which seem more vividly real to him than were the original data of sight. [7]

36 *Estuary with Rocks*, 1946
The British Council, London
This study conveys the emergence of the half-human, half-organic figures in landscape.

Many of the embryonic shapes found and re-created by him in the thirties were to continue to have importance, for, although at first they were used more or less as part of, or in, a scenic landscape, later these shapes were withdrawn, lifted out of their original environment, isolated, and used as a separate structure. There is evidence of illusionary human configuration in *Studies of a Landscape* (1936) and in *Estuary with Rocks* (1946: Plate 36). The emergence of the obscure half human, half organic structure can be envisaged sporadically as early as the late thirties. He was not to return in any conscious way to such a vein of discovery until the late forties and fifties when he attempted the *Standing Form* subjects.

In *Studies of a Landscape* we see already the genesis of an idea, later to be developed in a subject such as *Standing Forms against a Hedge* (1951). Although humans are rarely given a significant role except by their spiritual presence, in *Welsh Landscape with Roads* (1936) a broad, masterly painting, there is every evidence of both human and animal reaching for the horizon. The leg of the dancing mannequin breaks the otherwise monotonous line of the horizon. Sutherland kept the construction of human individuals unobtrusive in the thirties; he did, however, say that he felt better if humanity was in attendance. He was contradictory in this respect. Many years later, in 1976, looking up across a viridian field which was high above an estuary and coated with spray fertilizer, he saw that the skyline had been changed since the thirties by the addition of an oil refinery chimney, and remarked to me that there was a certain comfort in feeling that people were not too far away. But in those heavy umbelliferous undergrowths where he trod a lonely step, he hated to be disturbed; his mind, he said, and his eyes, had to be focused on what he hoped and anticipated was about to reveal itself. His walks did, however, bring occasional encounters with, say, a fisherman or a boat-builder, and although in essence he remained all his life a loner, part of the land, yet he was interested in humanity – the daily life of the ordinary man – and would always pause to pass the time of day.

There can be no doubt that the first encounter with the Pembrokeshire countryside changed Sutherland's life. It was a metamorphosis. There are constant reminders in his later work – the French subjects, the religious subjects, and his war scenes – that even when he had spent some years away from Wales, the sources of his inspiration derived from there. In Pembrokeshire he felt it his job 'to reveal the associated and almost

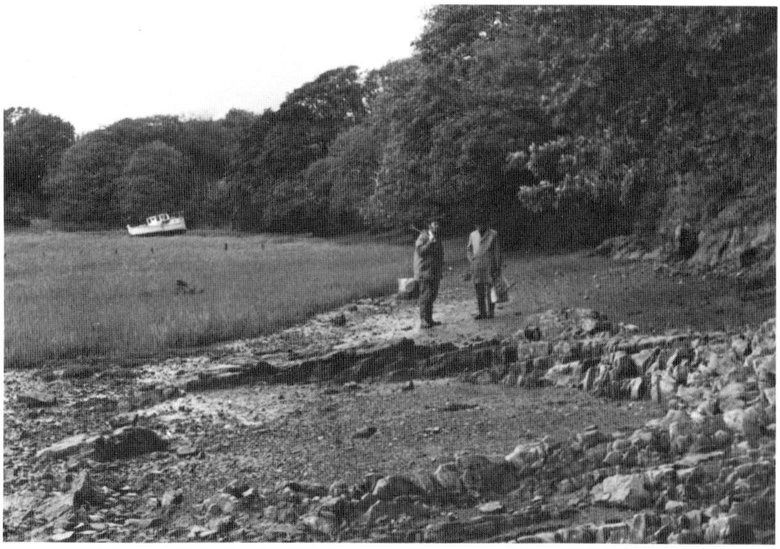

37 Graham Sutherland in conversation with fisherman on Picton shore
Photograph Gilbert Adams FRPS

hidden stresses and relationship which, in science, is done by X-rays; the pattern changes with the angle of the beam and the face of the crystal you shine on it.' [8] His stimulation came from characteristics he found within the shape. He would magnify significant features or reduce forms to a minute scale, according to whether they were of prime or subordinate importance to his requirements. The early designs he made in England, his experiments with patterns on squared-up pieces of paper, appear in retrospect to be a restless, anxious, exciting search for reassurance that it – his own individual way of interpreting nature – could work. The drawings have a somewhat hesitant quality, yet they are strong in concept. He had, after all, used line with great precision during his engineering training and his engraving days.

Pembrokeshire has a curious, cruel, mysterious atmosphere. It has certainly proved magnetic for Sutherland and for other painters. Through the tracery of entwining oaks an explosive light descends upon the ebbing tide of the Eastern Cleddau. From a marshy swamp a fan of runnels rises to the opposite shore at Landshipping. The dreamy silence, broken only by the curlew's call, the heavy flapping heron and the boat-builder hammering intermittently, heralds the area of Pembrokeshire where lies Picton, now the centre of Sutherland's gift to the nation. The Graham Sutherland Gallery at Picton Castle is embedded deep in the surrounding woodland. The gift, made in 1976, was in recognition of all that Sutherland felt he had derived from the Welsh landscape.

Chapter IV
WAR YEARS

With the outbreak of the Second World War in 1939 came the closure of the Chelsea School of Art and the end of Sutherland's regular teaching career. The war also terminated, in a sense, the first phase of Sutherland's regular visits to Pembrokeshire. He had already been faced with problems when his print market collapsed in 1930, as a result of the Depression. Now, only a decade later, circumstances forced him to limit his visits to Wales and, up to a point, his continual discovery of nature.

When war broke out, Kenneth Clark took the Sutherlands into his home in Gloucestershire. He was the chairman of the War Artists' Advisory Committee and it was he who suggested that Sutherland should become an official War Artist. Sutherland was appointed in August 1940. Among the other important artists who were employed for successive periods throughout the war were Edward Ardizzone, Edward Bawden, Muirhead Bone, Stephen Bone, Henry Carr, Leslie Cole, William Dring, Charles Cundall, Evelyn Dunbar, Richard Eurich, Barnett Freedman, Anthony Gross, Bernard Hailstone, Thomas Hennell, Eric Kennington, Henry Lamb, Paul Nash, Vivian Pitchforth. In taking up the challenge to depict scenes of war, as he did, Graham Sutherland had to face interpreting images quite alien to his familiar natural phenomena. But Sutherland was disciplined, diligent, determined and possessed of extensive vision and imagination, attributes which could readily be adapted to the horrifying situation. He reacted quite sincerely, with appropriate awareness, to the subject matter with which he was now faced, and produced five hundred works between September 1940 and November 1944. Roberto Tassi, in his introduction to the catalogue of the 1979 exhibition in Milan of Sutherland's war drawings, describes his earlier works, *Gorse on Sea Wall* and *Green Tree Form: Interior of Woods* (Plate 23), as 'great examples of invention'. In wartime, invention was not the point; the war paintings had at least to tell a story or convey an experience.

When confronted with this new pressure, Sutherland at first found it difficult to adjust. The artillery ranges at Melton Mowbray, Leicestershire, which he was asked to visit, did not overtly inspire him. A magnificent, fluid, steel grey watercolour *Breech Blocks in the Shop at Gun-Testing Range* (1940: Plate 38) proved, however, that he was more than adequately equipped to interpret mechanical subjects and adapt to new challenge. This painting demonstrates how effective had been his early training in engineering and it foreshadows the passion he later had for using machinery to form part of a large composition.

In September 1940 Sutherland was posted to Swansea, which had just

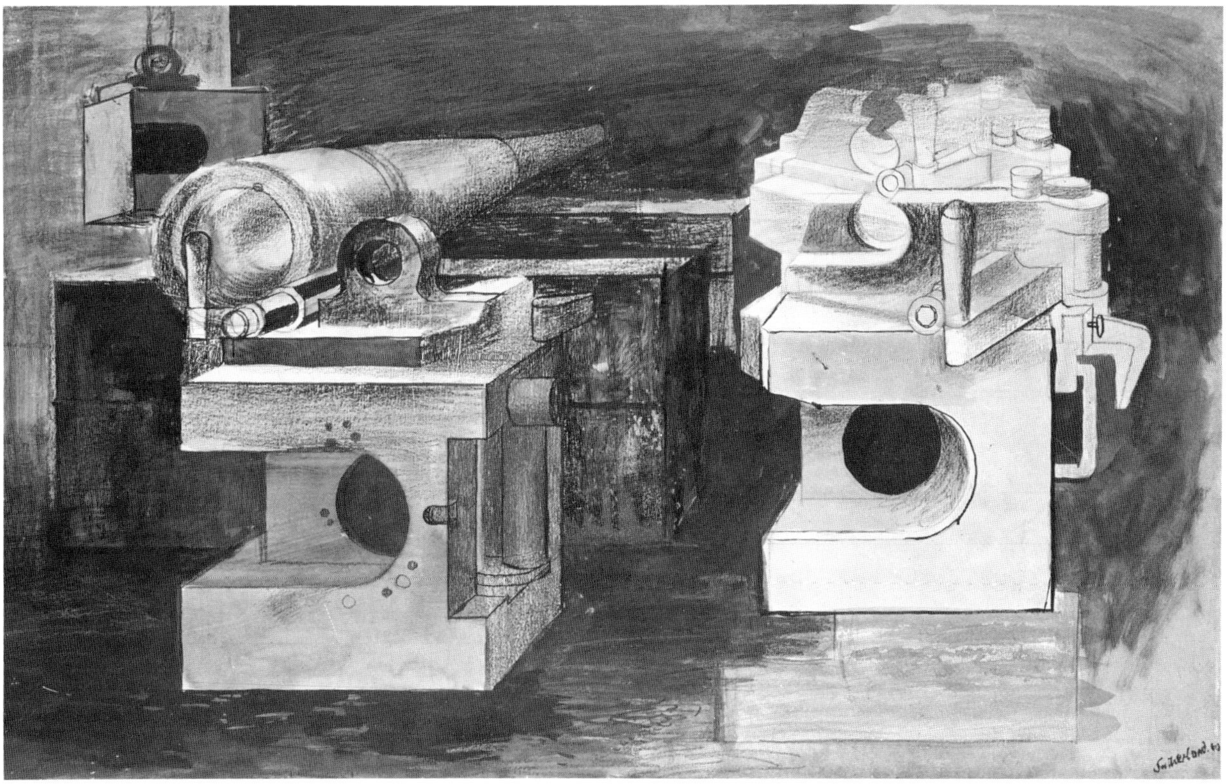

38 *Breech Blocks in the Shop at Gun-Testing Range*, 1940
Imperial War Museum, London

been heavily bombed. This gave him his first opportunity to portray solid Victorian architecture. Six or seven works were done – a large oil and several gouaches. In *Devastation – House in Wales* (1940), the delicious quality of colour curiously romanticizes the destruction. Back in London, however, Sutherland came face to face with the true nature of mass destruction in terms of the 1941 Blitz. The silent City, with its ruined office blocks, many of them shattered to the ground and tumbled into contorted positions, supplied him with a rich variety of subjects whose shapes had a certain parallel with the nature forms he had formerly discovered. These shapes became, in a way, an extension of subjects familiar to him, yet they provided an instant inspiration of their own. In common with others, he found himself living for the moment; every day had to be lived as though there were no tomorrow, and yet he recalled never feeling really desperate. He was receptive to challenge, even though at times it frightened him. And had he not experienced often a mixture of apprehension and anticipation, I doubt whether his work would have had such a powerful impact as it so evidently did.

He spent many days and nights in the City, wandering alone around the flattened area near St Paul's and experiencing the terrible smells and the silence, interrupted by bomb explosions and the intermittent sound of tinkling glass. The crumbling buildings offered him immense variety of forms to portray. The womb-like interiors of empty offices, the range of

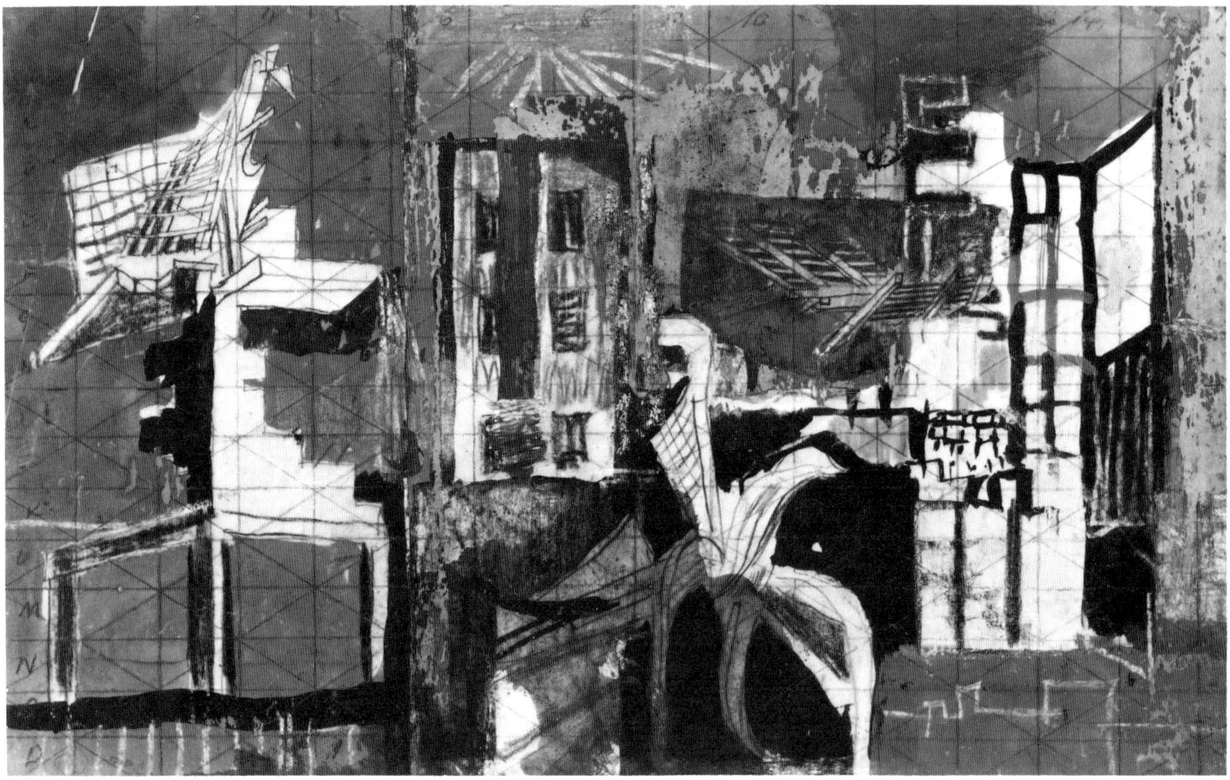

39 *Devastation*, 1941
Collection Mrs Graham Sutherland

patterns created by fallen, twisted girders, corresponded with the tangled roots in pre-war Wales. The cavernous underground tunnels, wriggling like snakes, were illustrated with more realistic and conventional perspective than was his previous nature work, and there was a conscious effort to convey the actuality of the situation.

Not only did the experience bring fresh inspiration to his art, it also provided fresh energy and drive. To accept the fact that he was earning a living as an official War Artist, a sort of war correspondent, he felt both that he had truly to earn that money, and that he had to seek a way to represent with immediacy the subjects assigned to him.

In *Devastation – City – Twisted Girders* (1941), one notes that he uses the subject as an opportunity to extricate his mind from man-made destruction and return to those nature-eroded shapes in Wales, painting with an already familiar palette of aggressive yellows and blacks. Where the relationship between the war and Wales is especially evident is in *Devastation – East End – Burnt-out Paper Rolls* (1941). In spite of the destructive element of his subject, Sutherland managed, as previously, to re-create a harmonious relationship between his forms in a composition using the perpendicular, horizontal and round forms – that same correspondence of geometrical shapes which had been his chief concern in his landscapes and which manifested itself in the major part of his work. When he moved to the East End of London Sutherland came face to face with human misery. The place had a profound effect on Sutherland's awareness. The sombre atmosphere of an evacuated

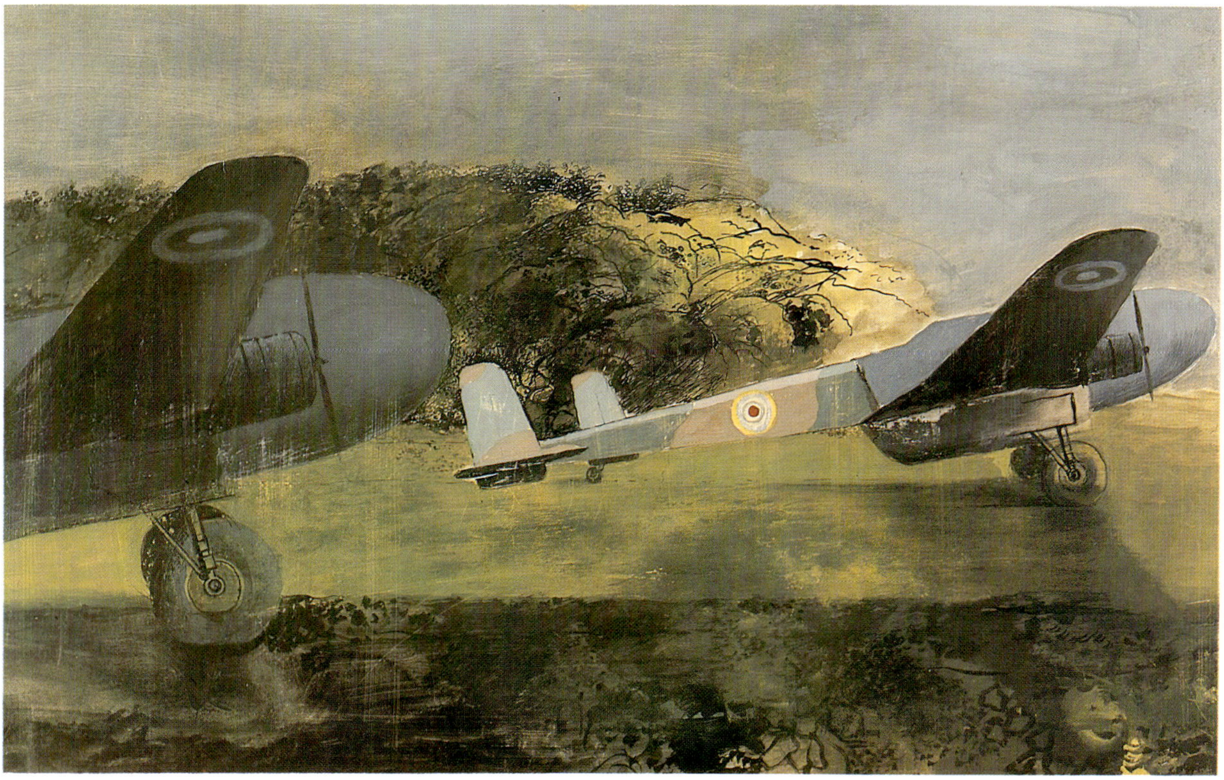

40 *Picketed Aircraft*, 1941
Imperial War Museum, London

community was hauntingly described with magnificent use of perspective in *Devastation – East End Street* (1941).

Activity in the tin mines in Cornwall was one area of production which supported the battlefield. At the suggestion of Kenneth Clark Sutherland was sent to Cornwall to record the activities. He never forgot the mysterious and beautiful qualities of that landscape. At the beginning he imagined he would suffer claustrophobia in the mines, although of course in Wales, exploring in search of subjects, he had deliberately chosen claustrophobic areas of undergrowth. He once described to me the hair-raising descent down a tin mine at St Just. When the lift, which travelled down at over fifty miles an hour, reached the fourteenth level below ground, he began to shake, not realizing at the time that a further three hundred metres had to be climbed down on foot. Still trembling, he managed it, and only afterwards was told that it would have been impossible to fall. In the galleries he realized it would not be difficult to lose oneself. The shafts, vaginal openings and declivities he encapsulated with vividness and imagination once he began to make studies of the scene. That Sutherland found each new experience a challenge is evident by the way he expressed with such forceful rendering each part of the mine and the activities of the miners. In these burrows of underground activity one could hear the muffled sounds of miners working away on other levels. The atmosphere was womb-like, humid, warm. Sutherland portrayed the instant labours of the miners crouched in embryonic position; he depicted man utilizing nature; in exploring the situation of

Right
41 *Tin Mine, Emerging Miner*, 1944
City Art Gallery, Leeds

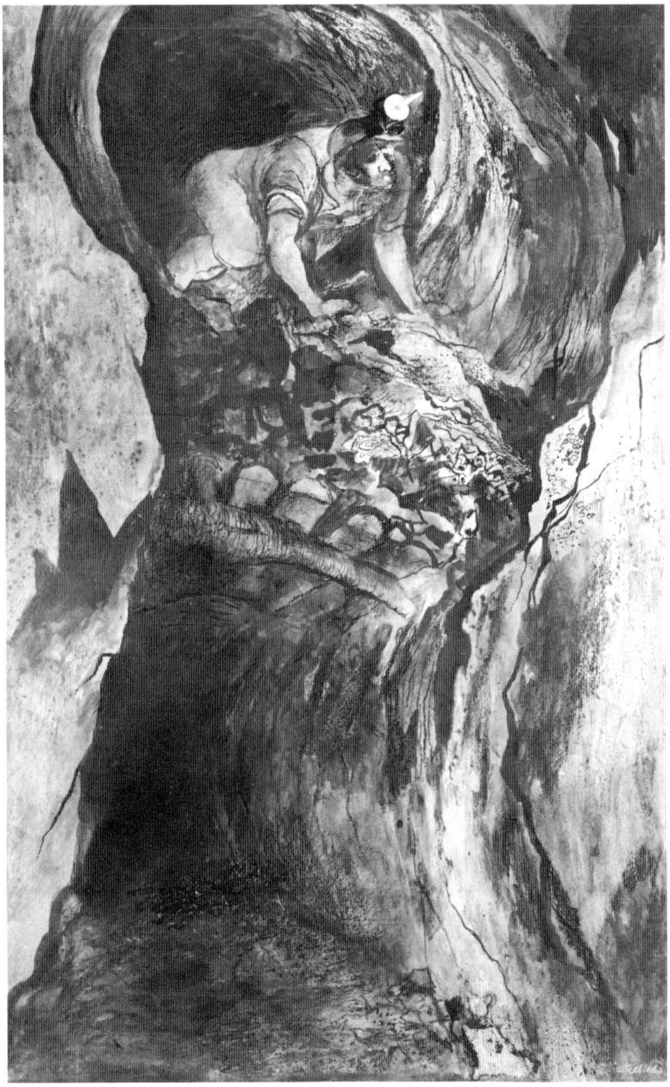

Below
42 A series of intricate forms in
Pembrokeshire
Photograph Gilbert Adams FRPS

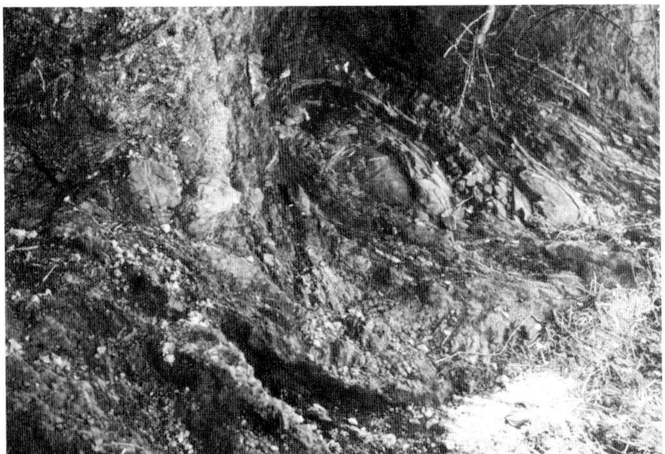

man at work, and one with his labours, Sutherland went far beyond his later study of personalities. The portrayal of human figures in the mine subjects, the first real use since his etching days of people in a situation, was made with complete compassion, sincerity and perception, whereas previously he had merely shown subordinate figures in a few of the earlier Pembrokeshire landscapes.

It was essential for Sutherland the War Artist to express the activities of man, especially in the tin mines, as without those figures the holes and chasms would have had neither scale nor meaning. The war effort was the contribution that each individual made, so the human figure had of necessity to be included.

Several paintings emerged during the period of Sutherland's war work, conveying his personal and profound endeavour to make a departure into the portrayal of people. These include *Studies of Gypsies* (1939), *Landscape with Figures* (1944), *Woman in a Garden* (1945: Plate 86), *Study for Woman with Apple* (1945) and *Woman in a Chair* (1945), together with some studies of his wife. *Man and Fields* (1944), *Triple-Tiered Landscape* (1944), *Smiling Woman* (1945) and *Woman Picking Vegetables* (1945) are others which suggest that these years were far more explorative and far-reaching in terms of his own private painting than Sutherland would have had us later believe when he discussed at length his *Standing Form* figures. ('Figures should be unidentifiable in landscape.') It was about this time that he seems to have recognized the importance of the ordinary man in the scheme of human endeavour. He had an obvious interest in individuals, selecting his friends and later choosing his portrait subjects with great care and discrimination, and it was at this stage that he appears to have accepted the role of humanity in the mass. Later, when he became seriously interested in the portrait, it was as if he moved into a close-up of the face. Many portraits were, of course, exceptions to this, and became the more successful. I find that Sutherland was able to create the most moving portrayal of tin miners. Their attitudes, their positions, were revealed as authentically human – whether they were crouching, drilling, resting in wall cavities, or examining the roof of a slope. Their faces had strength and character. Sutherland was happy for the time, coming to terms with the introduction of the human presence, and these studies of miners are among his most successful war efforts.

Whilst the difficulties of the war photographer's task must be dealt with on the spot, the painter has the opportunity to assimilate, often working up sketches into the final painting. The conditions under which Sutherland made his original sketches were often, however, of extreme discomfort. His output was prolific but many of the works were executed away from the scene, mostly in gouache and coloured chalks; this had always been his way of working in nature. Having gathered shapes and forms and atmosphere in his mind, he liked to detach himself from the scene and re-create subjects. They acquired none the less a sense of reality – of the actual moment of occurrence. He was extending the ideal of his landscape painting, that the work should retain the 'first *frisson* of an encounter'. When he was working at the steel furnaces at Swansea and Cardiff, he had an illuminating yet terrifying walk at the Port Talbot Steel Works along a narrow parapet with blazing furnaces either side. He described this experience to me with electrifying actuality.

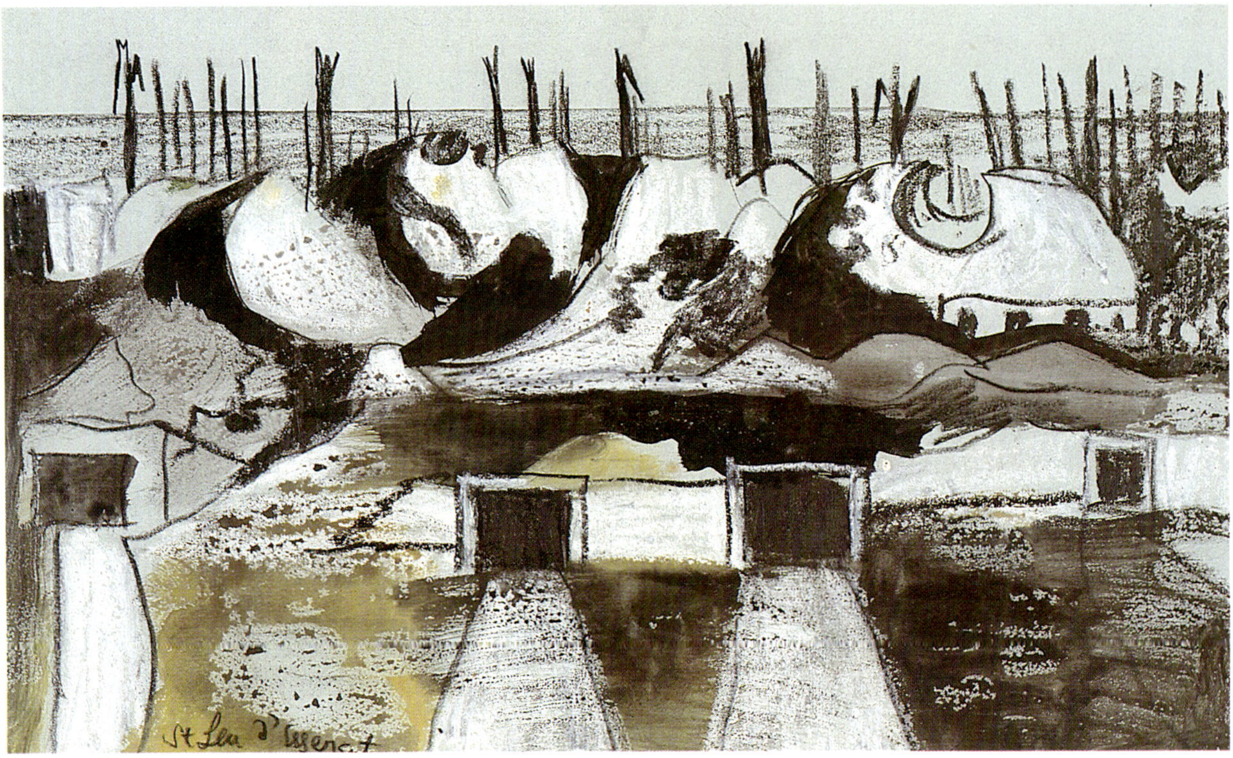

43 *A Flying-Bomb Depot, The Caves, St Leu d'Esserent*, 1944
Imperial War Museum, London

During 1943 he was asked to illustrate excavations of opencast coal mining near Abergavenny, but I find these rather sketchy and unhappy and to my mind they are the least successful of the war series. *Outcast Coal Production* (1943), a more formal and structured study, is, however, closely related to inspiration gained in Pembrokeshire.

Two later landscapes, *Landscape with Stones in Grasses* (1952: Plate 82) and *Rock Shelter* (1972-4), include in their composition the recollections of *Moulds: Iron Foundry* (1942) and *Tapping a Steel Furnace* (1942). Sutherland stored images in his mind and found them re-emerging like recurring dreams. He discovered a theme, shaped it, explored its possibilities and practical function in a composition and re-established its purpose in a subsequent design. We are seldom, however, left with the feeling that the final shape is overworked. Freshness and vigour are retained, the sensation is that of first experience.

Without comparing too profoundly Sutherland's war work with that of any of his contemporaries – for each artist was after all invited to render his own personal vision – one can see a striking similarity between the figure in *Miner Probing a Drill Hole* (1942) and Henry Moore's sculptural drawings of figures at this time. During 1944 Sutherland went to St Leu in France to record the effects of English bombing at Trappes. The relationship between his painting and Paul Nash's representation of battlefields is quite strong but there is also a clear distinction between Nash's delicate, free use of watercolour, and Sutherland's bold, black-and-white rendering relating inherently to the defined hilly landscape in Wales.

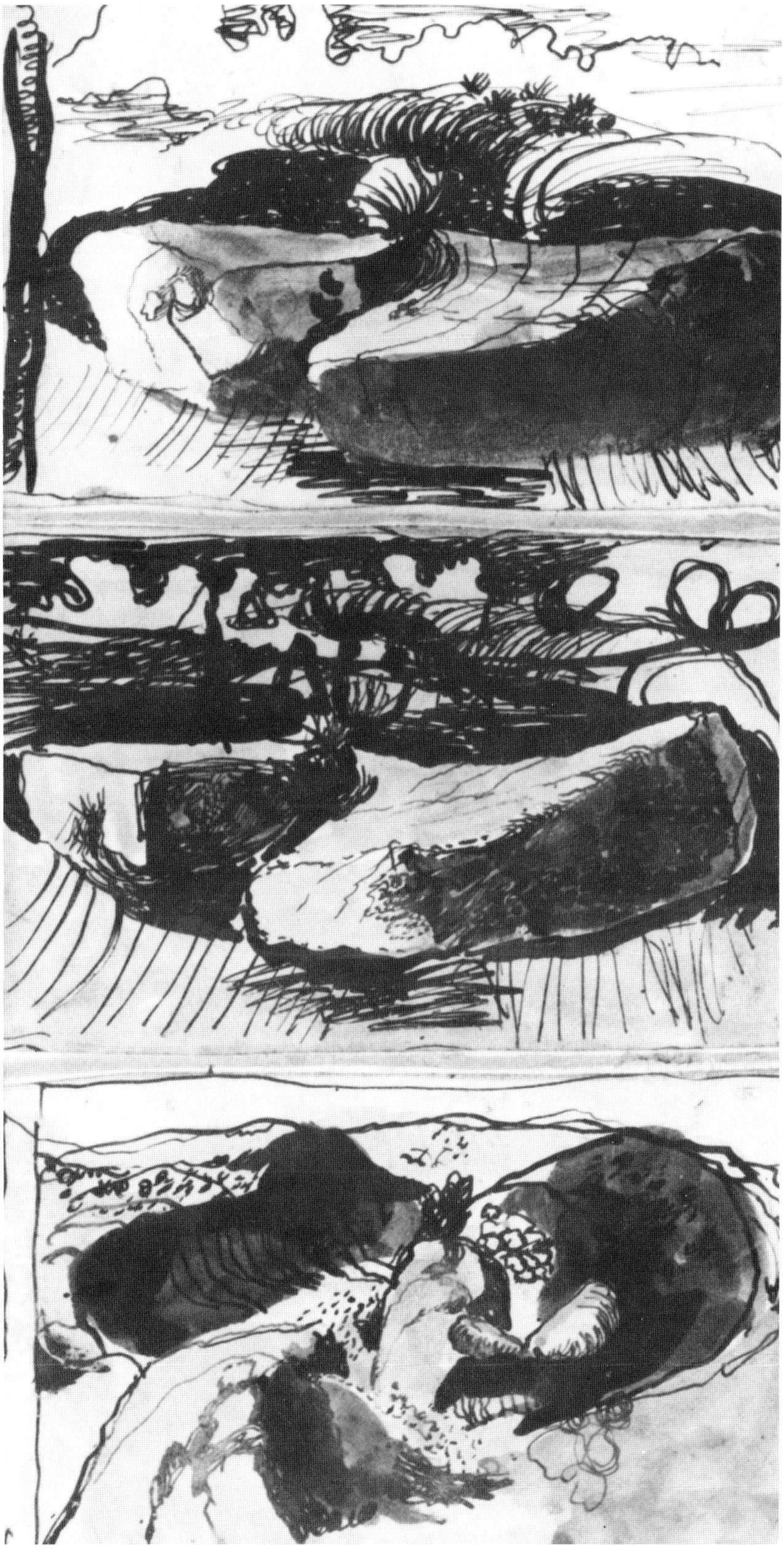

44 *Three Studies for Interlocking Stones*, 1940
Christie, Manson & Woods Ltd, London

Right
45 *Landscape with Pointed Rocks*, 1944
Christie, Manson & Woods Ltd, London

Centre left
46 *Estuary Foreshore*, 1946
Owner unknown

Centre right
47 *Landscape with Estuary*, 1945
The British Council, London

Below left
48 *Dark Hills with Hedges and Fields*, 1940
Hiram Winterbotham

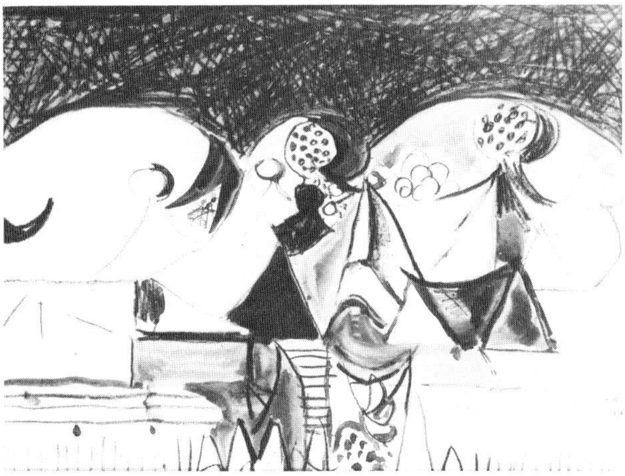

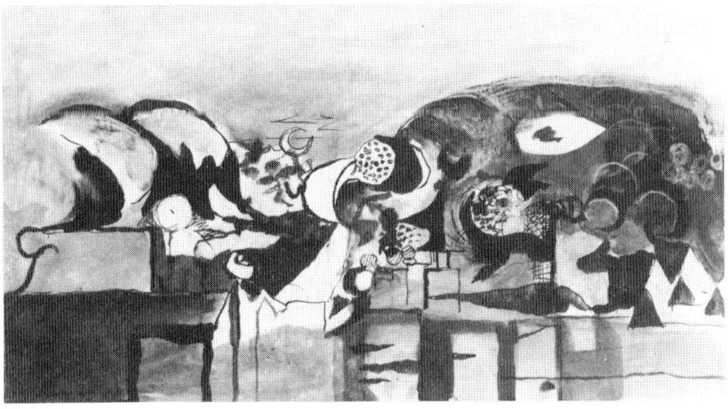

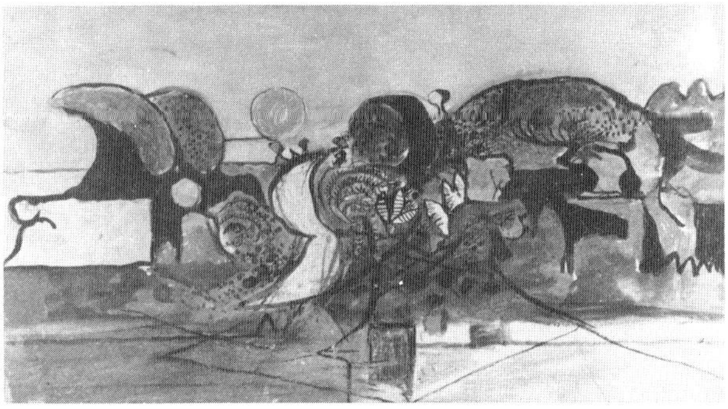

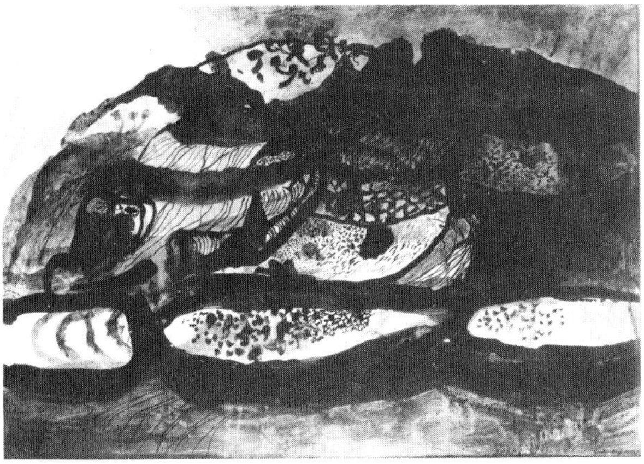

Right
49 *Study for a Mountain*, 1945
Christie, Manson & Woods Ltd, London

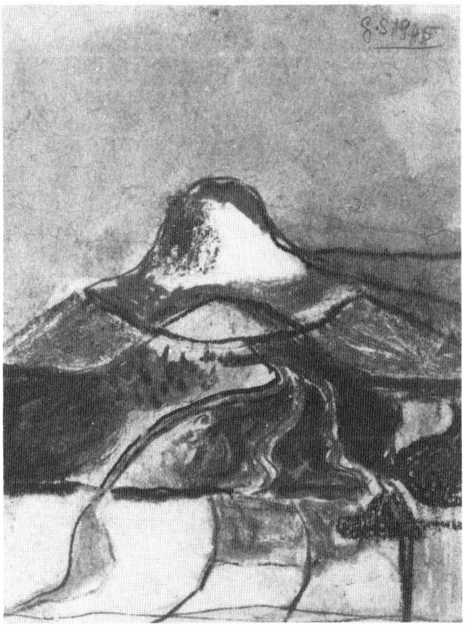

Noble Frankland, director of the Imperial War Museum, wrote in 1964 about the War Artists:

> The resulting artistic record naturally tends to conflict in exactitude of detail, and sometimes abruptly so, with the photographic record. It may, because of this, tend to conflict with the image of the war in the eye of the beholder. If this is so, it is because these works of art have no stereotype. On the contrary, they enshrine the individual imaginative responses of many artists whose differing impressions were inspired by their having witnessed, and in many cases experienced, the incidents they depicted. There is little doubt that this authenticity, which was always the primary criterion of the Ministry of Information's War Artists' Advisory Committee, will in time prove of greater value than what might perhaps have been the more immediate appeal of overstatement. . . . It is of interest to call attention to the extent to which the expressionism that is so noticeable a part of the best of the 1914-18 work has been replaced by a much more matter-of-fact reportage. The riven countryside, the blasted towns and torn men no longer appeared to produce in artists sophisticated by modern times that sense of outrage so apparent in the earlier war paintings of Paul Nash and C.R.W. Nevinson. [9]

During the war Sutherland made several visits to Pembrokeshire for the purpose of his own painting. Perhaps it was because he felt liberated on these visits, free from the constriction of having to make as near a

50 *Landscape*, 1939
Private collection, Italy

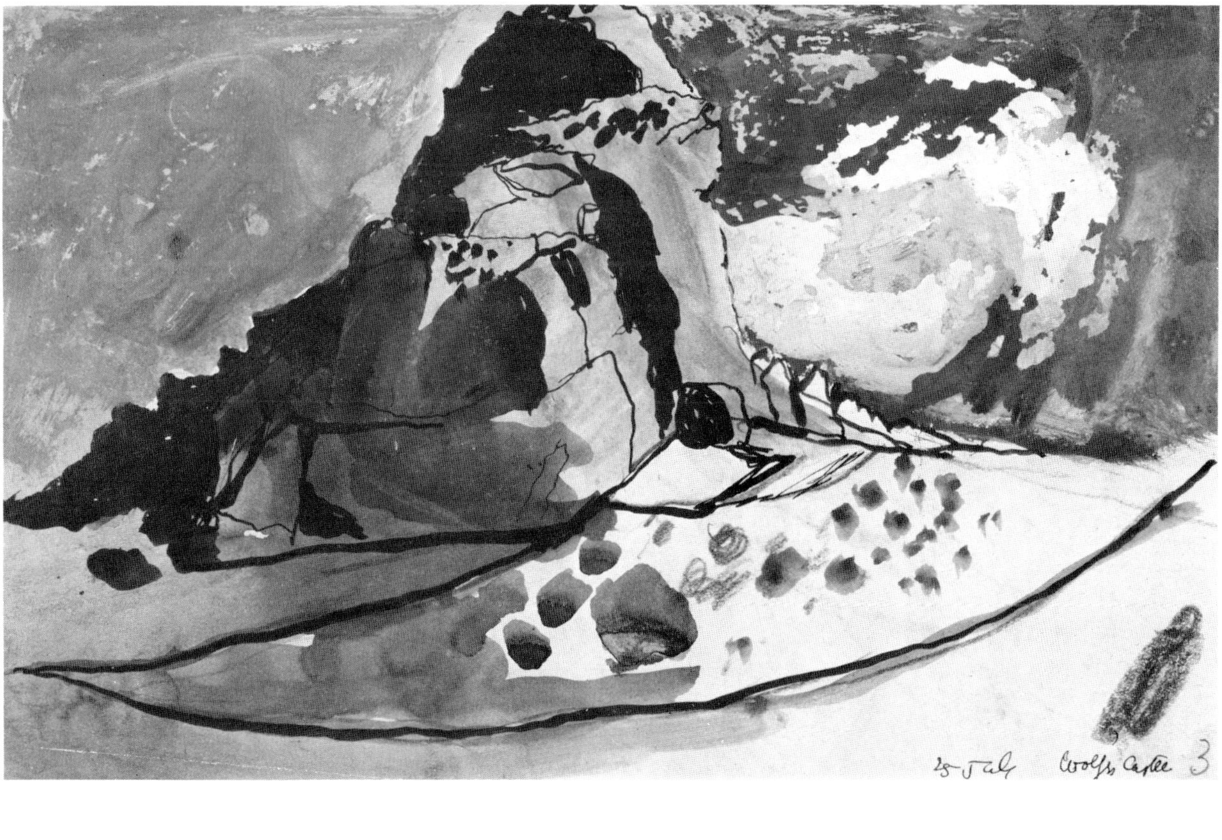

representation as possible of the war scene, that his palette was lighter, colour was used with greater sensitivity and more delicacy; deep alizarin, concentrated areas of black, ochre skies, light viridian, pale ultramarine, overrode the acid green, lemon yellows and cerulean – at least for the present. These Pembrokeshire paintings – made during the war – were emerging as less explorative, less experimental with colour; already Sutherland's work was becoming more assured. The war experience had greatly complemented his landscape work.

In 1938 Sutherland had had his first one-man exhibition of paintings at the Rosenberg and Helft Gallery, London, and in 1940 another at the Leicester Galleries, London, both of which proved at once successful. The British Council had organized an exhibition of contemporary British art for the British pavilion at the New York World Fair 1939-40, and invited Sutherland to hang. Slowly he was beginning to emerge as the foremost exponent of the contemporary neo-romantic movement in

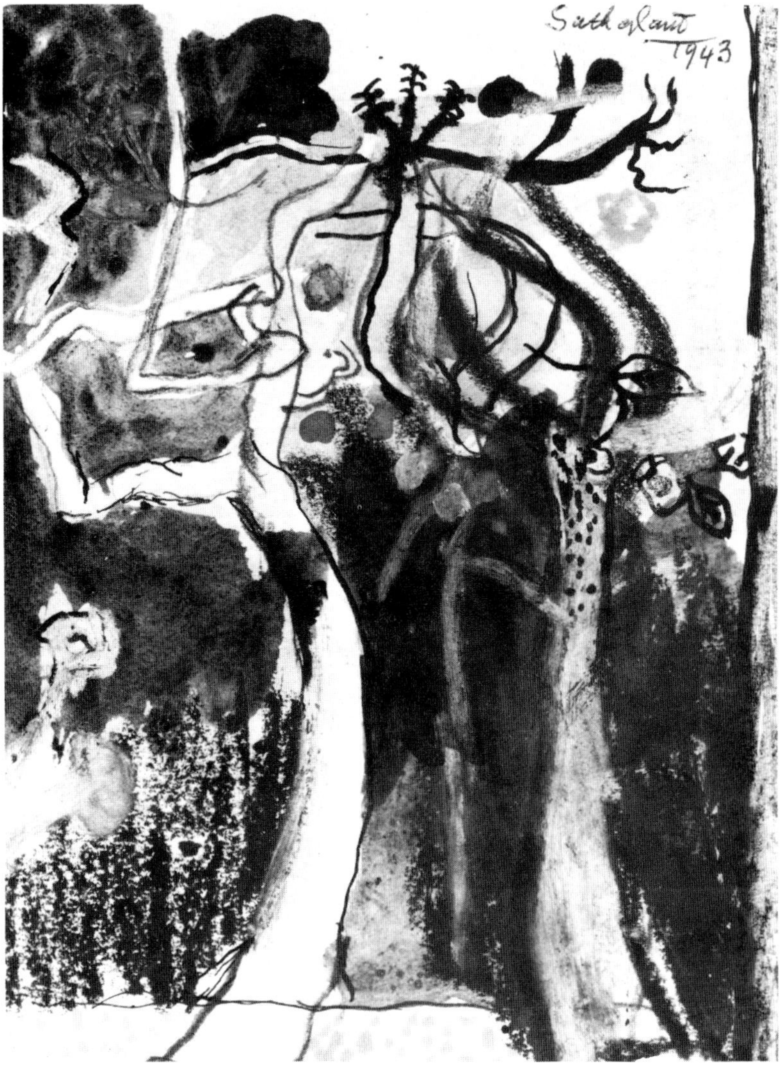

51 *Study for Trees in an Apple Orchard*, 1943
Christie, Manson & Woods Ltd, London

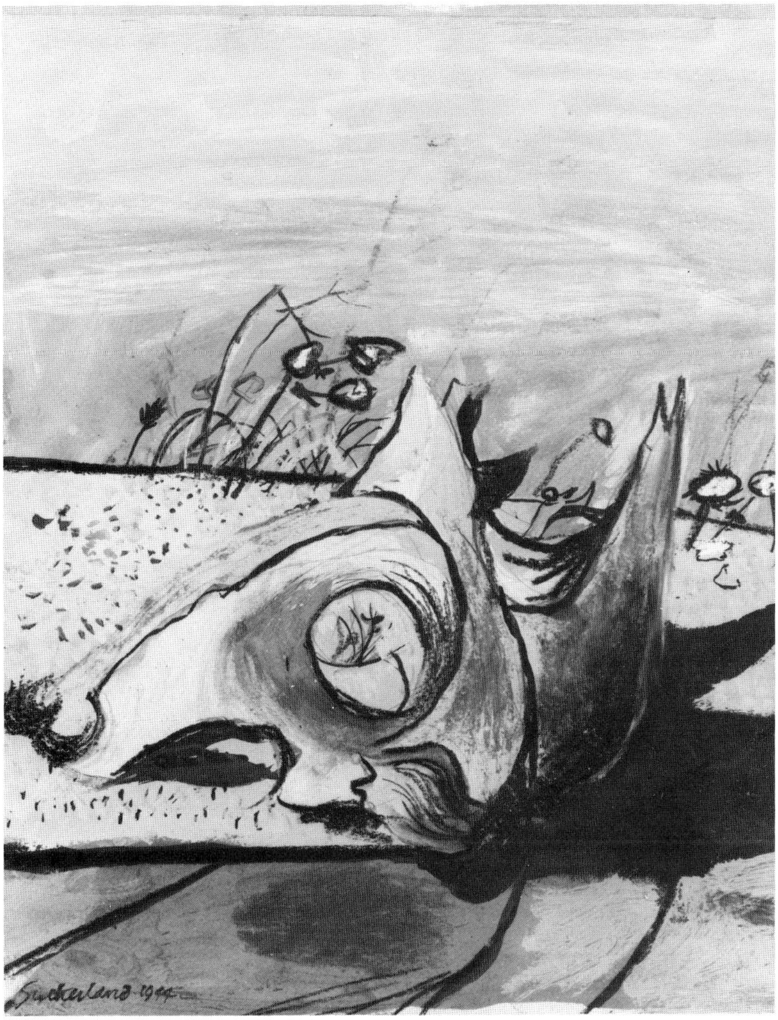

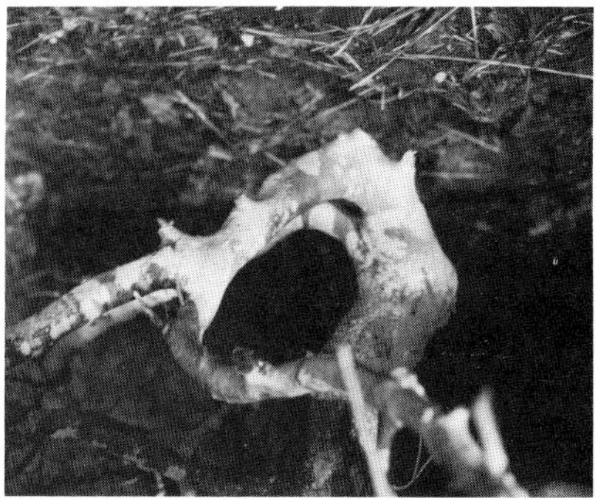

Left
52 *Untitled*, 1944
Owner unknown

Above
53 Tree form
Photograph Gilbert Adams FRPS

England. Robert Melville wrote, many years later, about the London exhibition, 'This French firm [Rosenberg and Helft] specialising in masters of the School of Paris might have shown tasteful English paintings in a French manner. Instead it showed the profoundly original paintings of Graham Sutherland and in so doing can claim to have launched one of the greatest painters the country has ever had.'[10] In 1944 he exhibited at the Redfern Gallery along with Paul Nash, Henry Moore and John Piper, and in 1945 at the Lefèvre Galleries with Bacon, Hodgkins, Moore, Matthew Smith. Sutherland's war drawings, together with his Welsh landscapes, were already showing signs of a maturing genius.

Chapter V
RELIGIOUS SUBJECTS

In February 1944 Canon Walter Hussey (later to be Dean of Chichester) invited Sutherland to paint an *Agony in the Garden* for the south transept of St Matthew's Church in Northampton. Henry Moore had already been commissioned to sculpt a *Madonna and Child* for the north transept. Sutherland's inspiration in this case came more from the vision of the patron, Canon Hussey, than from a place. Unhappy, however, about the particular subject suggested, Sutherland proposed that he should instead represent the *Crucifixion*. To what degree was this choice of subject influenced by the war?

How Sutherland's war work would have developed had he been sent to the Russian front, an opportunity he regretted missing, or been faced with documenting life in a concentration camp, is hard to envisage. Suffice it to say that he felt the Crucifixion had particular relevance to the experiences of the war years. After he had begun work on the commission he saw a series of photographs published by the United States Information Service which showed the terrible scenes of emaciated bodies in the concentration camps Buchenwald, Belsen and Auschwitz. Together with his own experience of wartime devastation, they moved Sutherland to deep contemplation and inspired much of his religious work.

For the next twenty years, from 1944 until the mid-sixties, one part of his creative process was directly concerned with religious subjects.

As we already know, Sutherland was continually appraising elements in nature; how they asserted their identity, providing fundamental stimulus for subjects he felt ready to pursue. Now more than ever he realized that they became important, not by being left in direct correspondence with their original environment, but by being lifted out of their habitat and given a new role.

Having accepted Canon Hussey's commission, happy that the war years had got him used to the idea of working to commission, he set about finding ways to give the figure of Christ authentic agony. The subject had, however, to be acceptable in terms of contemporary ecclesiastical dogma. Considerable personal debate took place. While on a walk in Pembrokeshire he reflected once again on the enormous implication of the Crucifixion:

> My mind became pre-occupied with the idea of thorns and of wounds made by thorns – on going into the country I began to notice thorn bushes and the structure of thorns, as they pierced the air in all directions, their points establishing limits of aerial space. I

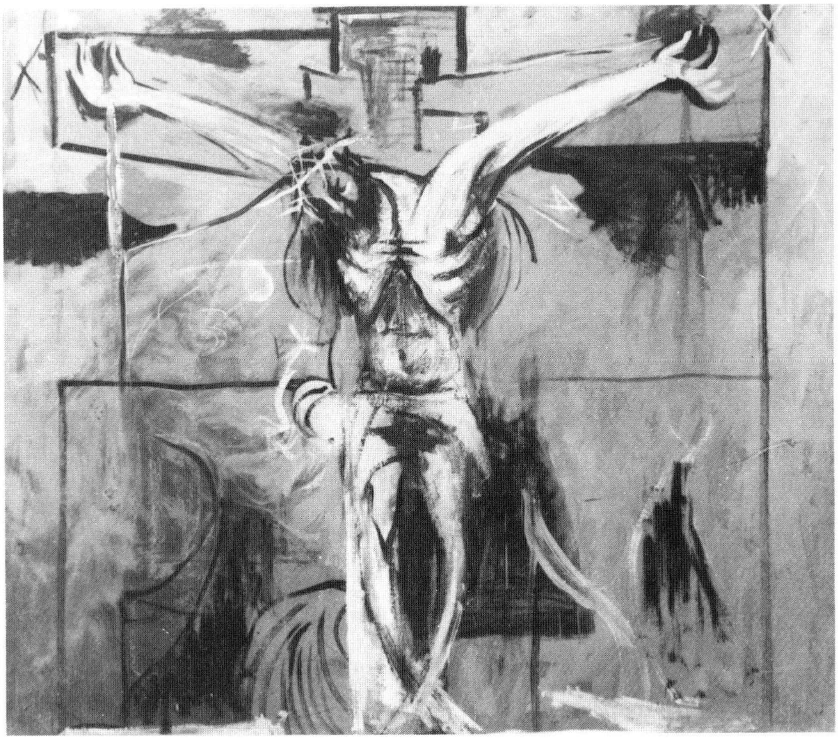

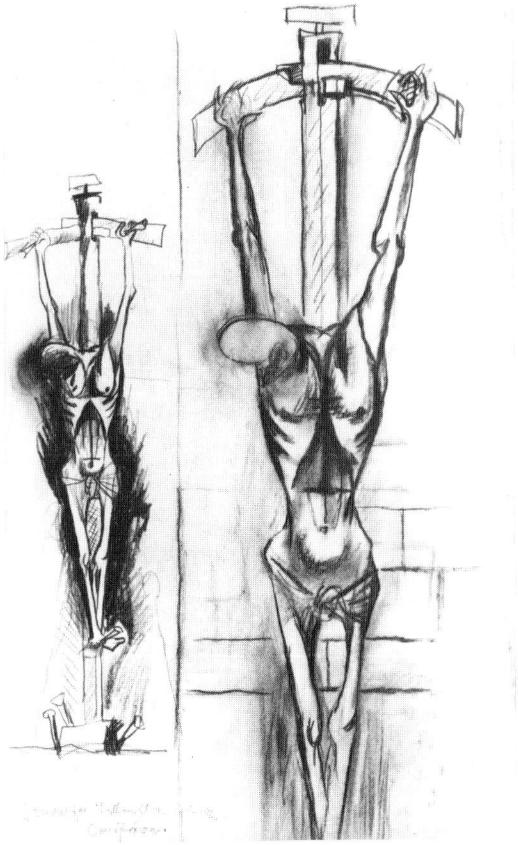

Above
54 *Study for Northampton Crucifixion*, 1946
The Tate Gallery, London

Left
55 *Studies for Northampton Crucifixion*, 1944
Collection Mrs Graham Sutherland

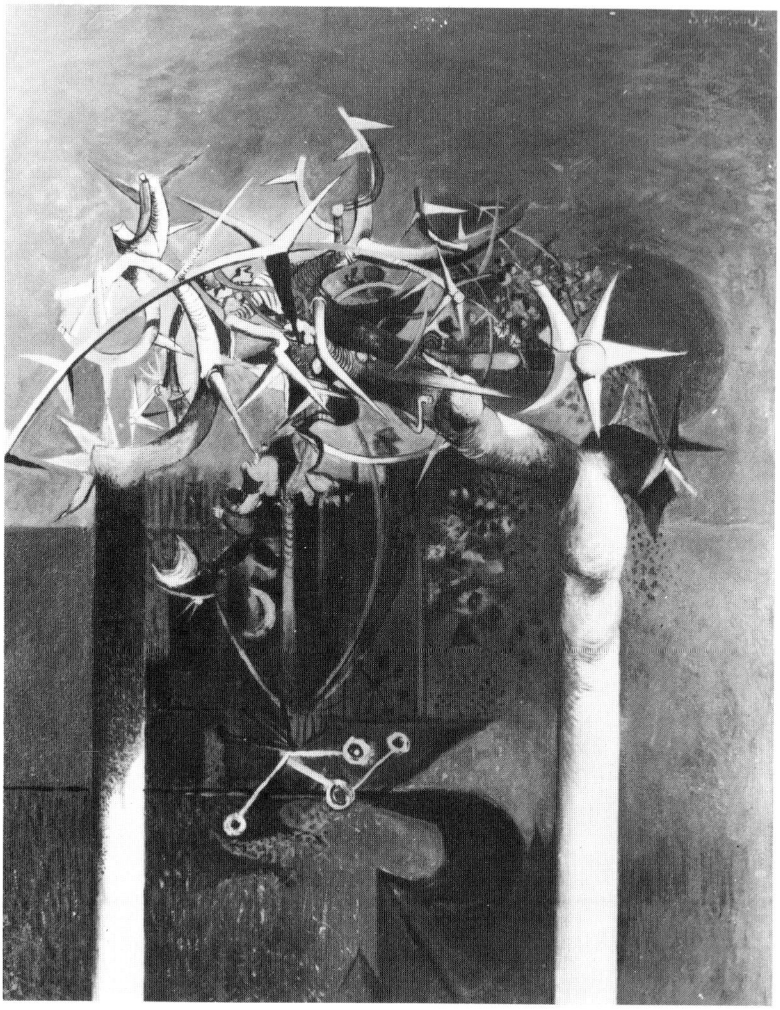

56 *Thorn Trees*, 1946
The British Council, London

> made some drawings and as I did so a curious change took place. While still retaining their own pricking, space encompassing life, the thorns re-arranged themselves and became something else – a kind of paraphrase of the Crucifixion and the crucified head – *the essential cruelty.* [11]

Subsequent reappraisal of the thorn trees lent substance and truth to his portrayal of the Crucifixion: the cruel nakedness, the corporeal reality of Christ, especially the upper part of the body, was conceived very much as the result of his statement that the artist

> . . .soaks up impressions and is very much part of the world. He cannot, therefore, avoid soaking up the implications of the outer chaos of twentieth-century civilization. By that token, subconsciously perhaps – and even lacking a tragic subject – tragic pictures will be painted. [12]

Certainly Sutherland, more than any other painter, gave us the true tragedy of the event.

The *Thorn* subjects were started at the same time as the *Crucifixion*, yet they embraced a longer period of evolution. In themselves they became one of Sutherland's major themes. Having found in them the vital clue to his Crucifixion, Sutherland went on to paint a whole series of thorn pictures. Through his profound study of thorn structures, and of nature itself, he gave the thorns new life and identity. Within the boundaries of Sutherland's imagination they became adorned with stature, structure, light, tortuous areas of shadow and incisive spaces of rich colour. To many they were far more interesting as subjects in themselves than when used solely as symbols in the *Crucifixion*. They were evolved as the substructure for the ellipses, they took on poised, statuesque, stabilized attitudes, they made allusions to tree forms, they produced the spiky connotation of metallic machinery; and eventually they became separate standing tree-like forms in themselves. Kenneth Clark said, 'His pictures of a thorn bush are more vivid and more personal than his *Crucifixion*,

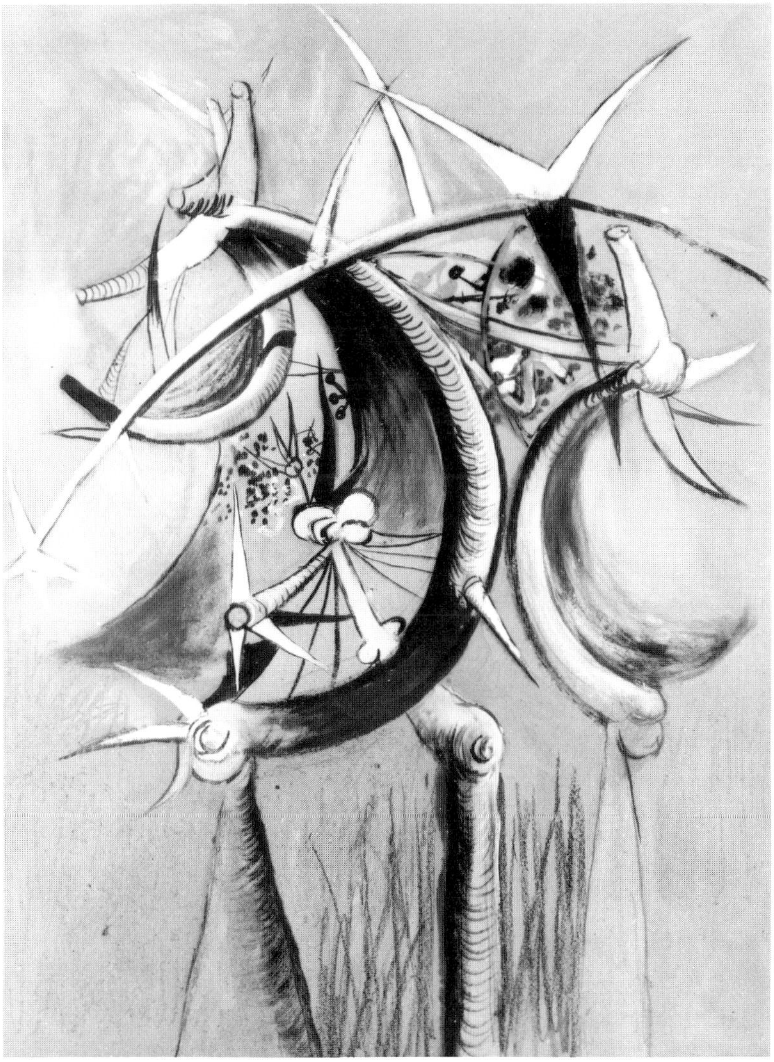

57 *Thorn Head*, 1945
Crane Kalman Gallery, London

simply because the subject has been expressed indirectly, through an image which has not already been deadened by use.'[13] Sutherland's life of permanent personal debate introduced so many contradictions that only by constant repetition and hard work did the subject become intuitively resolved. This dilemma never resulted in non-creativity, rather the constant debate created an evolution in his painting. Although he lived in debate with himself, he had the outward appearance of certainty. Repetition of certain themes was not the result of planned academic research, but rather of logical evolution and transition. When ideas were forming in his mind, their alternatives, too, were often presented to his thoughts, and became themselves of great importance.

The contributory studies made for the *Crucifixion* convey the complex debate which he experienced within himself: whether the subject should be represented along the lines of traditional Christian icons; how he could best adapt such principles to his own idiom without causing too much reaction at a time when religious feelings and susceptibilities were on the wane; how he could, nevertheless, represent a thoroughly modern interpretation. The depiction of the Crucifixion has, over the centuries, carried a tradition which provides a challenge to any contemporary painter who has spiritual integrity and respect for the great masters of the past. Sutherland accepted this challenge and produced in his own idiom a work which depicts the awesome meaning and stark horror of the event. The Crucifixion to him was the supreme sacrifice. He once described to me the hopelessness of world events, and in so doing unconsciously explained much of the torment illustrated in his work.

Sutherland was invited to execute a number of other commissions on the basis of his first great hieratic statement. There followed *Deposition from the Cross* (1946), *Christ carrying the Cross* (1953), *Noli Me Tangere* for Chichester Cathedral (1960), and a *Crucifixion* for St Aidan's Church, Acton (1961). His most important contribution to religious art, commissioned in 1952 and taking ten years to complete, was the giant tapestry, the largest of its kind, *Christ in Glory in the Tetramorph* (Plate 59), for the new Coventry Cathedral. The invitation was initiated by Basil Spence, the architect of the cathedral, and to accept it seemed a major act of religious affirmation.

Many drawings were made and several designs were submitted; and in the eight years prior to the weaving, just as with the Northampton *Crucifixion* (Plate 58), Sutherland experienced continual personal debate as to how the final image should be shaped. In the late forties and fifties he had much greater opportunity to see and extend his acquaintance with examples of Christian art around the continent of Europe; he was now spending increasing amounts of time in the South of France. Byzantine mosaics, Romanesque art and architecture considerably inspired the progress of the Coventry cartoon. There was also the comforting allegiance of contemporary painters who had depicted religious subjects this century: Picasso, Matisse, Rouault, de Maistre and, the most illuminating of all, Stanley Spencer. A Herbert Art Gallery and Museum leaflet outlines the development of the commissions.

> From the start Sutherland knew that he had agreed to undertake a difficult commission which would be beset with pictorial problems. The Church authorities had earlier compiled a statement defining the

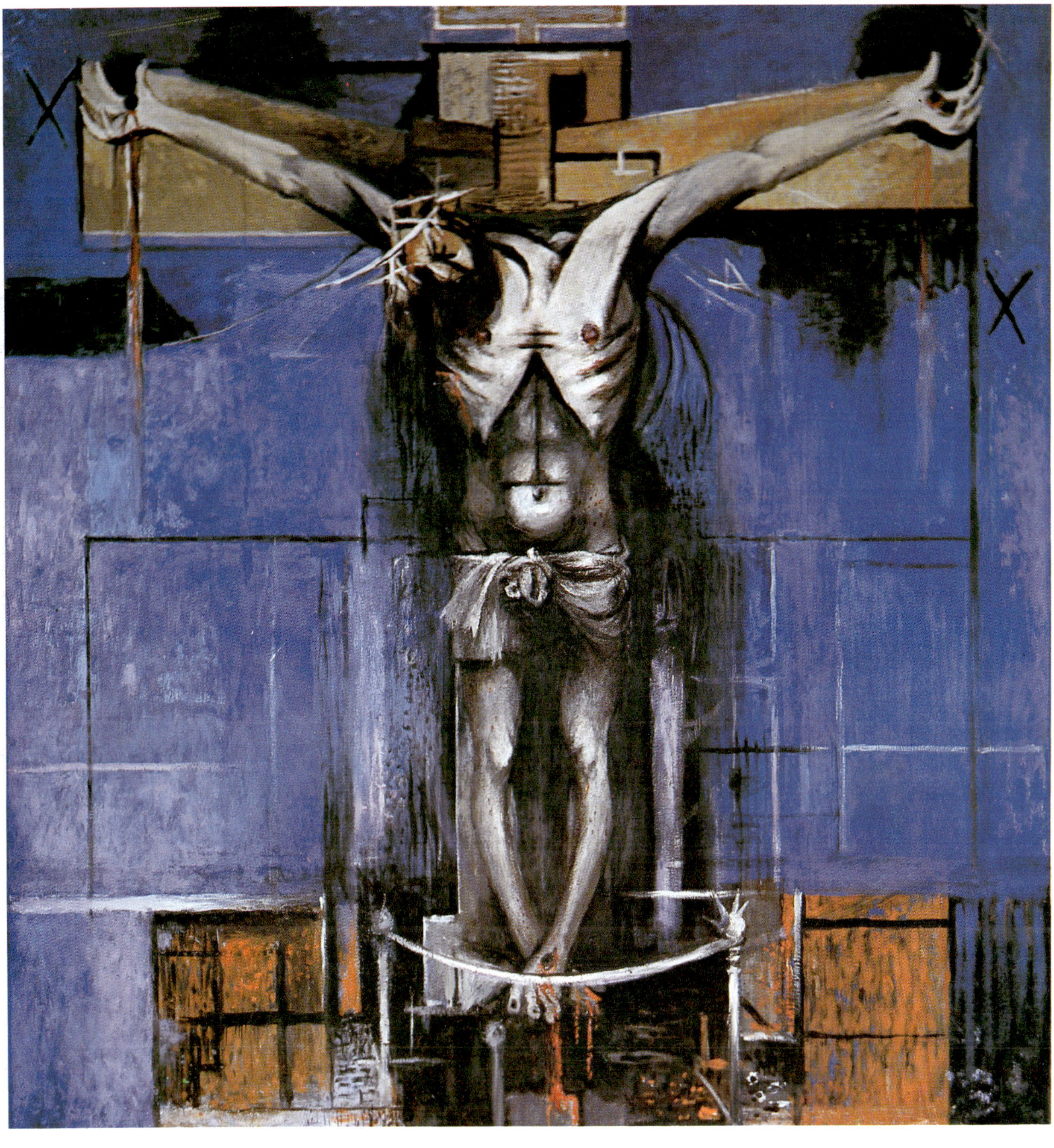

58 *The Crucifixion*, 1946
Church of St Matthew, Northampton

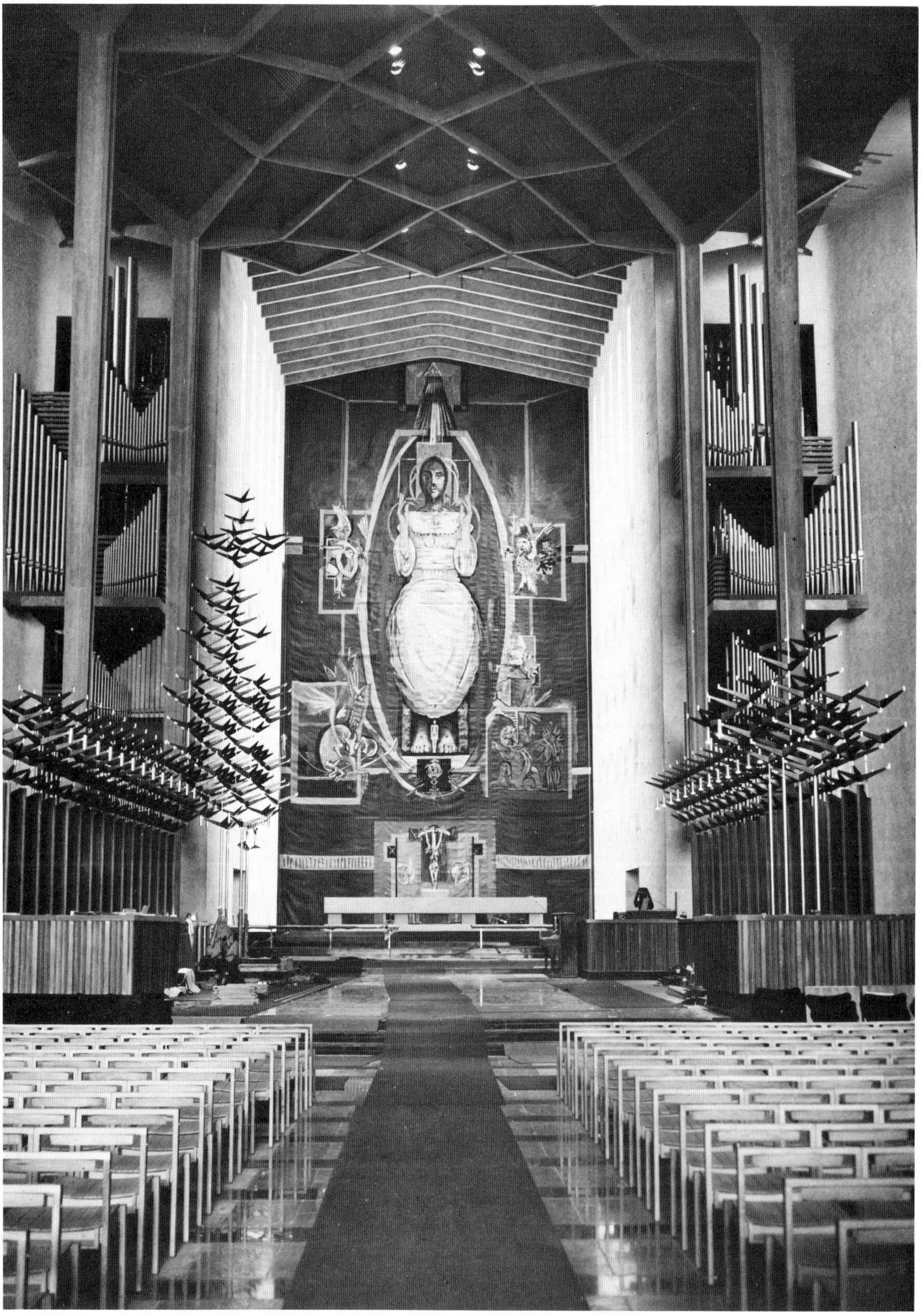

theological content that the design should incorporate and adhere to. The task was to depict the risen Christ seated in Glory in a heavenly environment, and surrounded by the symbols of the four Evangelists which are the Man of St Matthew, the Lion of St Mark, the Calf of St Luke and the Eagle of St John. And as the Cathedral was to be dedicated to St Michael this Saint was also to be included in the design. The subject comes from a passage in the Bible which meant that Sutherland had in effect been asked to illustrate Revelation, Chapter IV, vvs 2, 3, 6 and 7.

The Biblical text had long been a traditional source for religious works, especially those of the medieval period intimately connected with religious architecture. Sutherland was certainly aware of such outstanding examples as the 11th Century marble plaque of the tetramorph in the Ambulatory, St Sernin at Toulouse, France, the 12th Century Pantocrater in Monreale Cathedral, Sicily and the 12th Century Tympanum at Chartres Cathedral, France. These Romanesque and early Gothic works all followed strict doctrinal formulae for representing the subject, and differ only in style and detail. Sutherland was expected to continue with this tradition in Christian art but with the subject interpreted in a 20th Century style.

Executed in either pencil, ink, crayon, chalk or gouache, or a combination of these media, the studies may be divided into five basic areas: (1) the tapestry design as a whole, (2) the figure of Christ, (3) the side panels, (4) the lower panel and (5) the details. Each area Sutherland thoroughly explored, rejecting and accepting ideas, before arriving at the final cartoon. He very quickly established the format for the whole tapestry which is essentially a combination of Romanesque and Gothic iconography, and only in the various constituent parts did he make alterations during the six years of the design's evolution.

For the figure of Christ Sutherland made numerous sketches of various poses based upon art historical examples, and even photographs of the Pope [Pope Pius XII] in order to establish the most appropriate 'body language' which was crucial for the 'Spiritual' effectiveness of the design. In the details of Christ he paid considerable attention to the robes, head, hands and feet. And to a lesser extent the figure between Christ's feet and the chalice below.

Similarly, Sutherland made many studies for the symbols of the Evangelists and St Michael, although it seems that he arrived at the basic forms for the calf, lion, and St Michael at an early stage as these parts are not drastically altered between the first and final cartoon, whereas the man and eagle differ considerably. In fact Sutherland admitted that he found the eagle presented a particular problem in searching for a form that would 'balance' the other three symbols. With the exception of the Man of St Matthew, he found it necessary to make studies from life of the calf, eagle and lion in order to acquaint himself with these animals' characteristics.

The principal departure in the design from his earlier plan concerned the lower panel which was originally intended to be a triptych of the Virgin's life, (the annunciation, the visitation and the pietà). He abandoned this idea in favour of a single image of the

Opposite
59 *Christ in Glory in the Tetramorph*, 1962
Coventry Cathedral

pietà which appeared in the first cartoon, but on the advice of the Church authorities changed this to the crucifixion which appears in all subsequent cartoons. [14]

When it came to the overall arrangement of the cartoon, he deliberately sought to base the whole on natural organic growth, using a leaf shape as a sort of egg form establishing the proportion of the figure. This is similar in concept to the oval mosaic of *The Last Judgement* in Santa Maria Assunta at Torcello. The Sutherland figure relies on a series of ovals, or leaf shapes, separated by squares and culminating in the head. In his conversation with Andrew Révai about the Coventry tapestry he said:

> I wanted the figure to be real, yet not real. I wanted it to be slightly ambiguous; a human form, but with overtones of a nature form. . . . Nearly everything in the design is in a sense ambiguous. [15]

When asked whether the church authorities exercised any restraint over the work, Sutherland replied, 'Ultimately it is the measure of one's power of expression if one can, while submitting to the rules, transcend them.'[16]

In correspondence with Douglas Cooper, Sutherland described seeing Egyptian 'mummy' pictures, bound by tape to coffined figures. He set out to make boxes round the central figure, binding them to it by strips of 'brass tape'. (The oval mosaic at Torcello also looks as if it is bound with tape.) The scaffolding, from which burst the emblems of the Evangelists, balanced the overall lobulate. Faced with the problem of robing the central figure, Sutherland made drapes on a clay model and spent many hours changing the direction of the folds until suddenly, as if he had come across some hidden juxtaposition of patterns in nature, the folds fell into an acceptable arrangement and looked right. He verified this in conversation with Andrew Révai.

> I believe that, in the same way as by constant observation of nature, the lucky chance falls into one's lap, so, in using a model in this way one may be able to produce a much more mysterious realism using the forms as they actually happen and interpreting them rather than inventing them . . . . Translating the thing that actually happens in fact.[17]

For the head Sutherland amassed a collection of photographs. Some showed cyclists, close-ups of eyes, faces depicted in Egyptian art. He studied portraits by Rembrandt, and examined, too, his own features. He had been commissioned to show Christ the Redeemer enthroned in the glory of the Father, who was to be represented as light unapproachable; he was told that Christ's attitude, 'though serene, should indicate His present active saviourhood of men on earth – eg He may be shown blessing, helping, ruling, giving the sacrament, especially drawing humanity up into Himself.' The face does contain a feeling of great power, serenity and magnetism.

As we see in Sutherland's other work, he was concerned primarily that images should have balancing properties, stabilizers for the uprights, the one lending the other movement. There should be high notes and low notes and the whole should seem symphonic. The emblems for the four

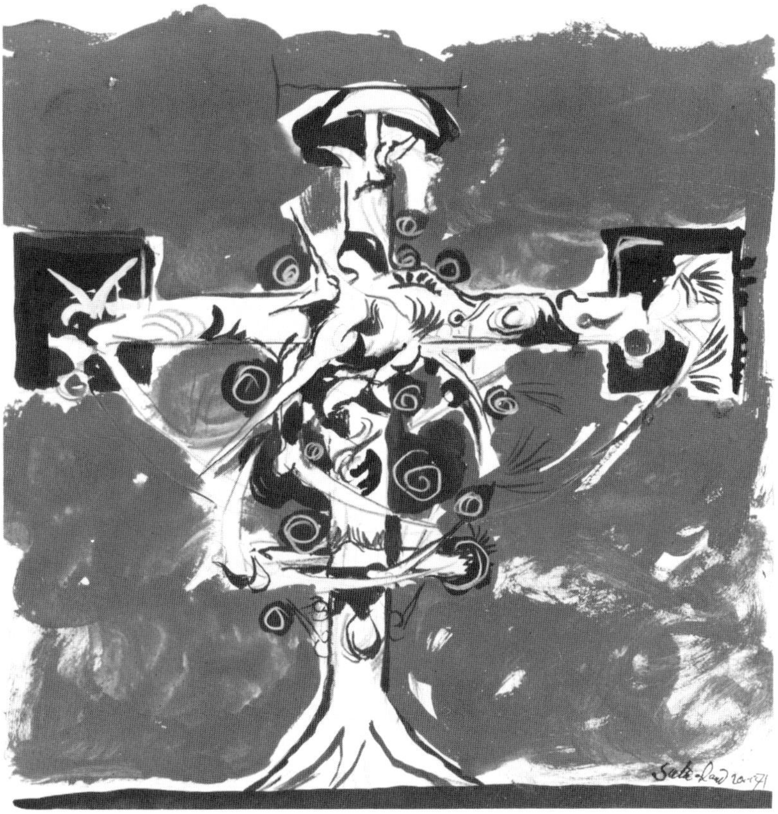

60 *Thorn Cross*, 1971

Evangelists, creatures about to take flight, were contained in a series of rectangles overlapping one huge rectangle with the action of several horizontals to preserve the whole in harmony. Had Sutherland relied on his own concept of this subject, the result would have appeared much more ethereal than that which was eventually conceived. He submitted his first cartoon to the bishop in 1953; twice he had to redesign his original composition, following it in 1955 and 1957 with two cartoons which were formally submitted to the Reconstruction Committee. The many animals which he cast for the tapestry became subjects in their own right and can be seen in the Herbert Museum in Coventry.

As the tapestry was:

> . . .to be woven in a single piece, measuring approximately 74 feet by 38 feet (23m × 12m) and weighing over one ton, a loom 40 feet wide was required. Only a few tapestry workshops could accommodate a work of this size, and the firm of Pinton Frères at Fellatin near Aubusson, France, under the artistic direction of Madam Marie Cutoli, was chosen for the enormous task.
>
> Sutherland's final cartoon had arrived in France in February 1958 and shortly afterwards a contract was signed with Pinton Frères. The first steps towards the tapestry were to make a photographic enlargement of the cartoon which the weavers could use as a pattern to guide them in their work, and to commence the hand dyeing of

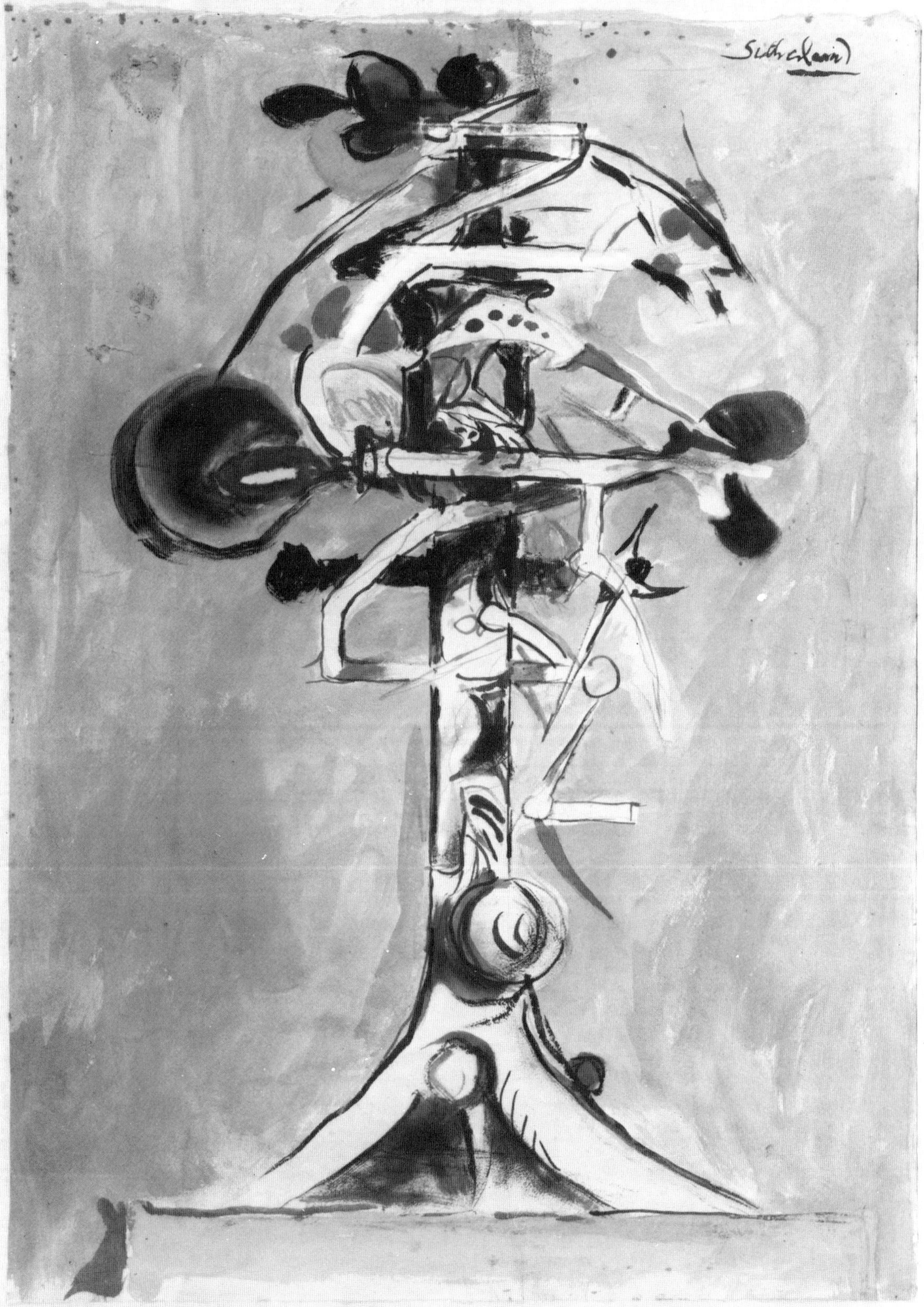
Sutherland

the wools of which more than 900 different colours were to be used in the making of the tapestry.

Towards the end of 1958 a trial tapestry of the Eagle of St John was begun and completed several months later. This piece was to provide the artist and the weavers with an example of how the finished tapestry could look, and what, if any, changes to the design would be necessary. From this Sutherland was prompted to make corrections and simplify areas on the photographic enlargements to assist the weavers. By far the greatest amendments were made to the head and arms of Christ which Sutherland completely reworked in order to obtain the correct shape and detail which were lacking in the cartoon.

This done, the work on the whole was begun and occupied twelve weavers for a full year before the tapestry was completed early in 1962. On March 1st the tapestry was flown to England and installed in the Cathedral prior to its consecration on May 25th 1962. [18]

It was inspiration on the part of Basil Spence to conceive that Sutherland would be the right person to design the tapestry, for Sutherland's mystical relationship with nature, combined with his devout and spiritual response, integrity, determination and courage during the ten years of execution undoubtedly make the tapestry a far greater achievement than was imagined when it was originally conceived.

Sutherland was inspired as always by nature, and it is interesting to reflect on how natural forms influenced the structure of his religious work. My belief is that Sutherland was so positive in his conviction that nature rules a world which man cannot ultimately destroy, that his religious works have a dominating power which we have to admire and respect and which made him amongst the greatest painters of Christian art this century. Nature was the constant source of his inspiration. He did not break with that emotional contact – he always respected nature and saw things through nature. It was not necessarily always the visual power which gave him purpose, but rather the spiritual presence. When sometimes he was emptied of inspiration, he felt a physical nudge on the shoulder – a religious impulse. This may have been unconscious, yet I am sure the very non-realization of the fact created in him the energy to progress.

Opposite
61 *Thorn Study*, 1954
Christie, Manson & Woods Ltd, London

Chapter VI
SOUTH OF FRANCE

Had anyone suggested to Sutherland before the outbreak of the Second World War, that he would live semi-permanently in France, or indeed anywhere but in the British Isles, his reply would probably have been very dubious. Essentially a painter of nature, he found the 'stuff' available in English and Welsh natural landscape sufficiently stimulating, enjoyable and profitable.

The ascendancy of a painter is not always obvious. His work may become so varied that the viewer wonders into what field he will develop, or alternatively it may become stereotyped, non-progressive and static. Sutherland's art developed on the one hand as a result of outside influences, the collapse of the print market, and the war; on the other hand it was shaped by his instinctive response to Welsh and French subjects. In conversation with Noel Barber he said, 'I think I made a major step forward three years before going to France regularly. Even before going abroad I owed a profound debt to Picasso and Matisse. People claim to see a certain broadening of quality resulting from my many visits to Venice . . . I am conscious that I learned a very great deal both in France and Italy, but the direct influence was largely subconscious. It took the form of a heightening and lightening of colour.' [19] Sutherland was very much at the mercy of his critics and his public who attributed his lighter palette and brighter pictures to his move to the Mediterranean, yet his series of *Thorn Trees* begun in 1945 (Plate 56) shows that this was not so. However, when Sutherland was sent to France in 1944 to chronicle the effects of war he found himself aware of, and receptive to, an extra dimension – other possibilities and advantages that might be available to him. A visit to Paris in 1945 gave him the opportunity to extend his until then very limited knowledge of French painting, and two years later his wife's ill health and need for sunshine prompted the first of several moves to the South of France.

In 1947 he met Picasso and Matisse, and said of the latter, 'One would have to be blind not to profit by the new role of colour invented by Matisse and his new conception of space, rough colours and line.' The friendship of both these painters strengthened his respect for their work and considerably benefited his own. Ready to extend his own visual experiences, he was beginning to broaden his vision and become enormously receptive to external influences. 'The immediate advantage of going abroad was, for me, firstly a matter of museums and churches, and secondly I was able to see the country in which Van Gogh and Cézanne had painted. To see Provence for the first time is to know

Opposite

Top left
62 *Two Standing Forms against a Palisade*, 1949
The Art Gallery of Toronto

Top right
63 *Blue Standing Form (Form on a Pedestal)*, 1952
Christie, Manson & Woods Ltd, London

Centre left
64 An early version of 'Form in Reeds' (1952), 1949

Centre right
65 *Standing Forms II*, 1952
Tate Gallery. London

Below left
66 Standing form in Pembrokeshire
Photograph Gilbert Adams FRPS

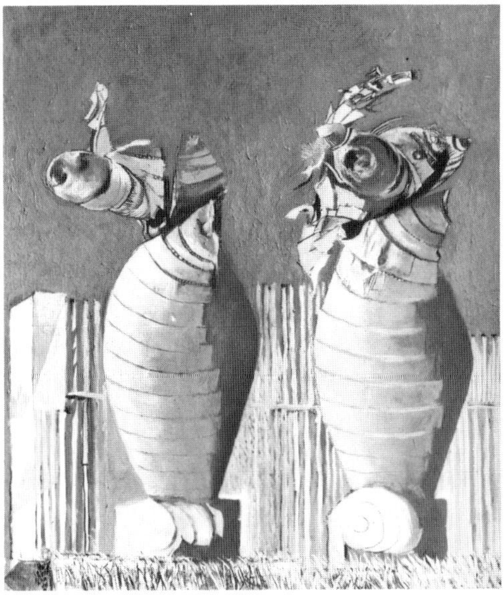

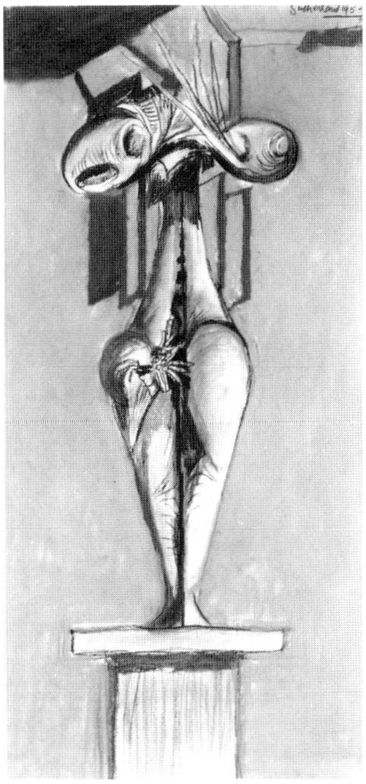

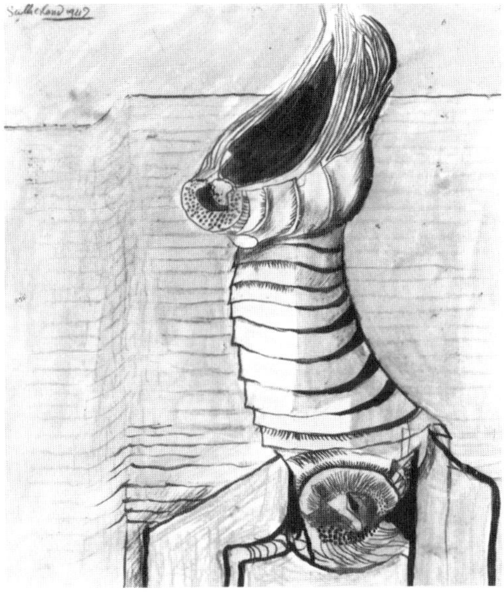

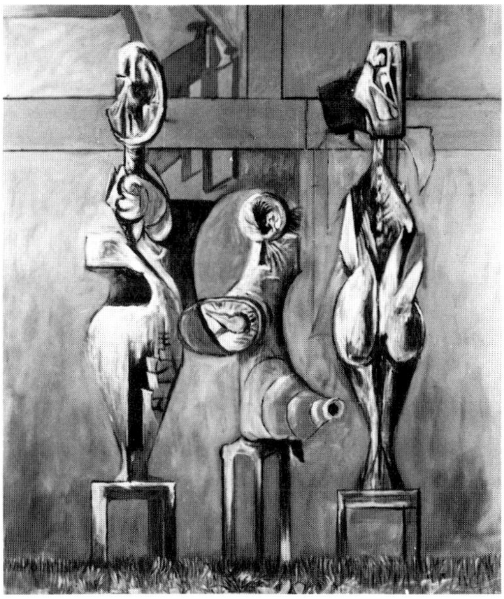

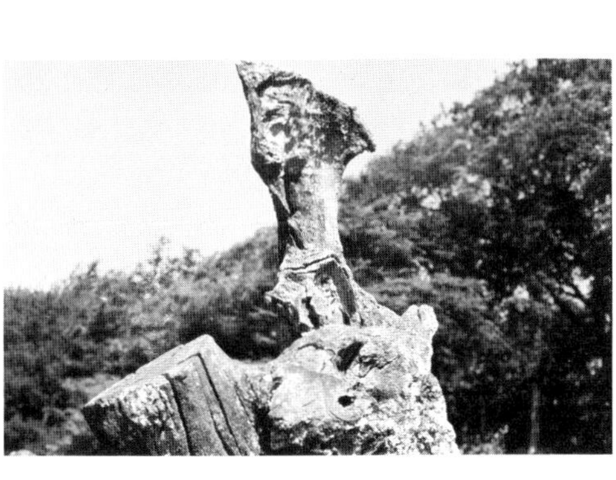

Cézanne properly for the first time and the painting of Van Gogh had suddenly a new excitement.' [20] He was as always inspired by contemporary painting, much of which reassured him of his own ability to develop and create decorative images. In turn he himself inspired many young painters and sculptors, especially when he taught at the Slade School in the fifties.

In a way it was inevitable that a painter such as he should have eventually moved to France, for he had been attracted by the work of the cubists, abstracts and surrealists, and there, in the 'hot basin' of the Mediterranean and in Paris and its environs, they were working: Braque, Léger, Villon, Kandinski, de Chirico, Miró, Rouault, Derain, Matisse and Picasso. The latter two, as he said, ultimately had a profound influence on his work. Sutherland owed a debt to Picasso even before going to France as he had seen exhibited in 1938 Picasso's *Guernica* and its attributive studies and was deeply affected. Although Sutherland found communication with Picasso difficult on first acquaintance, he developed an immense admiration for him. To Matisse he constantly referred as 'this great genius'. He was a giant, Sutherland told me, not only for his use of colour and line but because of his indomitable courage in working even after he had undergone a most serious operation.

In France Sutherland found a new vocabulary of forms, but one can see clearly that many were extensions of the earlier obsessions with organic matter. The place added greatly to his sophistication and personality, lessening though, it seems, his primitive perception. Philip Hendy, reviewing Sutherland's painting in 1948, wrote:

> Though his evolution as a colourist is a history of little more than a brief ten years it has been a succession of distinctive colour phases, each growing out of the last, but suggestive of a new emotional development, and altogether making a colour evolution bolder, more rich and more varied than any other modern English painter, except Matthew Smith. The particular gaiety of this latest phase must be largely due to the French light; but it has not unbalanced him, or changed his course, as it might with an artist with less of personal poetry or with a less determined theme. [21]

Sutherland remarked to me that of course he painted bright pictures much earlier and if one looks at *Landscape with Estuary* (1945), one must concede he is right.

Had Sutherland gone to France to soak in the atmosphere of her light and see the work of the French school rather than to concern himself with a new range of nature-based subjects, the above passage could equally well have described the maturing, illuminating process of his tried and tested Welsh subjects. He admitted after several preliminary visits to France that he preferred to work there. The light was better, and he liked the sun on him, French food and the French people. He found here freedom after the incubation of war, and he enjoyed 'the precarious tension of opposites'. This was a time when he felt he wanted colour to be liberated. Philip Hendy did, however, make it clear that the impact of the light in southern France had only hastened a process which was already well advanced:

> Most painters of passionate feeling have proceeded from the relatively dark to the relatively light. It is partly perhaps the natural action and reaction between technique and expression. As technique develops, expression becomes easier. With ease of expression comes some relaxation of the emotional tension which has demanded expression. More light in the soul brings more light on to the canvas. Sutherland is no exception. His pictures have always seemed to represent the resolving of some inward personal conflict distinct from the more general necessity which all artists must feel to link themselves with nature, to reconcile the perplexities of transient and self-bound man with the continuity and vastness of the universe. [22]

With the period of intense activity and variety begun in the late forties, Sutherland did not lose sight of his English origins or of his pre-war years. Inevitably the South of France subjects echoed the Welsh theme. The new shapes depicting thorns, vine pergolas and datura flowers, constantly reflected wriggling tree roots. The subjects lost the hesitant linear quality of his excited earlier discoveries. They began to assume a poised, statuesque, elegant, aloof appearance. Sutherland seemed to paint with greater self-confidence; the war was over and it would seem that he was being swept along by new ambition, stimulated by new landscape and further travel. His compositional arrangement became more a question of simplified statements – single objects brought into direct contact with the viewer.

The continental influence on Sutherland provided us with an impression of objects displayed frontally, often on a pedestal-like form, which gave

Left
67 *Standing Form against Hedge,* 1950
The Arts Council of Great Britain

Below
68 *Three Standing Forms,*
lithograph, 1953

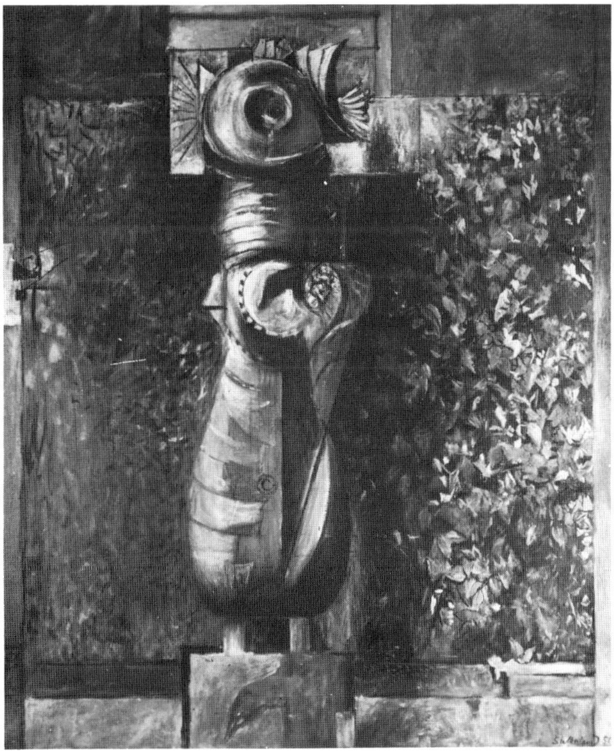

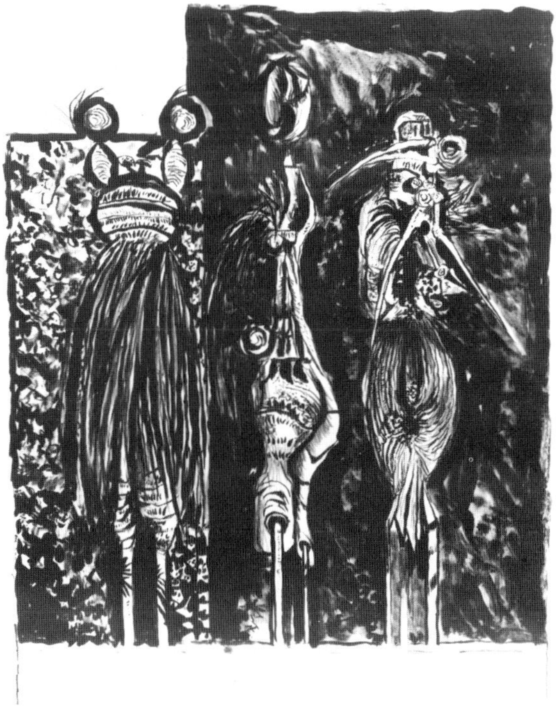

Opposite

Above left
69 *Reclining Stone Form*, 1948
Owner unknown

Above right
70 *Vertical Stone Form*, 1951
Owner unknown

Below left
71 *Study for Stone Tower*, 1977
Private collection, Italy

Below right
72 *Stone Tower*, 1977
Private collection, Italy

them a static quality. Sometimes he set his subject – monument, plant, insect – upon a platform, using a low horizontal as the balancing force; sometimes it was on a high pedestal with wobbly, spindly legs. The *Standing Forms*, the presences, evoke a former deity; increasingly the monstrances and monoliths were created with stylized reference to dramatic statements, unlike the spontaneous innovative subjects of Pembrokeshire. The figures he evoked were sculpted postures designed and arranged in three dimensions, expressing volume and mass. He gave them added proportion and radiance by using vivid ochres, reds, purples and ultramarines. Sutherland was working simultaneously on portraiture at this time, and soon on the Coventry tapestry. Many painters would have considered the 'nude' at such an important crossroads in their life but Sutherland wanted to retain a certain remoteness in the landscape subjects, no doubt to counterbalance the truth he required when revealing a portrait. One has to admit, however, that the *Standing Forms* and *Figures* do have a voluptuous, sensuous and often sexual connotation. They are far more vividly illustrative than the naked body. Indeed, they became more real and sensitive than the human figure. He seemed at the time to divide human structures from organic structures, though he did produce a conglomeration of anthropomorphic and machine subjects demonstrating the complexity of the painter's reasoning powers. 'I began to see a curious similarity between machine forms and nature forms.'

According to Bryan Robertson, 'In France, Sutherland orchestrated a tough new raucous kind of colour – orange, purple, red, green – his images from nature were only extensions in bright daylight of previous subjects gathered in Wales.' [23] I believe, however, that the blacks became then less dominant, and there emerged a delicious new range of colour, not raucous but pastel pink, alizarin mixed with white, mauve, orange. light blue, lavender, scarlet, emerald, chrome and yellow. He began to handle subject, colour and composition with greater discretion, the most evident development being his use of greatly flattened pictorial space, as Douglas Cooper suggests. The respect he had for Picasso and Matisse was beginning to be expressed in his own painting. Philip Hendy, describing Sutherland's work at this time, wrote:

> It was plain that here was a poetry of feeling which was worthy of a more adequate means of expression than he had at his command. It was not merely the need of technique in the practical sense; his vision seemed then to lag sometimes behind the impulse of expression. There was always the passionate sympathy with nature, always the original intensely individual mysticism; but the symbolism by which they were expressed was erratic in degree of clarity or articulation. [24]

Sutherland was not a copyist of natural history or a botanical illustrator, he only chose to use nature as his source of inspiration, his means of expressing spiritual mysticism, and he used it in a remote manner. Anyone who is acquainted with these nature forms in their stark reality has no difficulty, therefore, in understanding the Sutherland motif, the significant forms he drew out of their environment. We cannot attempt to compare Sutherland's nature painting with the super realists – such illustrators as Dürer, Stubbs, Audubon. His was a mystical symbolism,

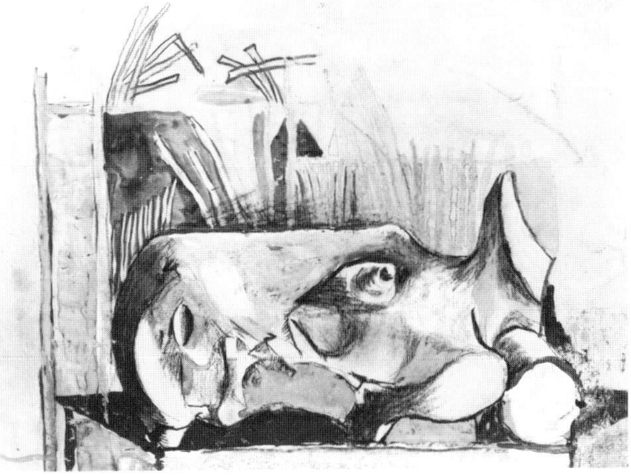

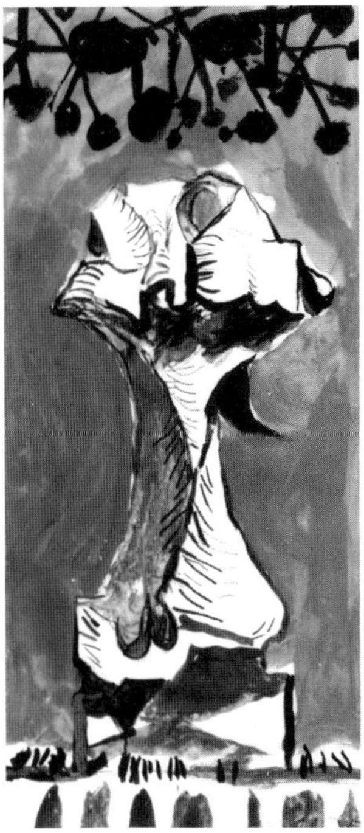

but one which is not difficult to apprehend if we are in tune with nature.

The association between the structured natural form in *Hollow Tree Trunk* (Wales, 1938) and the naturally structured form in *Standing Forms* (France, 1952) was such that both are really in the end only variations on a theme – the nature theme.

For the substance of his paintings in the late forties Sutherland, as was his habit, relied on what was immediately around him, although conceptual images of certain former visionary experience in Wales, his studies of maize, palm fronds (see *La Tenda*: Plate 77), pergolas, fruit and vegetables and occasionally the amphitheatrical effect of a nocturnal garden, convey only an extra dimension of nature-based subjects. The most interesting example of this can be seen in *Datura* – dated 1949, France – a Mediterranean plant which he also seems to have spotted in

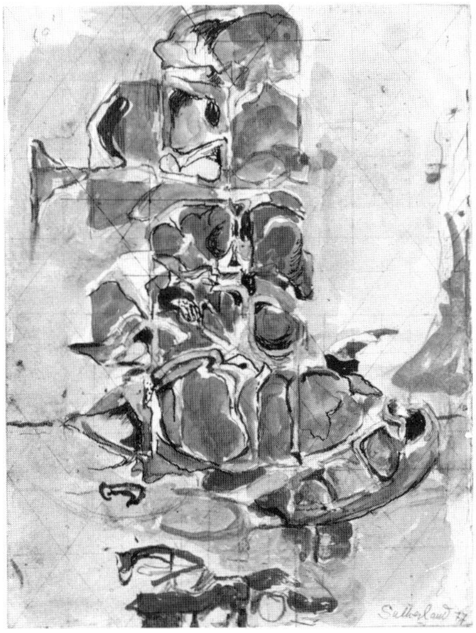

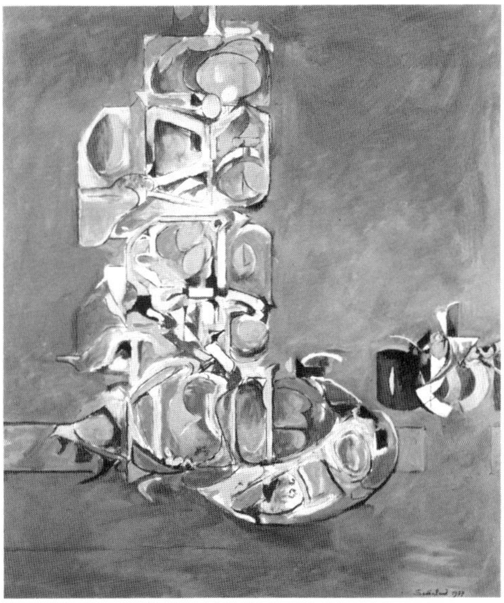

Wales (as illustrated in *Viaggi con Sutherland*, produced in 1971 for special customers of Olivetti). The so-called 'French subjects' were subconsciously and overtly the accretion of visual recollections. They had a dual role. They had their source directly in a particular place, yet they could quite easily have antecedents elsewhere.

The weaving movement of 'pretty' vine pergolas engendered the same motivation and energy to depict it as did the tentacled wriggling oak root on the shores of Picton beach. It was always the inexplicable inspiration derived from peering at movement and juxtaposition of shapes which created in him the desire to consider a new vein. But as he said to Barber, 'Then the "mind" must take a hand and the rest of the time between that first inspiration and the completing of the work is a question of putting what intelligence one has to the task of governing and controlling and refining that which has been pure inspiration into something which works and which becomes a picture.' [25] The *Standing Form* subjects were the transformation of early organic forms into ones with sexual implications – a sculptural translation from *Horned Forms* (1946). The monuments, however, still have their origins in the strange metamorphosis between organic and inorganic material. After the striking figure work he produced in his engraving period, and his evocative portrayal of tin miners during the war, Sutherland now had to move towards the truthful portrayal of the human personality – the portraits. He did so by way of those devious stand-in human forms, and when asked *why* he never painted figures in a landscape, he replied:

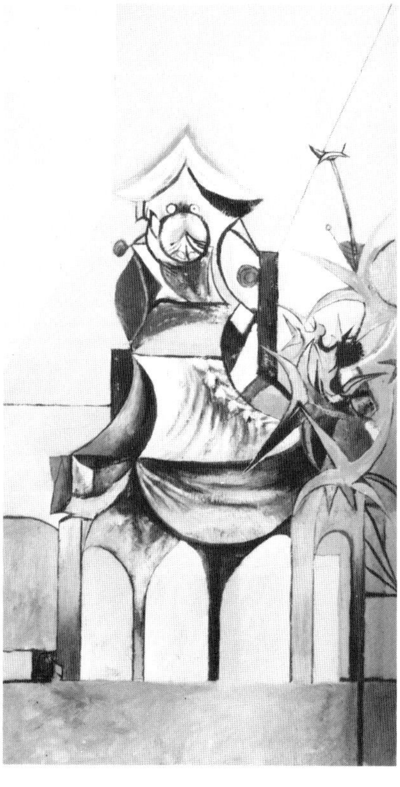

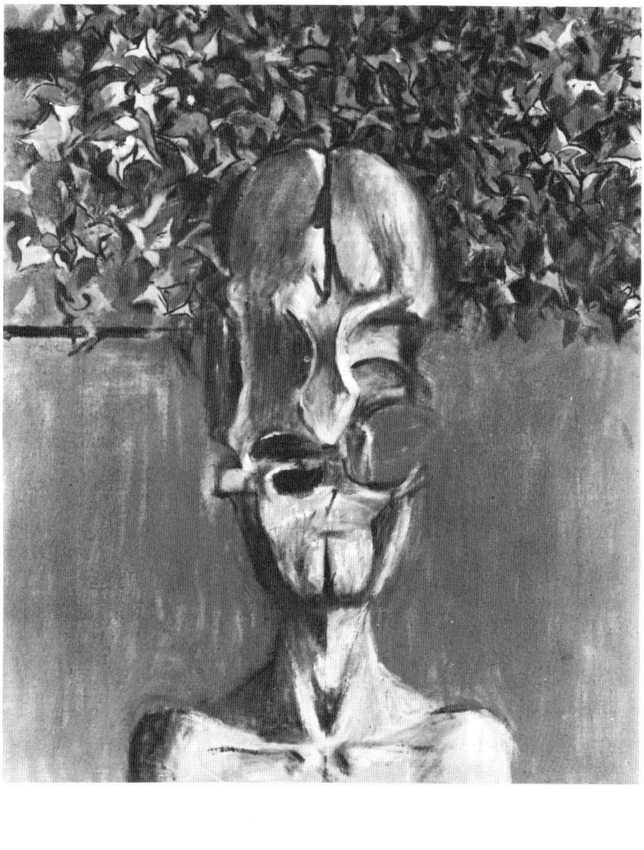

Above
73 *Chimère II,* 1946-7
Private collection, London

Right
74 *Head against Bougainvillaea*, 1951
Collection Mrs Graham Sutherland

> Once a figure is in the landscape it's nameable. When I deal in natural forms, they are much more remote. I want to keep a distance from naming something whether it be a figure or tree. I want to keep it a little away from its origins and there is more scope for doing this if I use natural objects which are rather hidden and remote. For instance, I simplified the elements of tree forms. Trees have extraordinary beautifully varied and rich shapes which detach them from their proper connotation as trees; one doesn't think of them as trees really; rather as figures. They have the same urgencies as figures in action. The individual detached forms are nearer to human forms. A tree is anchored to the ground, could be picked up and moved, if necessary, and lifted out of the ground. I like things not anchored to the ground. They should be ready to lead a separate identity.[26]

He was, he said, concerned with deflecting reality even if reality bounced back. The forerunner of these formalized and stylized stand-in portraits can be seen as far back as the early forties in paintings such as *Association of Oaks* (1940) and *Tree Forms* (1943). Although he tried to portray nature and, one would say, succeeded, he maintained that 'nature in the raw is almost impossible to represent'. It was almost as if he were evading representing the actuality of nature in order to make nature-based substitutes.

What is also curious is that the *Standing Forms* seem more suited to his inventiveness, ingenuity, persistence – his constant need to create an individual metaphor or to keep, as it were, the viewer in suspense. The outstanding range of his invention succeeded in attracting both viewer and critic. What, in the *Chimère* subjects, lay behind the rather grotesque thorny creature whose shapes and patterns in themselves were sufficiently decorative? Was this sort of half animal, half human, feline configuration designed to shock? Sutherland liked to shock not only his public but also himself – he liked an element of surprise. But, shocked or not, we cannot help liking *Chimère I* (1946), a dramatic invention from a gnarled bole.

Having noticed that a tree takes on a human association and having suddenly seen it stare back at him, Sutherland developed the genesis of a shape, half natural, half human, which was then reincarnated into a figurative, separate standing form. *Chimère II* (1946-7: Plate 73) has prickly thorns and cat-like characteristics, but is monumental. To make a monument out of very little became Sutherland's chief challenge and forte. It is interesting to see how he progressed towards his human representation via the *Chimère* subjects. They may appear to have little to do with Sutherland's portraits, but here nevertheless was a simple key which opened the door to portraiture. He appeared ready to shape the portrait, yet diffused his energies from things seen in nature, through the quasi-human substitutes and his elliptical shapes, to the portrait. The shapes that were being achieved in sculpture by Giacometti, Richier and Henry Moore, Sutherland and Francis Bacon were developing concurrently in two-dimensional painting. At the Venice Biennale of 1952, which included paintings by Sutherland and work by the sculptors Chadwick, Armitage, Butler, Moore and Paolozzi, none of the selection committee, which included Herbert Read, had the least idea before seeing the exhibition of the relationship between the sculpture and Sutherland's paintings. It was the juxtaposition of his paintings with the sculpture which was a revelation. Curiously a similar thing occurred in 1948 when works by Henry Moore and J.M.W. Turner were shown together at the British pavilion. One could see and appreciate for the first time the tunnels and holes in Turner's painting. Sutherland, in conversation with me many years later, said that he would ideally have liked to have been a sculptor; whether this was on account of the enormous respect he had for Henry Moore or, as he said later in interview with Bryan Robertson, because he liked something which one can touch, slap on the bottom, is questionable, but the sculptural paintings feature quite largely in his repertoire during the late forties and fifties.

In France, it seems that for the first time Sutherland began to use plausible areas of shadow. Objects were seen in a garden – a hot overhanging Mediterranean garden with pergolas, deeply shaded by bougainvillea; a person half-seen, haunted, formed a striking image, almost incongruous when seen in relation to the primitive Pembrokeshire organic shapes. The images were lifted from their ancestral context and re-presented as a different, separate symbol, given a different mood.

While the tonal balance in Sutherland's painting was becoming more restrained, *Standing Form against Hedge* (1950: Plate 67) represents the coexistence of the dendroid, man and machine, the assembly of his visual experience. There is a brief period, 1950-1, when Sutherland experimented with elliptical shapes, shapes reminiscent of the Brancusi workshop; cephalic forms were rotated from face-on to oblique. His friend Francis Bacon was simultaneously producing a series of those monster paintings designed, it seemed, to disturb. Writing at the time about these figures, Sutherland said:

> For myself, I believe that a new vision must grow out of reality – that the mysteriously intangible must be made immediate and tangible. What do my standing forms mean? They do not, of course, mean anything. The forms are based on the principles of organic growth, with which I have always been pre-occupied. To me they are monuments and presences. But why use these forms instead of human figures? Because, at the moment, I find it necessary to catch the taste – the duality, the essence of immediacy – of a figure standing in a room or against a hedge in its shadow, its awareness, its regard, as if one had never seen it before – by a substitution, I find at the moment that I can make these qualities more real to myself in this way. It happens that I find these organic forms best for my purposes. They themselves are emotionally modified from their prototype. They give me a sense of the shock of surprise which direct evocation could not possibly do. Also, in these pictures I am trying to return these forms after drastic rearrangement and emotional and formal modification to the field of purely visual response – to throw them back as it were, into the original cradle of impact. [27]

Sutherland was continually being asked to clarify his painting so the intellectual process of discussion about his work became increasingly a part of his job. He viewed the Press with deep concern and was always considerate and courteous in his dealings with them.

> In painting, by a substitution – by personification, by a paraphrase or a special way of putting things, we can shed a succinct light on the

nature of things and emotions, enabling us to know more about their essence and causing them to hold more than their original meaning – I want to give the *look* of things to my emotionally modified forms.

It is a question of bringing out the anonymous personality of things; at the same time they must bear the mould of the ancestry. There is a duality; they can be themselves and something else at the same time, they are formal metaphors. If I feel I must paraphrase what I see, it is because to do so gives me a new valuation of things. [28]

Kenneth Clark, in his contribution to the catalogue for the British pavilion at the Venice Biennale of 1952, expressed his view of Sutherland's work:

He does not, like the 'abstract' artist, give up imitation in favour of a new pictorial reality; on the contrary, he imitates objects with most literal acuracy; only these objects do not usually exist. This is due partly to the moment of vision in which they were identified, and partly to his skill in endowing them with the structure and articulation of living things. It is reasonable to ask whether Sutherland will always require these strange substitutes for the ordinary visible world. Would he not gain something if the shapes which appear so vividly to his imagination and the shapes he sees so accurately with his outer eye, drew closer together? The answer is that at the present his freely created forms give his work an added vividness similar to that of metaphors in poetry. [29]

Sutherland was commissioned in 1950 by the Festival of Britain Committee to design, for the Festival to be held in 1951, the giant *Origins of the Land*, which then became the property of the Arts Council which presented it to the Tate Gallery. The painting contains many of the motifs expressed in his smaller works. The motifs are brought in like musicians

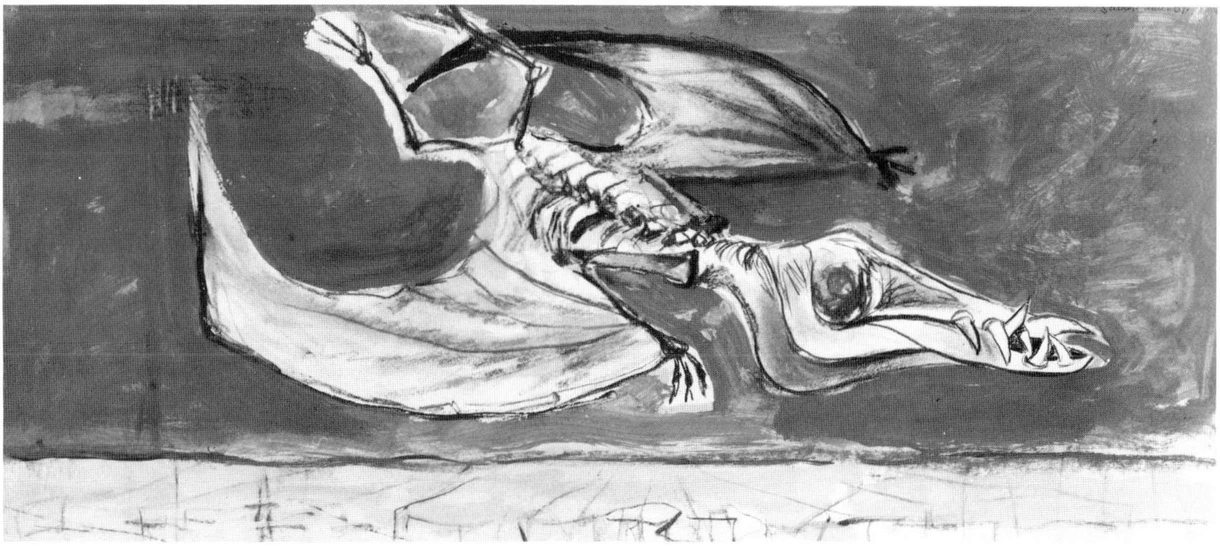

75 *Pterodactyl: Study for 'Origins of the Land'*, 1951

assembling for an orchestral concert. The canvas was executed in the rooms at the Tate belonging to the then director, Sir John Rothenstein, who lent them to Sutherland. An amalgam of ideas had been formulated, shaped by his deeply rooted respect for natural shapes; these were then re-created and reproduced in the giant canvas. Studies for *Red Monolith* (1937, Wales) and *Standing Forms* (1949, France), the setting Pembrokeshire sun, the three forms, the contained oval, the wriggling arabesque lanes, the swooping pterodactyl, all were woven into the final design, as though he took pleasure in showing the public the culmination of his studies. The colour, tone and balance of the work have a close relationship to Arshile Gorky's *The Betrothal II* (1947). Sutherland's composition was the bringing together of many stimuli. It seems as though romantic unstructured phases had been resolved, and an intellectual process had begun to develop. Sutherland conveyed a disquieting feeling soon after, when he said:

> I would like to have been born in the Renaissance when they did not have to go through the double action of working and presenting oneself . . . [30]

but throughout his life he always presented himself with integrity.

Other subjects, as exciting in their way as the thorn subjects, were his conscientious developments of spiky, metallic, extending, piercing palm palisades, rich in tone and delineation – vivid, dominating and brave in colour. No wonder Philip Hendy wrote, 'More light in the soul brings more light on to the canvas'; and we here owe a debt to Matisse who inspired and encouraged Sutherland to be brave with colour. The flat areas of pink, red, orange, yellow and turquoise heralded an exciting new colour phase.

From the thorns and palms, the pergolas, the maizes, the chimeras and ellipticals, Sutherland proceeded uninterruptedly to the ambience of Mediterranean coastal gardens. Objects and humans emerge in half night when the cicadas begin their guttural chatter and there is a sort of haunted stillness in the air, heavy with the sweet smell of humid bougainvillea and honeysuckle. We look into, through and beyond Sutherland's new garden subjects. The feeling of what lies beyond becomes more pervasive. In *Path in Wood* (1958: Plate 79), the bird swoops in to rest, yet only for a moment. In *La Primavera* (1975: Plate 110), the opening in the wall provides the excitement of anticipating what lies beyond – again the bird alights, yet seems poised to fly off once more.

Sutherland moved from the presentation of hidden elements in gardens to a long period of preoccupation with lithography, using well-tried and tested forms (themes). These were extended into reproductions, more than life-size, of birds, beasts, suspended forms and hanging forms, people, lions, bees, insects, flowers and conglomerates. In lithography he managed to achieve an extremely subtle delicate colour harmony and tonal range which defies comparison in this century. In Roberto Tassi's *Graham Sutherland: Complete Graphic Work,* Eleonora and Valter Rossi describe Sutherland's enthusiasm for aquatint.

> Sutherland became fascinated by aquatint from the moment we proposed it to him. The artist approached the medium with curiosity

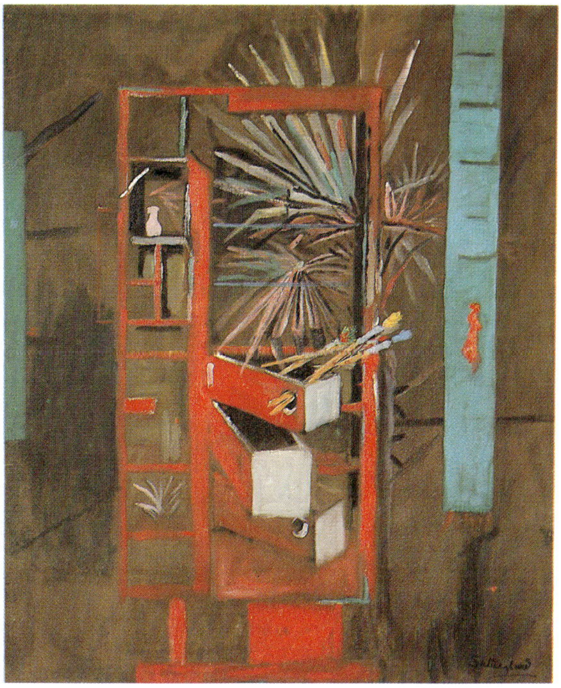

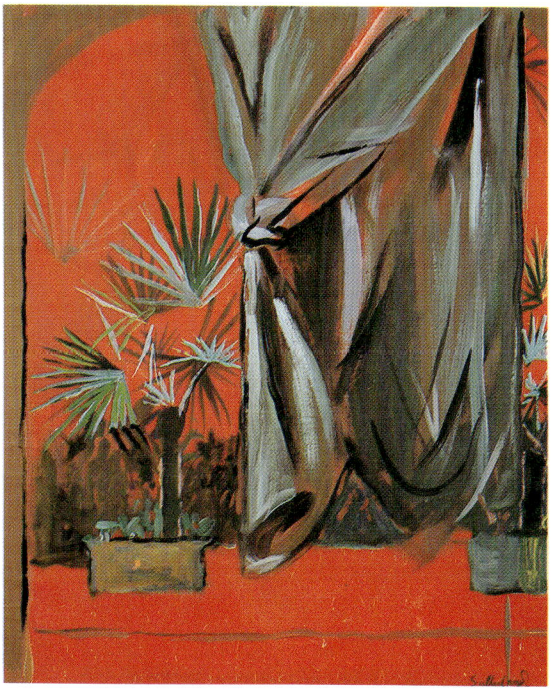

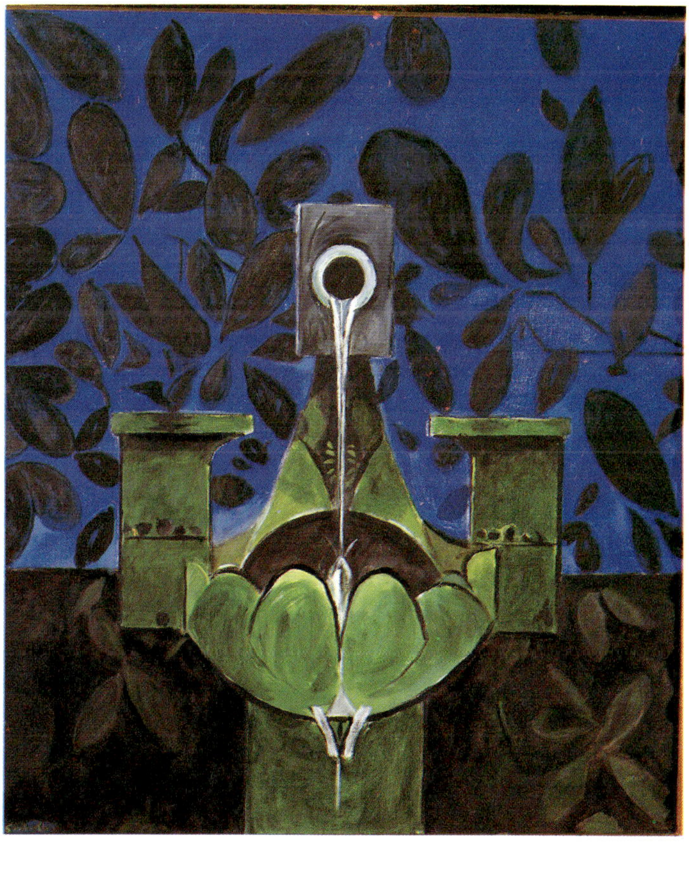

Above left
76 *The Artist's Studio*, 1965
Private collection, Italy

Above
77 *La Tenda*, 1965
Private collection, Italy

Left
78 *La Fontana (The Fountain)*, 1964
Private collection, Italy

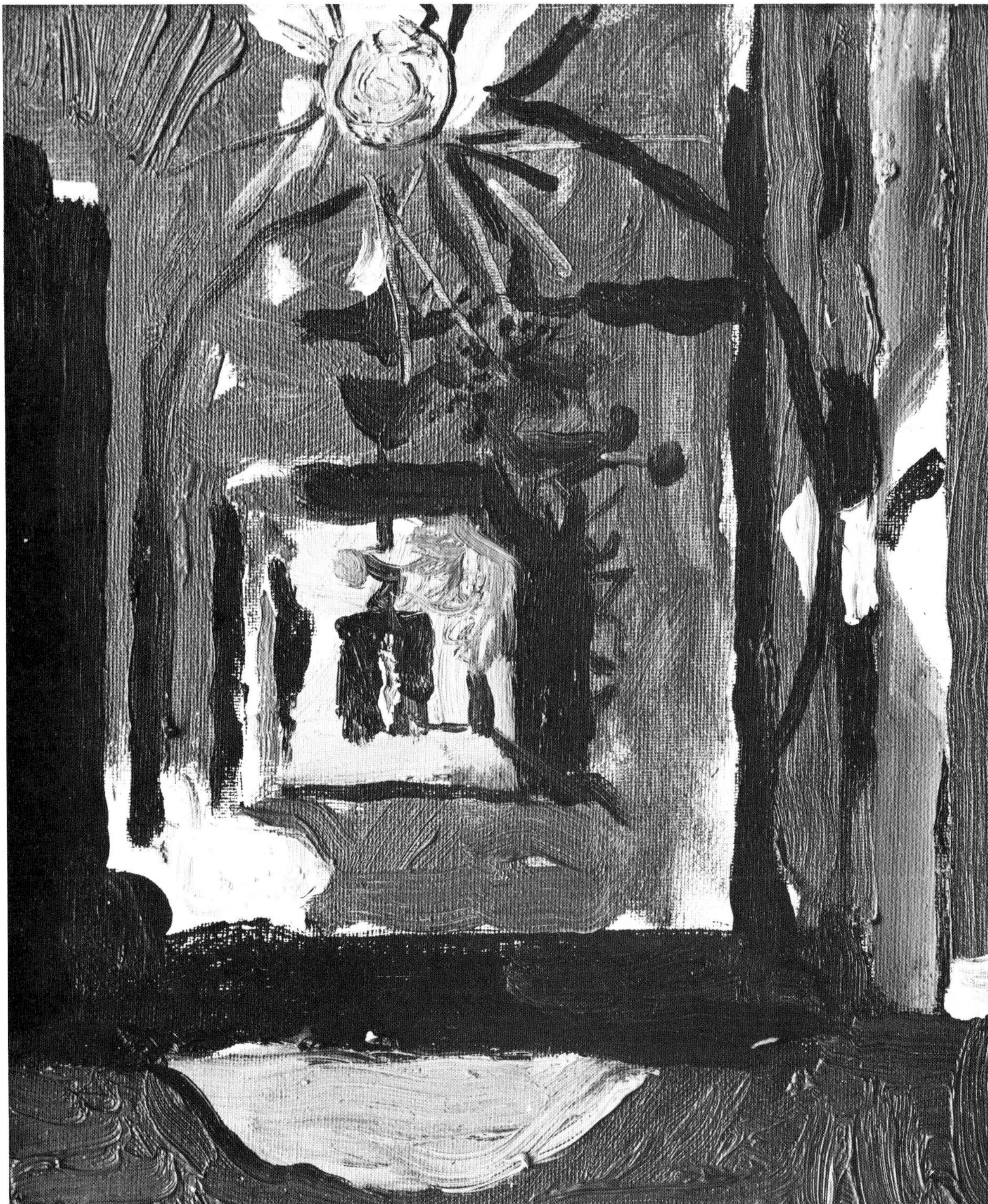

79 *Path in Wood*, 1958
Southampton Art Gallery & Museums

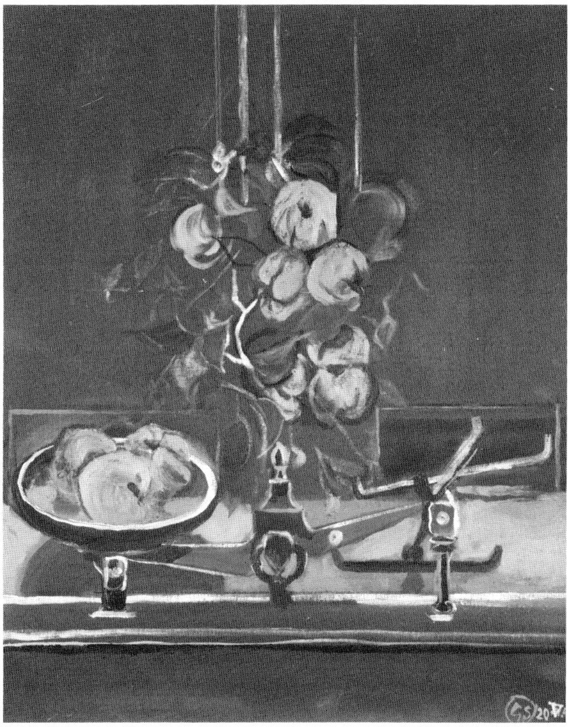

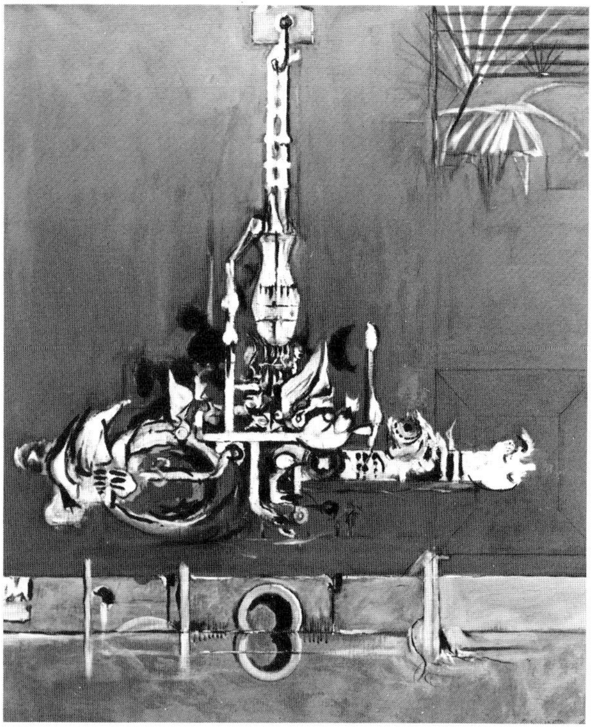

> and excitement; he tested it fully in order to evaluate its application to his own pictorial idiom. His past experience as an etcher helped him to appreciate a vital and innovative technique. This he approached with modesty; from the very first proofs of the Bees series, we were able to achieve fascinating results. As Sutherland began to master the medium, everything started to fall into place; line gave vigour; colour glowed with light by absorbing and reflecting it; blacks became alive. This newly acquired extension to his graphic experiences introduces us to the mysterious realm of Bees. [31]

Above left
80 *Still Life with Apples and Scales*, 1957
Crane Kalman Gallery, London

Above
81 *Hanging Form over Water*, 1960
Southampton Art Gallery & Museums

Sutherland began to weld together all his inherent themes and personal experiences of man, machine and nature. Animals became portraits, portraits became animal-like, standing forms became flowers, rock forms became machine forms. Birds in flight developed into humans diving, the conglomerate contained the complexity of living matter, stones and rock faces were translated into heads. Some subjects even became hybrids. In spite of the imagination and invention of Sutherland's subject matter, his style and compositional arrangement remained intact. He never failed where colour was concerned, always balancing and harmonizing the most vivid colour. The animals were weighed, measured, captivated, imprisoned, mechanized, symbolized. Kenneth Clark said, 'His creatures are trying to claim full human status. They have begun to change their habitat, they no longer appear against a cloudless blue on fearful crimson, but emerge surprisingly from a naturalistic background of bougainvillea. The contrast is a shock, like of those light-string images in the metaphysical poets of the 17th century; but this may be his ultimate intention.' [32]

Sutherland wrote:

> It has been said that my most typical images express a dark and pessimistic outlook. This is outside my feeling. The precarious tension of opposites – happiness and unhappiness, beauty and ugliness – so near the point of balance, are capable of being interpreted according to the predilections and needs of the beholder – with delight or abhorrence, as with those of bitter-sweet fruit. [33]

A number of interior paintings and still-lifes emerged during the fifties and sixties. *The Fountain* (1964: Plate 78) was portrayed richly and lucidly at night, and is a painting which conveys the rapid meridional transition from day into night – when indigo night sky percolates through leafy forms. The prolific output of work which Sutherland managed to achieve during the years in France was confidently decorative, spectacular and exciting – we are always, however, obliged to recognize his love of nature and his rooted obsession with certain themes. If one takes a look at *Landscape with Stones in Grasses* (1952: Plate 82) one sees that it is developed from the embryo of an idea used in *Breech Blocks in the Shop at Gun-Testing Range* (1940: Plate 38); the fiery furnaces of war are remoulded from a work such as *Moulds: Iron Foundry* (1942) and re-used, along with ideas used in the cross and thorn series, in a painting such as *Braziers* (1967) with its strong backcloth of datura, and again in paintings such as *Rock Hut* (1974: Plate 83), *Study of Rock and Flames* (1975: Plate 85) and *Hollow Tree* (1977: Plate 84).

Many exhibitions of Sutherland's work were held throughout the fifties

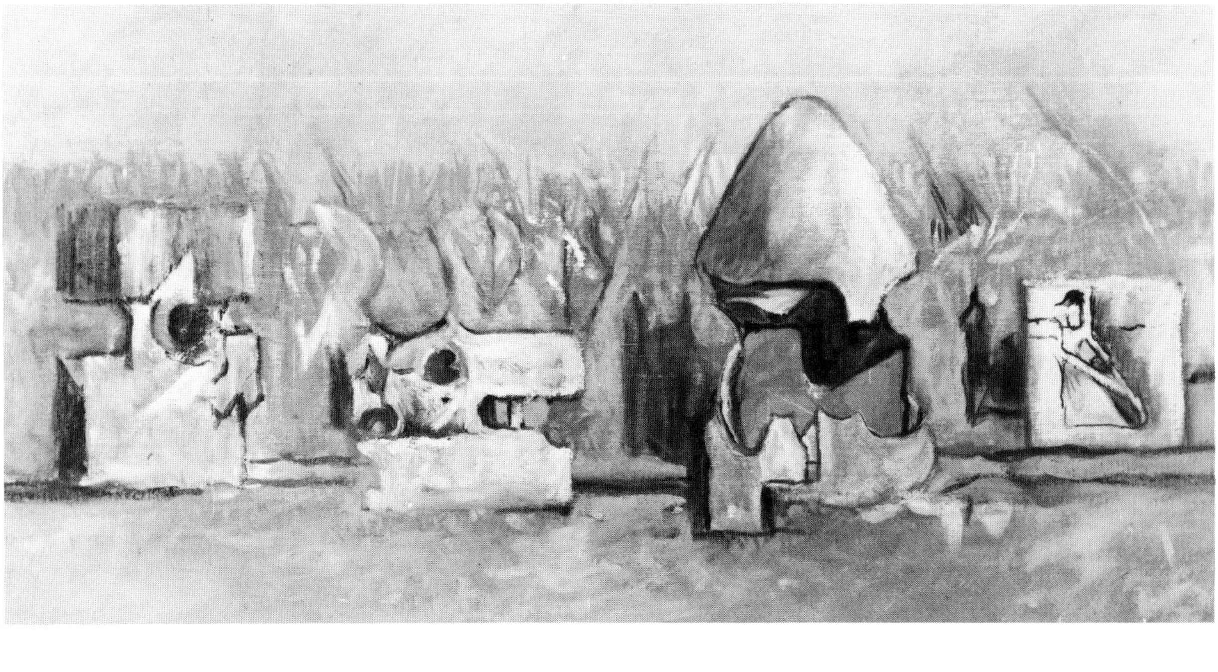

82 *Landscape with Stones in Grasses*, 1952

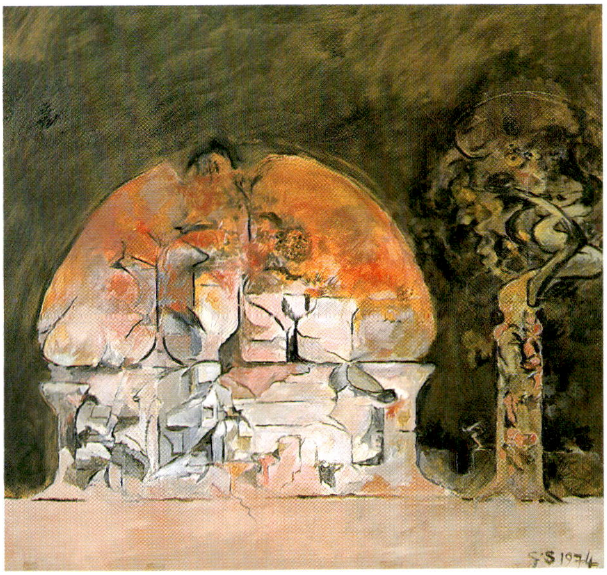

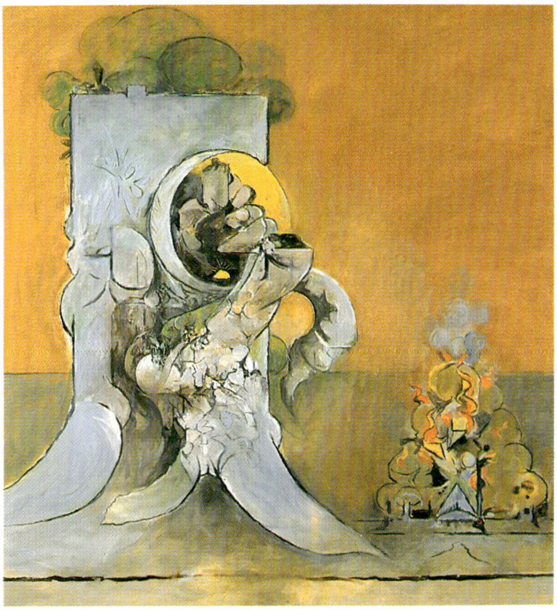

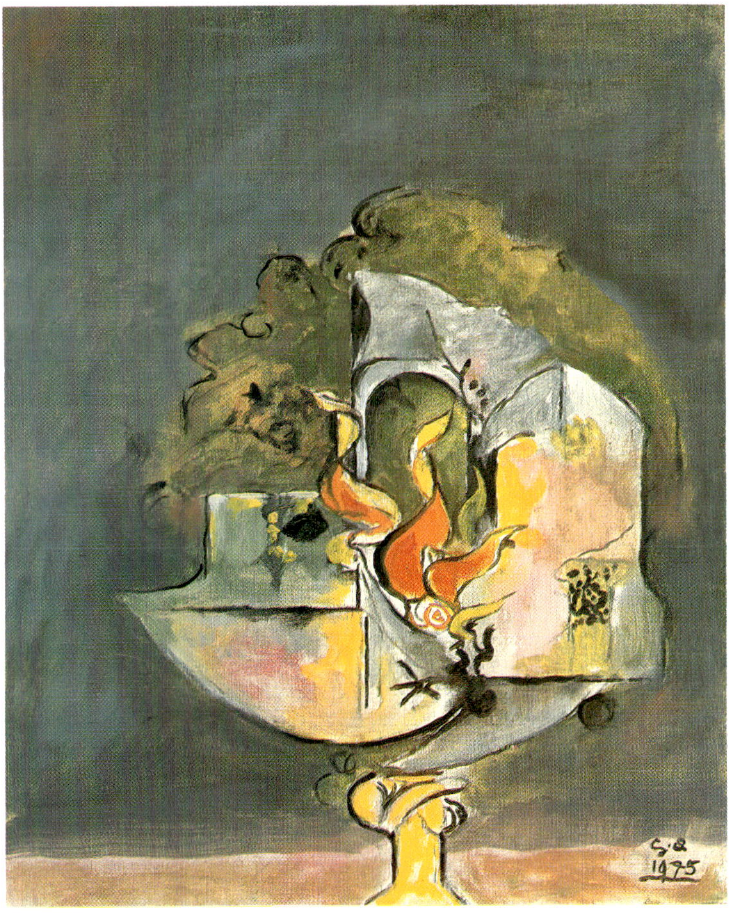

Above left
83 *Rock Hut*, 1974
Private collection, Italy

Above
84 *Hollow Tree*, 1977
Private collection, Italy

Left
85 *Study of Rock and Flames*, 1975
Graham and Kathleen Sutherland Foundation, Picton Castle Trust

and sixties in all parts of Europe, the Americas and South Africa. The Italians became his principal patrons and still remain his most enlightened collectors. At the time of the 1965 Turin exhibition, Luigi Carluccio, in his preface to the catalogue, spoke of 'Il nostro Sutherland', suggesting that he had been adopted by that country.

After several successive visits to the South of France to paint, he eventually bought, in 1955, La Villa Blanche, near Menton. One of Le Corbusier's collaborators did the internal designing of the house with Sutherland. A feature of it is that there are no skirting boards. 'The cube,' Sutherland held, 'must be kept pure without embellishment.' He was keen to introduce this idea in the design of the Picton Gallery. As the years passed, and traffic and pollution increased, he found that the most precious thing he could have in life was silence and peace, so whenever there was money to spare the Sutherlands bought hectares of land, orange and lemon groves; and towards the end of the sixties they began to spend more and more time peacefully in Pembrokeshire – reawakening a spirit which had never really died.

Chapter VII PORTRAITS 1949–1979

In 1947 when Sutherland was in France he met Somerset Maugham whose face instantly appealed to him as the possible subject for a portrait. It was as though he recognized immediately all the craggy indentations of organic discoveries which could be translated in terms of the human face. Was it now going to be possible to portray a penetrating psychological truth? 'I am dependent on what I see,' he said. Perhaps what he saw in the human frame he would analyse too deeply for the sitter's comprehension.

Has there been another portrait painter this century who has revealed with such rich perception a character's personality? Sutherland went deeply into the *personality* of his subject – 'I paint the person in the way he

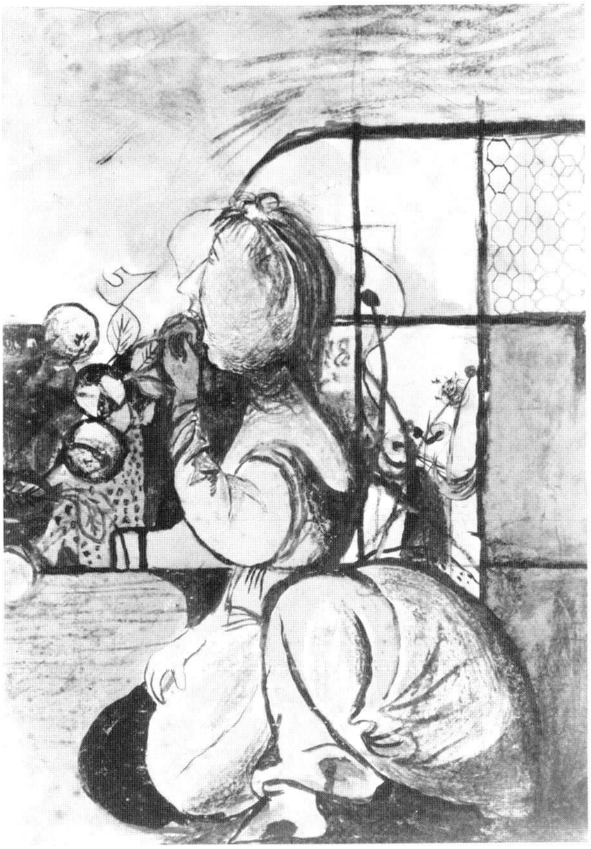

86 *Woman in a Garden*, 1945
Christie, Manson & Woods Ltd, London

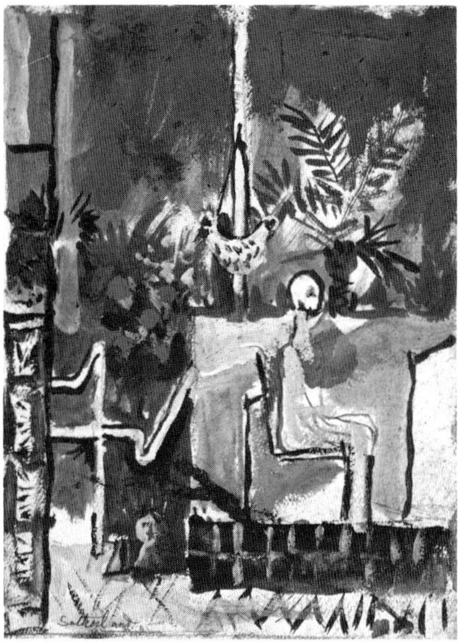

87 *Landscape with Figure*, 1961
Private collection, Italy

Although Sutherland was mainly preoccupied with integrating mechanical and organic forms within a theme and to a certain extent was concerned with the role of the animal as a subject during this period, we do see occasional reference to the figure in landscape as is shown here. It was not until the late '70s, however, that figures really become an integral part of the landscape.

or she presents himself' – not forcibly but spontaneously – 'It depends on what they show me.' It is clear that he was an analyst of character rather than merely a painter of his subject.

Although the immense importance he attached to his *Forms* delayed his embarking upon portraiture, it is at least evident that they contributed to this new departure when it came. He was then nearly fifty.

At Goldsmiths' he had not especially shone in the figure-drawing class, but he did make some acutely sensitive studies of figures during his engraving period. Then came the intense vibrant studies of tin miners and the series of figures already discussed in Chapter IV. *Study of Gypsies* (1939), *Woman in a Garden* (1945: Plate 86) and *Study for Woman in Chair* (1945) convey great promise and these studies together with the drawings he made of his wife Kathleen, provided a solid foundation for the intuitive development of the portrait. It is obvious that he was preparing the way for, or wondering whether he could eventually achieve, the live portrait. In retrospect he said, 'Landscape forms present themselves, and portraits seem to be the natural progression from the Standing Forms'. [34] If he was to extend his work into exploration of the complexity of human landscape he must pursue it only with the same penetrating scrutiny we have seen concentrated on the rocks, trees and stones.

Portraiture at this time had become a somewhat outmoded genre. The photographic portrait had gained increasing popularity and excellence during the twenties and thirties, while those whose work was selected by the Royal Academy made little impact by comparison with their forefathers. Sutherland viewed the world through a personal lens which magnified geological, biological and human structure, and, having recognized his own ability to portray a truthful yet individual metaphor in landscape, he left the actuality of nature to illustrators.

It was fortuitous that Somerset Maugham, having heard of Sutherland's enthusiasm, invited him to paint the portrait. When faced with the commission (1949), Sutherland became uneasy and wondered whether he could do it. 'I was reluctant and at first refused. I certainly didn't want to become a professional portrait painter.' They reached a mutual understanding that if Maugham liked it, that would be fine, but that the portrait should be executed without any pressure of sale or purchase – 'If it can be regarded purely as an experiment I would very much like to try.'

When he came to consider the portrait, technique, accuracy and precision of draughtsmanship were fundamental prerequisites (*vide* John Hayes) and it would have been impossible for someone like Sutherland to paraphrase a person or to represent them in abstract form.

> There are two basic ways of doing a portrait; one is to make an interpretive paraphrase of the movements of the forms of the head from sight, but largely from memory, or through a series of studies each gradually approaching the paraphrase. If your feelings for and memory of the person are strong enough, the likeness, however distorted, will not only never be eradicated, but actually enhanced. [35]

The intense, incisive qualities, the folds and creases, in Maugham's face contain striking similarities to the Pembrokeshire rock erosions. The

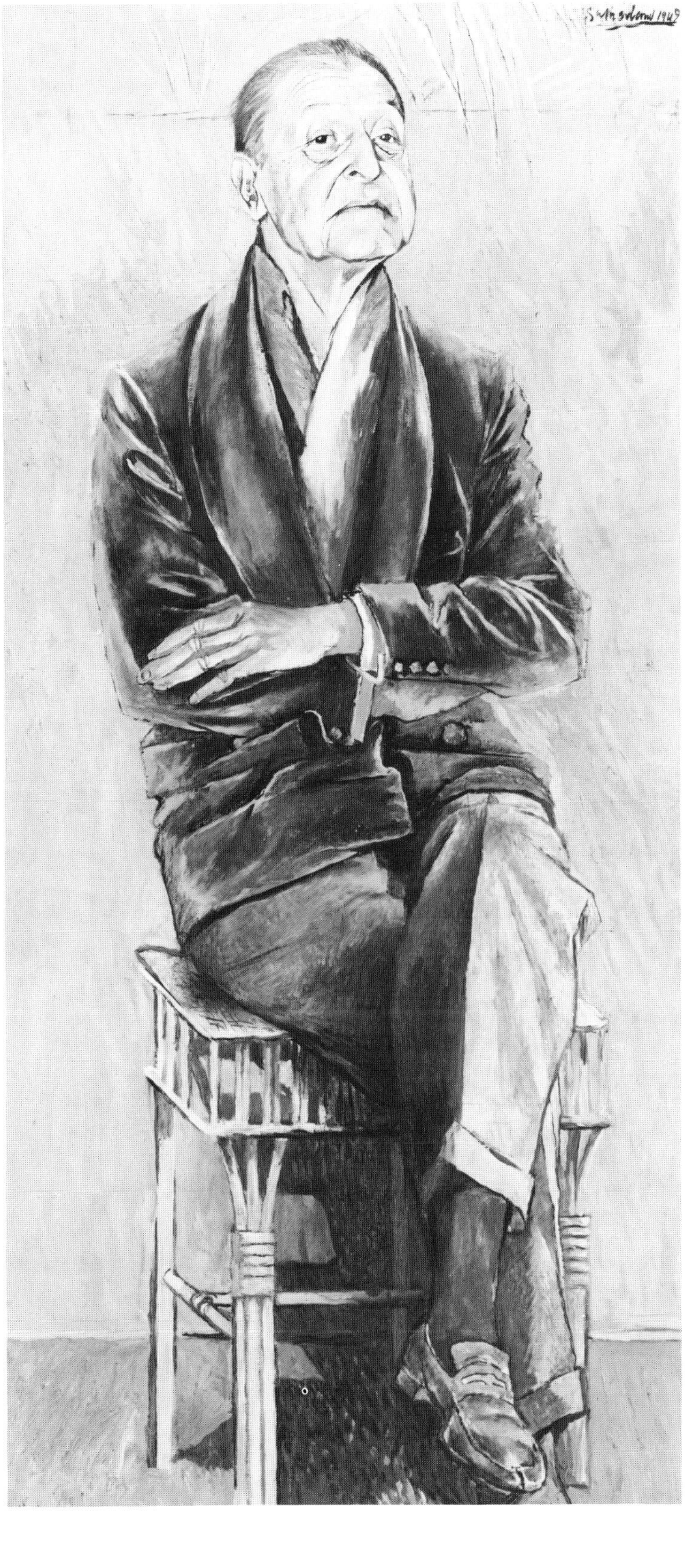

88 *Portrait of Somerset Maugham*, 1949
The Tate Gallery, London

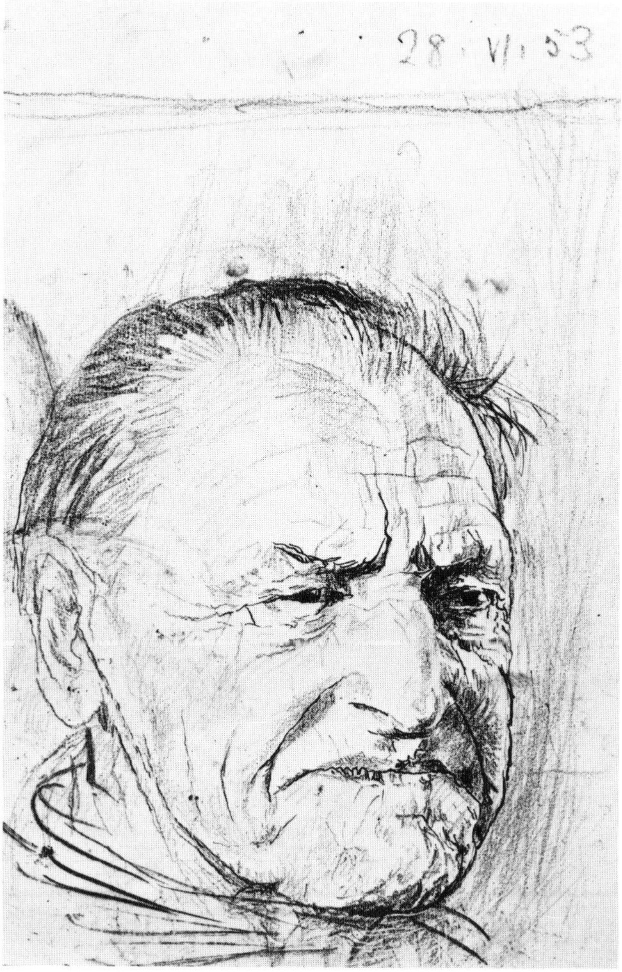

89 *Study of Head Facing Half-right (Somerset Maugham)*, 1953
Collection Mrs Graham Sutherland

characteristic similarities are, however, best conveyed in the lithographs Sutherland did of Maugham in 1953 (Plate 89). These were commissioned by Collins for their publication of *Cakes and Ale*. Sutherland could not have been faced with a more challenging set of features. The Maugham portrait is remarkable. It was his major work after departure into a new genre, and it has all the qualities of exploration into great detail. It was inevitable that he should be apprehensive – 'I go in fear and trembling' – yet the result showed that his fears were groundless. In Sutherland's subsequent drawings of Maugham, reference to the Welsh landscape is much stronger. The gnarled look of a serpent-like tree root such as he had exposed in *Study for Gorse on a Sea Wall* (1938) is reinterpreted in *Study of Right Ear* (1949). It is increasingly apparent that the use of line and colour in the former foreshadowed the Maugham study, although I believe the latter to be drawn more confidently, intently and analytically.

> You can have as much latitude and freedom as with any other forms in nature. The other basic way of doing a portrait is to render by analysis, or a notion or memory or all three, what you see in front of

> your eyes, or what you remember. This does not mean you make a copy of what you see. Far from it. But on the whole it is a matter of accepting rather than imposing. It is also an art of letting the subject gradually reveal himself unconsciously, so that by his voice and gaze, as well as by his solid flesh your memory and emotions are stirred and assaulted, as with other forms of nature. [36]

The most moving and sensitive of all Sutherland's portraits was undoubtedly that of his friend Edward Sackville-West (1953-4). The distressed, suffering body sinks within its clothing. The pallid face, which in later years upheld an enormous Haile-Selassie-type beard, did little to convey the spry little man, the great wit and aesthete that he was. In the first portrait Sutherland gave the head a modelled, sculptural quality with delicious tones of white; whereas in a second portrait, Sackville-West is featured achromatic in pyjamas against a dung-coloured background, a royal-blue diagonal breaks the otherwise pallid demeanour (Plate 90).

The third portrait which conveys great strength and modelling is that of

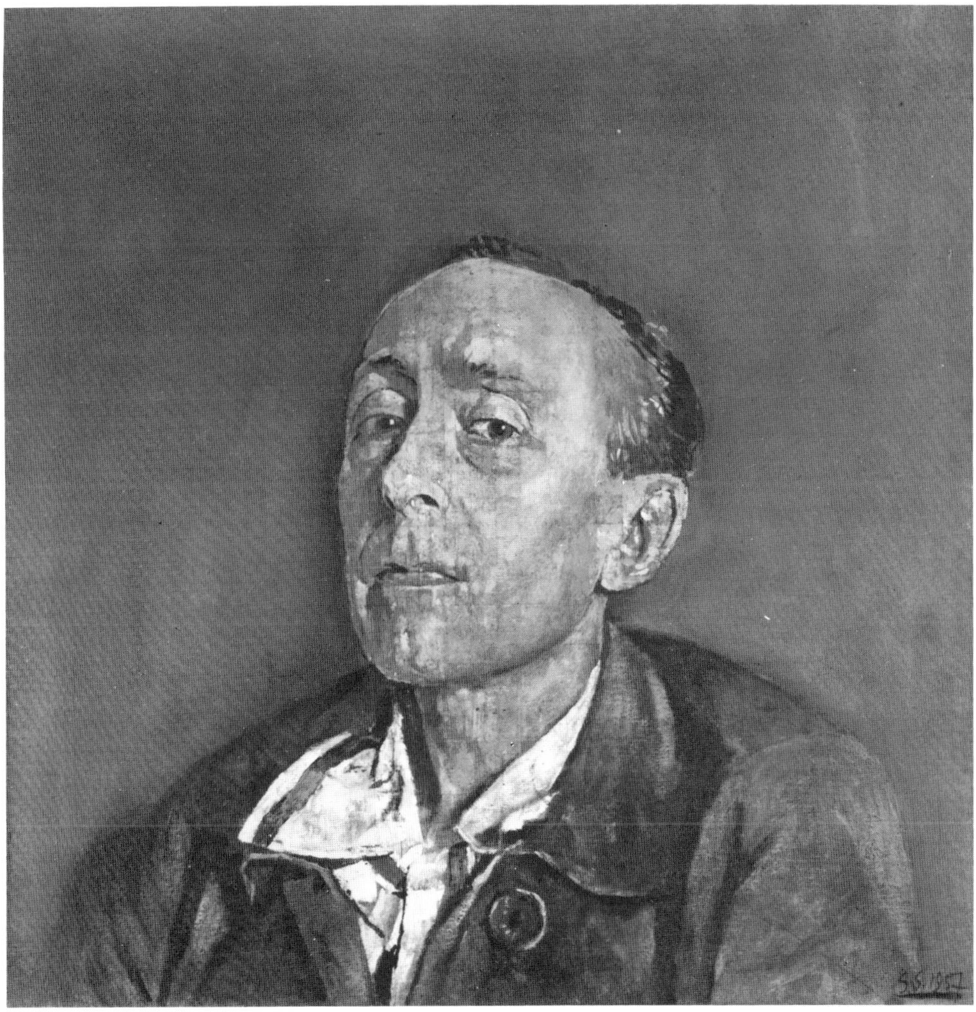

90 *Portrait of Edward Sackville-West*, 1957
Birmingham Museums & Art Gallery

the newspaper proprietor Lord Beaverbrook (Plate 91). Looking down on the sun-parched upper head, Sutherland was able to cut into the features with great force. In all these and in the portrait of Helena Rubinstein (Princess Gourielli), a great sense of drama surrounds the sitters. One is able to feel the intense authority which they commanded in their different spheres. Through landscape Sutherland became a stronger exponent of the human and through the human he was to give his landscape images greater presence. Sutherland explained this stage of development in 1951.

> I feel that now we can perhaps enlarge the field of painting by setting our emotional paraphrases of reality – they themselves have been conceived more optically – within the ambience of optical reality. Perhaps one of the reasons why I have recently tried to do portraits is that it is possible that I feel the need to narrow the gap between my 'stand-in' monuments and the real human animal. I cannot say for certain. It is difficult to say where the things which one is involved with at the moment are likely to lead one. [37]

When asked whether he approached his potential sitters in the same way as landscapes, he affirmed that he regarded them very much in the same way, as objects in a landscape. He did, however, have to concern himself with the whole question of the psychological presence of a person, which, he said, was infinitely more potent than any tree could be, though the initial exploration was much the same. Sutherland relied enormously on the reciprocal communication between himself and his sitter.

> I am drawn towards a paraphrase in some degree or other in order to display more vividly the inner life and mystery of the subject. But the human face and body is [sic] even more complex and mysterious. One is dealing with a sentient, breathing thing, and in order to obtain flavour, let alone the essence, I feel at least for the moment – that I have to be as absorbent as blotting paper and as patient and watchful as a cat. [38]

Not only were words vital, but laughter and smell – the whole aura surrounding a person had to be right. This, combined with the way his sitter revealed himself, his personality, constituted the vital ingredients for moulding the character. 'All I do ask of them is to take a pose which is uniquely significant for them.' He was asked in 1978, at the *vernissage* of the Churchill drawings at Picton, whether he would consider doing a posthumous portrait of Winston Churchill, having only six months earlier discovered that the portrait he painted in 1954 had been destroyed. His reply was that he did not think he could do a portrait without the atmosphere of the person being present, and that, especially in Churchill's case, he would miss his laugh.

When similarly asked to do a posthumous portrait of the late President Kennedy of the United States, he debated for a while but in the end declined as the aura of the President would be lacking. He did, however, manage to portray for Roberto Sanesi, the long-dead William Blake, and, in 1955, he painted for the São Paulo Museum a portrait of the eighteenth-century admiral Lord Nelson, which was commissioned by

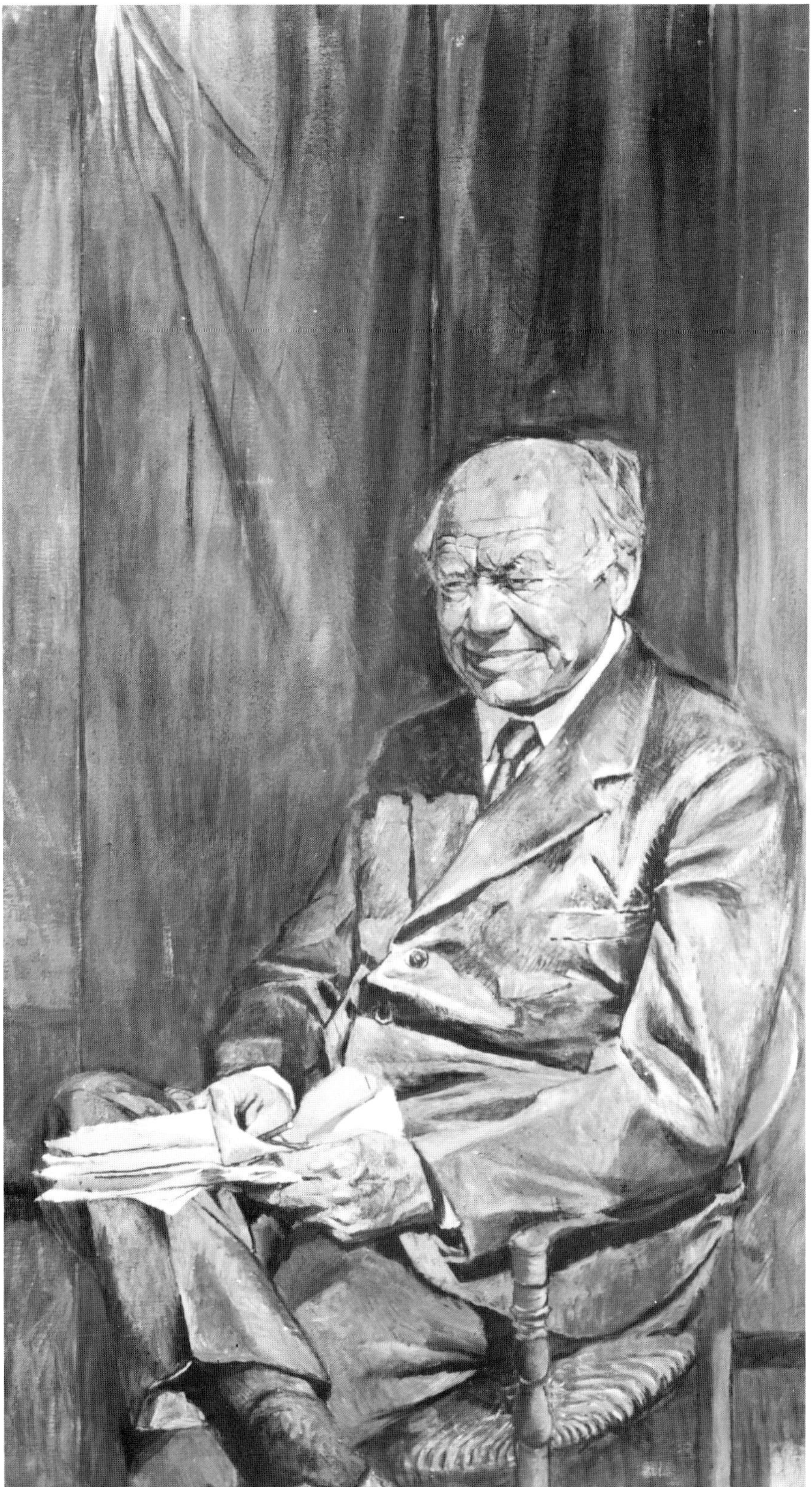

91 *Portrait of Lord Beaverbrook*, 1951
The National Portrait Gallery, London

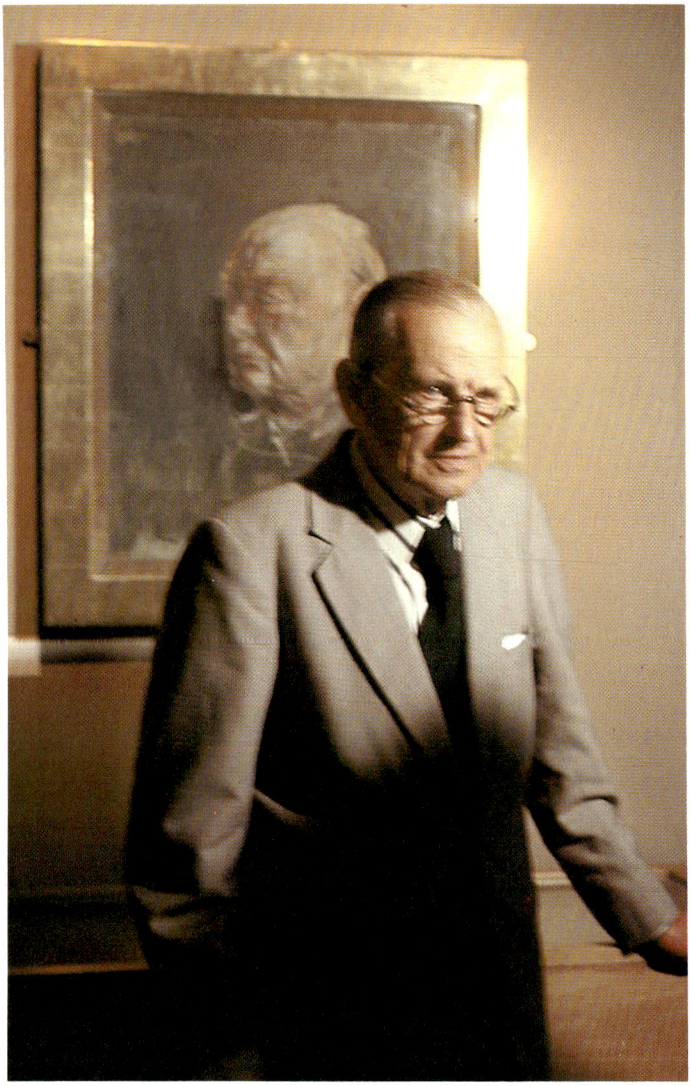

92 Two studies of Graham Sutherland with his *Study for Portrait of Winston Churchill* and reproduced portrait of Winston Churchill which was destroyed
Photograph Gilbert Adams FRPS

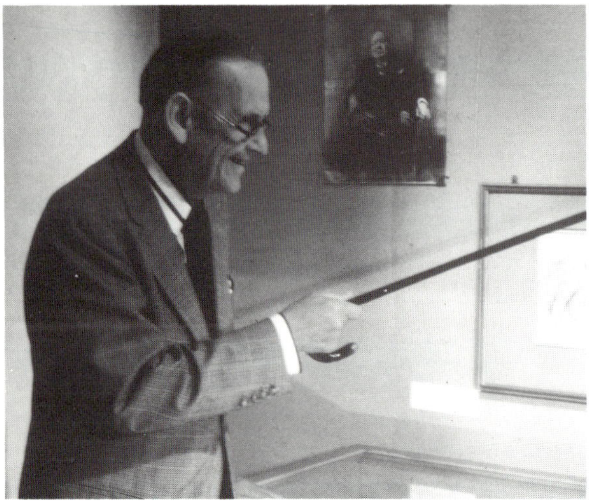

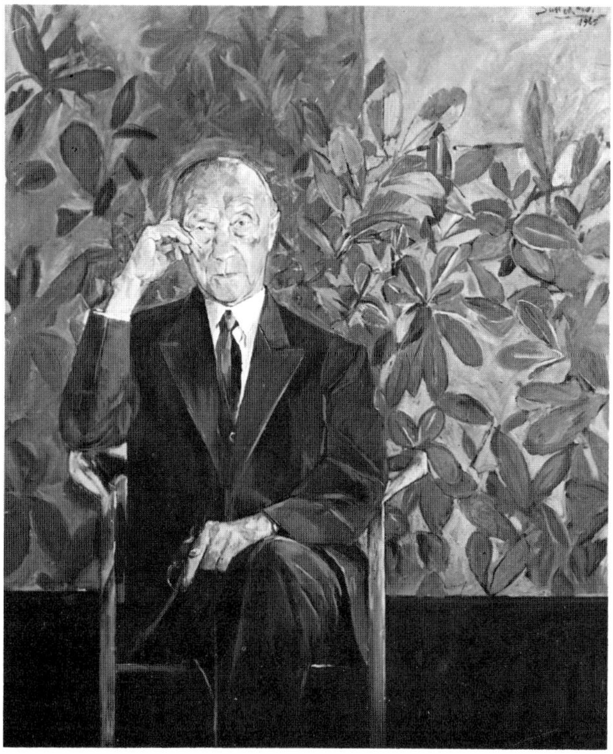

Left
93 *Portrait of Dr Adenauer*, 1965
Konrad Adenauer Stiftung

Below
94 *Sketch for Portrait of Dr Adenauer*, 1965
Konrad Adenauer Stiftung

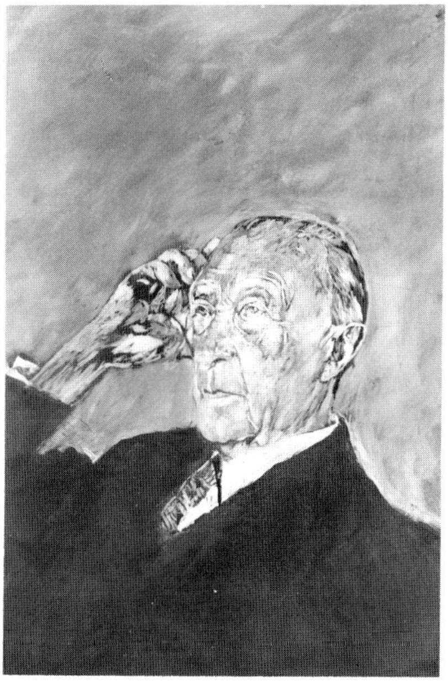

M. Chateaubriand, the Brazilian Ambassador to London and benefactor to the arts.

Sutherland's determined integrity and insatiable desire to produce a truthful revelation of his sitter will, without doubt, place him amongst the most profound exponents of the portrait in the twentieth century. He made many drawings and often preparatory oils before the definitive portrait.

> Usually I do a whole series of drawings, not always very miniature drawings, but finally I reach a stage when I think I've got enough material; it depends so much on what my sitter can give me. Then I take these drawings back to my studio and, hoping that I've seen enough, start work. [39]

In spite of copious notations and references as to idiosyncrasies, typical gestures, movement, colour of complexion and clothing, the final work still retains a freshness and vigour. Every feature had its purpose in the design of the human landscape. Colour of countenance eventually determined the scheme and tone of the clothing, as is evident particularly in the bucolic cheeks and spotted, pillarbox-red cravat of the Marquess of Bath. Sutherland liked to get as physically close to his sitter as possible to scrutinize expression and analyse form. As in landscape, he isolated areas of intense interest and suppressed elements of lesser importance. He attempted to give a suitable background: the suggestion of his beloved Italian garden for Dr Adenauer (Plate 93) and parkland for Lord Bath. He painted the final portrait away from the sitter. 'I find it distracting to have somebody in front of me – for the very reason that I gave for not painting in front of nature.'[40] (See Chapter IV, p.51).

Sutherland maintained that 'if you falsify physical truth, you falsify psychological truth' and set out to convey with total sincerity an accurate description of the sitter. It was most probably the very achievement of this truth in the Churchill portrait that the Churchill family found so disturbing. News in 1977 confirming the destruction of the portrait, commissioned by members of both Houses of Parliament for Churchill's eightieth birthday in 1954, won far greater public attention and sympathy for Sutherland than the presentation itself had done. To anyone brought up after the war, the Churchill that Sutherland portrayed was the person to whom we owed undying respect. The tragedy is that it was painted far too late, when Churchill had lost his dynamic manner. One has much sympathy with Sutherland, who had to portray a man of such greatness after he had suffered a stroke and was in bed, at times half asleep. Sutherland had to portray truth at a specific time; hence it is not hard to understand how he failed to please a proud family. Having asked Sir John Rothenstein if he had seen the portrait, Churchill asserted, 'I think the time has come for an artist to give some consideration to the *subject* of a portrait instead of looking over the wilderness of his subject hoping to discern there some glimmer of his own genius.'[41] I believe the photographic portrait by Bertram Park of Winston Churchill (Plate 95) will demonstrate, however, that Sutherland's approach was totally sincere; when Churchill asked Sutherland, 'How will you paint me, as a cherub or a bulldog?', Sutherland replied, 'It entirely depends what you show me, Sir.' (Letter to Lord Beaverbrook). 'As far as portraiture is concerned, he was an admirer, on the one hand, of the great draughtsmen Holbein and Ingres; on the other of Titian and Tintoretto and the leading painters of the Spanish school, El Greco, Velasquez and, above all, Goya; most of these artists contibuted to his style at some point and in some

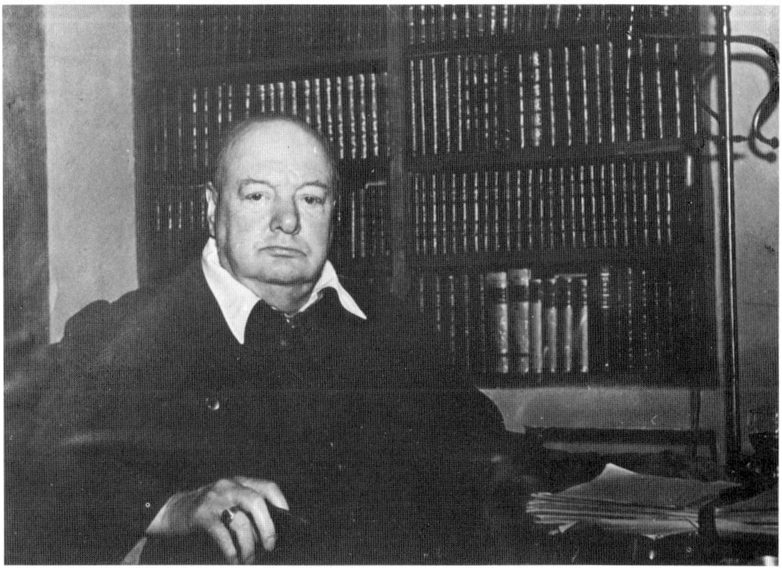

95 Winston Churchill, 1947
Photograph by Bertram Park
Collection Gilbert Adams

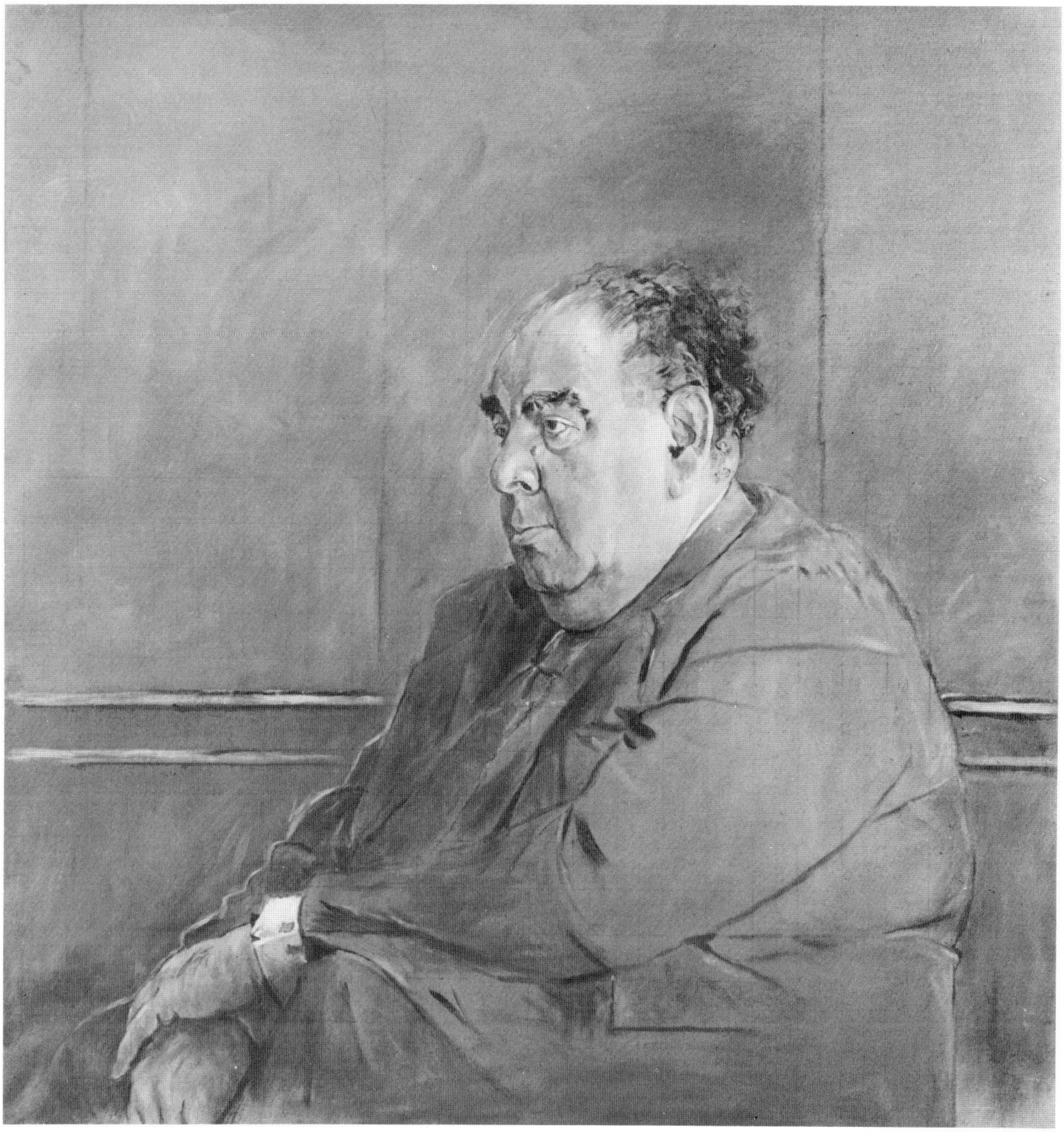

measure, though rarely specifically. But from the outset, his approach was governed by his own work in other fields.' [42] Where we see profound reference to masters in portraiture is in Sutherland's portrait of Kenneth Clark; both the study of the head in profile and the definitive portrait clearly resemble Piero Della Francesca's painting of Federigo da Montefeltro, duke of Urbino. Similar reference is made in Sutherland's portrait of Lady Marion Philipps. About Rembrandt, to whom I have already alluded, he said, 'Rembrandt's use of chiaroscuro was surely not simply a means of obtaining mystery: it was as much to isolate areas of acute interest and to suppress the elements of lesser interest.' [43]

96 *Portrait of Lord Goodman*, 1973
The Tate Gallery, London

As with the tree forms and *Standing Forms* Sutherland relied on a space

Right
97 *Self-Portrait*, 1977
Private collection, Italy

Below
98 Graham Sutherland
Photograph Gilbert Adams FRPS

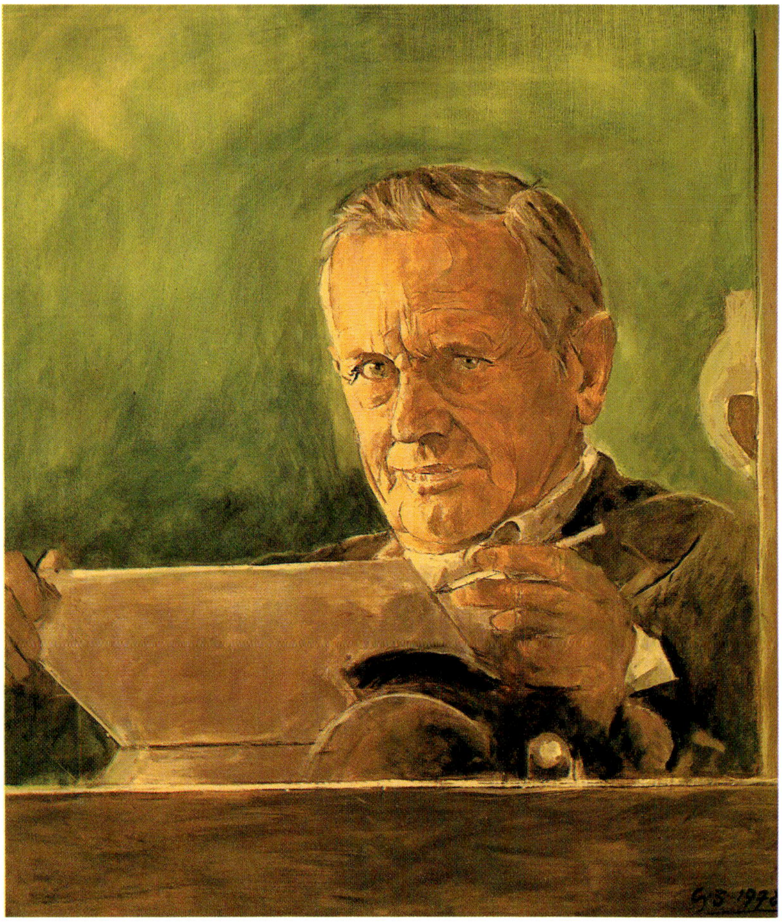

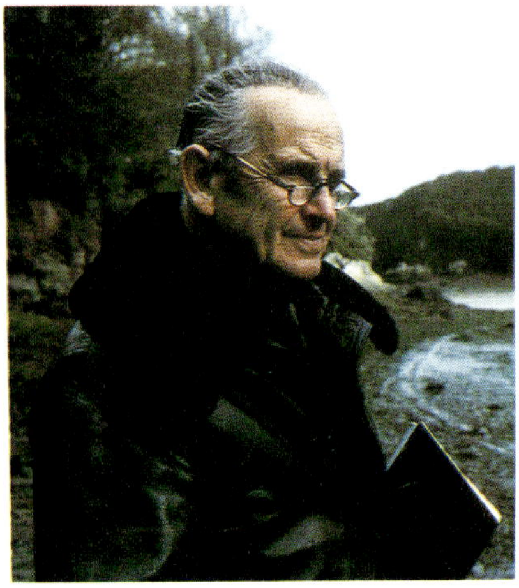

outside the main area of interest to stabilize movements and 'help preserve the equilibrium'. Here is an interesting feature whereby the relationship between the vertical, horizontal and oval are in perfect balance with one another. It undoubtedly originates in the momentous new awareness experienced by Sutherland near St David's early in 1934 (see *Stones in an Enclosure*: Plate 31) and it is most clearly demonstrated in the definitive portrait of Dr Adolf Jann, where the horizontal and vertical movement of the seat complement the oblique position of the sitter. Sutherland was very much concerned with the vertical portrait when considering Maugham, his first portrait of Sackville-West and his friend Giorgio Soavi; for which he used the pedestal as the balancing formula, whereas for Dr Adolf Jann, Arthur Jeffress (Plate 99), Max Egon (Prince von Fürstenberg) and Mark Longman, the subjects were contained within the round. He would wait, while movements and gestures before him coalesced, until the whole arrangement was stabilized. Thus he was able to establish the scheme of things. The same principles of composition and design were used in the Sutherland portraits as were adopted in the Sutherland landscape motif. He attempted to fuse all characteristic directions, movements and gestures into a rich and perceptive design.

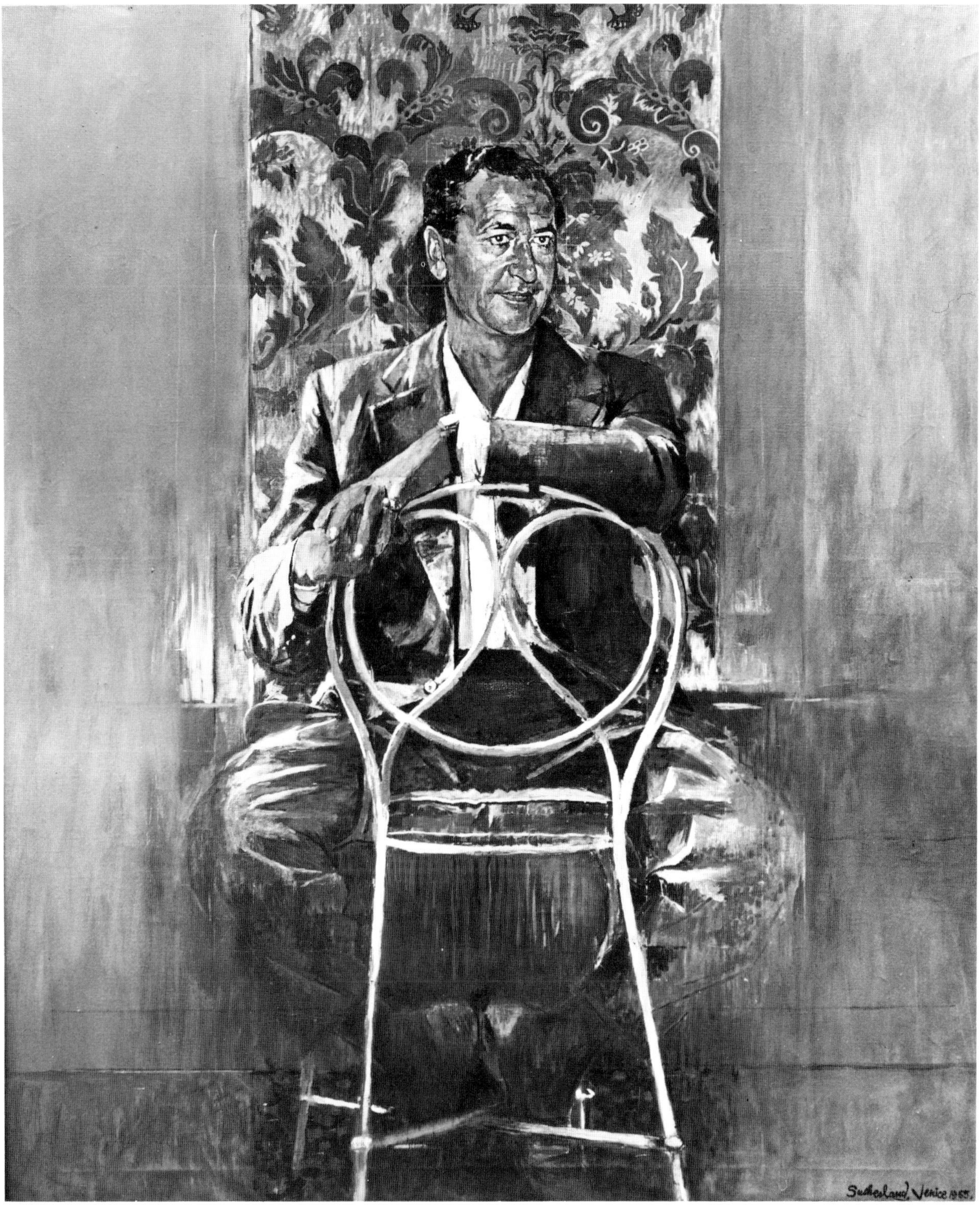

99 *Portrait of Arthur Jeffress*, 1955-6
Southampton Art Gallery & Museums

'There are some people who require endless studies, and sometimes even then I cannot find the exact equivalent of their look, even though I may know them well and have a perfectly clear idea in my mind as to how they do in fact look.' [44] Many of the methodical contributory studies he made for his portraits of Churchill, Somerset Maugham and Max Egon have been preserved. These often had the inspired effect of Matisse, where economy of line presided over detail, and colour composition was all-important. Sutherland drew with intensity and conviction, his brush moulding lines as if his hands shaped clay. There is intense power in the Sutherland portrait and it was with powerful people that he was principally concerned. He responded to the fascinating achievement of people in high office. In retrospect it is understandable that portraits should have become a part of Sutherland's *oeuvre*. If his ability to embark on the portrait does seem surprising, one only has to consider the delightful quality of his earlier drawings of his wife and his evocative rendering of tin miners.

I think Sutherland's portraiture may best be summed up by the well-known art historian who proclaimed at the National Portrait Gallery's exhibition to celebrate the Queen Mother's eightieth birthday, where a range of portraits and photographic studies spanned her life, 'The Graham Sutherland portrait sketch is the only one that's any damned good.' It elicits her personality; it includes motifs of horny shapes, the fleeing bird and the craggy indentations of organic structure, but it was lent graciously by the Queen Mother herself as a favourite of hers.

Chapter VIII
PEMBROKESHIRE
1967–1980

Increasingly during the later nineteen-sixties Sutherland made simplified statements; he painted larger and produced in one massive hunk of a form a marriage between the embryonic figure – the oval, the round, the conglomerate – and various fascinating intricate constructions and turmoils within the entrails of that form; luxuriant growth, voluptuous fertility, burst out into the air. These were paintings less rigorous in exploration – more contrived in end result. He fused nature with the mechanical; human with organic. His designs became increasingly structured and methodical. The principal objects, trees and noble boles, captivated the viewer; posts shimmered, reflected in water, heron took off from mudflats. Far from becoming repetitive, as Douglas Cooper suggests (*The Times*, 28 February 1980), his imagery was still based on the amalgam of ideas and *objets trouvés*, which provide important props in the overall design – ideas gathered from a lifetime's appraisal of nature. Reconstruction, planning and balance became more formal. *Form over Picton* (1971) and *Picton* (1971) are both works which appear richer, more dense in atmosphere. *Trees on a River Bank* (1971) conveys the setting of the sun and the early rising of the moon. A few works such as *Picton* (1971) began to show a close affinity with Max Ernst's *Après nous la Maternité* (1927) and *Paysage au Gemme de Blé* (1936). The forms – their construction, tone and mood – yield evidence of ever closer scrutiny. We are invited to share Sutherland's wonderful store of discoveries in Wales. It seemed as if the years of exploration were over. He had found a new formula and point of departure.

The constant love of estuaries and inlets, sea shore and coast, is rarely defined on a scenic scale. *Floating Forms* (1972), *Form in an Estuary* (1972) and *Undulating Form* (1973) typify the close-up peering approach of the painter. He was always looking *into* objects, *into* landscape.

The long absence from Pembrokeshire – in person, not in spirit – ended in 1967 when Pier Paolo Ruggerini wanted to make a film of Sutherland at work. 'Let's go to Wales,' suggested Sutherland, and so they went, stayed in Haverfordwest and all ate, he remembered, delicious fish in Milford Haven. The Italians fell in love with Wales, and Sutherland was ecstatic at returning. Having thought that he had discovered almost everything about Pembrokeshire before he took up residence in France in 1955, he now realized that he had been wrong. Subjects which had appealed to him before his departure and indeed had continued to inspire him throughout his time in France, now seemed even more vital and attractive and certainly were to prove the essence of his painting for

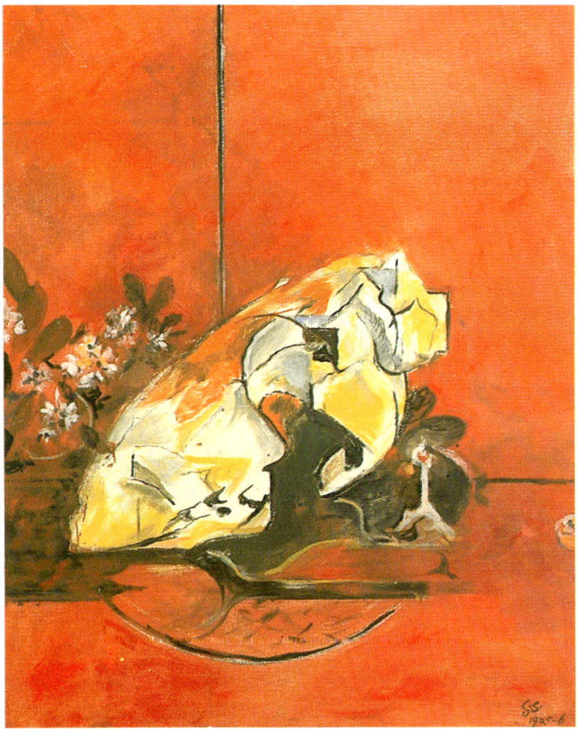

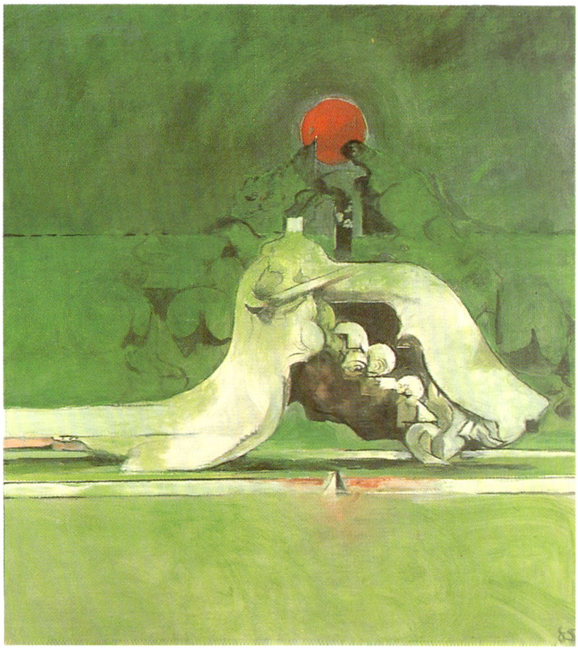

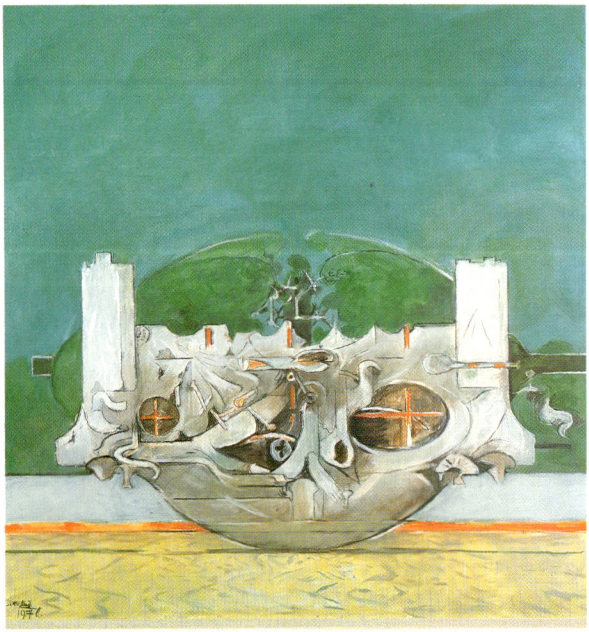

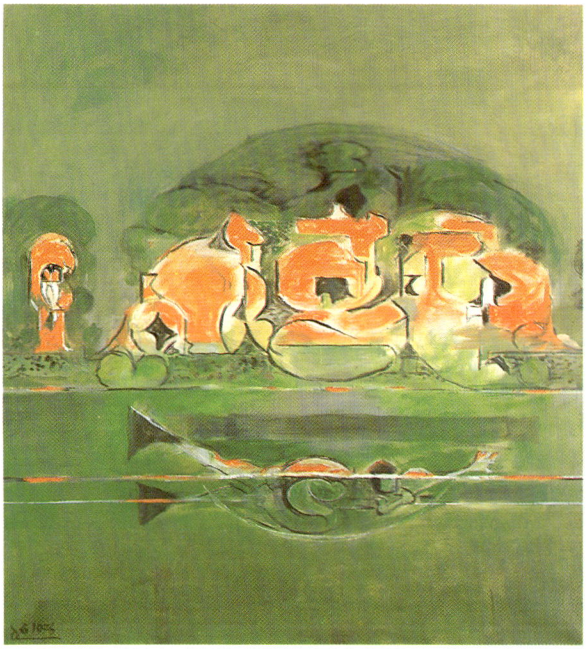

the next thirteen years. The galaxy of shapes and forms was to become even more of an obsession. In 1942 he wrote to a friend:

> I have confined myself to writing about a particular area and I do this because it was in this area that I learnt that landscape was not necessarily scenic, but that its parts have an individual figurative detachment. I found that this was equally true of other places which I visited later, but the clear, yet intricate construction of the landscape of the earlier experience coupled with an emotional feeling of being on the brink of some drama, taught me a lesson and had an unmistakable message that has influenced me profoundly. [45]

I think one can say that it influenced all his subsequent painting. Since the time he wrote that letter his ideas, his visual anecdotes and his manner of working had hardly changed, as is shown by his letter to 'G' (Giorgio Soavi) in 1972.

> If you really want to hear about it, you will probably want to know about my routine. But to tell the truth I must say one must not analyse oneself too much – otherwise there is the strange risk of 'pouring the baby away with the bath water'!
>
> But all right: I submit to discipline – to the disciplines practised by my predecessors. I am, I have to admit, a tireless worker – with regular hours. But the matter is far more complicated than that. I am dependent on what I see.
>
> Now I have to explain a little further – the creative process is something like this: I may go for a walk. There is everything around me. I look: certain things that one sees, almost by accident, seem to strike me more than others.
>
> Out of the thousand things I see – *one* juxtaposition of forms – above all others seems to have a meaning. I don't always understand what I am doing – or what I am likely to do. You might say that at this stage I am hemmed in and compressed – even thwarted. My mind is receptive – but vacant.
>
> I make notes following the first *frisson* of an encounter. Gradually an idea emerges: there is the knowledge that, almost in spite of myself – something significant has arrived.
>
> When I say I am thwarted, at first, I mean in the sense of Petrarch: 'The enclosed flame burns more fiercely' and if it grows – be it ever so little, it can in no way be concealed.
>
> The wonder is awakened: for me the objects have to be of a distant and recondite order in order to increase wonder.
>
> The preliminary stage – the direct contact, leads, then, to something else, controlled and ordered by the mind. The difficulty is to preserve the feelings of the first encounter – to realize that one must retain the freshness of instinct – to realize perhaps that what one has seen in a 'moment' – somehow by thinking and feeling, studying and restudying *might* become a work of art.
>
> Therefore, in the studio one remembers: one's encounters become redefined, paraphrased and changed into something new and different from that of the first encounter – yet the same. [46]

Opposite

Above left
100 *Dog Rock*, 1976
Graham and Kathleen Sutherland Foundation, Picton Castle Trust

Above right
101 *Untitled*, 1976
Graham and Kathleen Sutherland Foundation, Picton Castle Trust

Below left
102 *U-Shaped Form with Blue Sky*, 1976
Graham and Kathleen Sutherland Foundation, Picton Castle Trust

Below right
103 *Swimmer*, 1976
Graham and Kathleen Sutherland Foundation, Picton Castle Trust

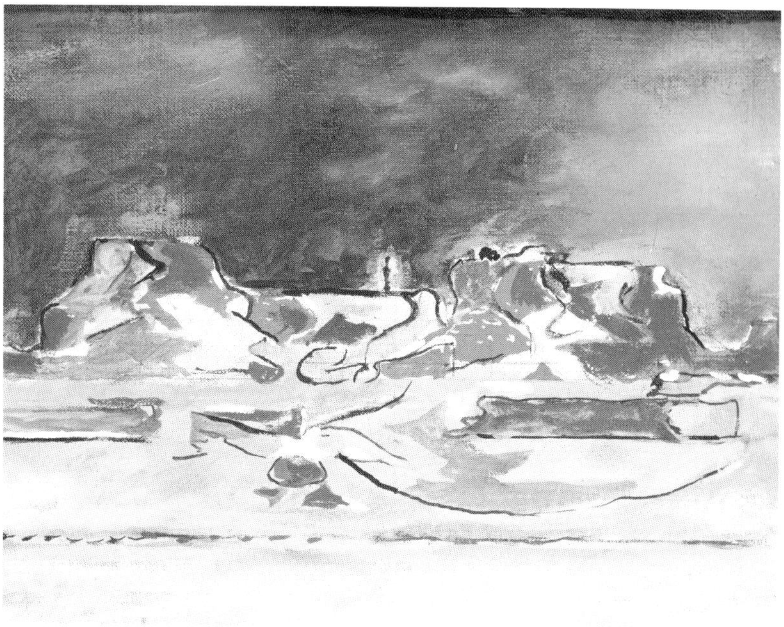

104 *Landscape II*, 1971
Graham and Kathleen Sutherland Foundation, Picton Castle Trust

An encounter with the Welsh landscape is an experience that had come to a number of Sutherland's contemporaries: Augustus John, Henry Moore, John Piper, Michael Ayrton and Paul Nash. When this observation was made to Sutherland, he wrote in reply:

> Most painters endeavour to present a *scenic* view. This is not the aim of Sutherland. He wishes to dig deeper – to isolate objects he sees – to make a paraphrase – a rebirth. In translating organic forms and shapes in this way it may be that he educates the observer into seeing the complex rhythms of his images for himself. [47]

The interrelation between Piper's Welsh scenes, Michael Ayrton's nature themes, Paul Nash's surrealistic reconstructions of nature and, a little later, Keith Vaughan's landscapes, conveyed a spirit blowing in the direction of a break by certain English contemporaries with conventional scenic views. Undoubtedly the last, for the time, of the British romantic artists, they showed that nature provided the raw material for a work of art; by being given separate status the work of art still remained akin to nature. At the time of their first visits to Wales, none of these painters had achieved international recognition but they were, in their amalgamating of organic forms and discovery of a Celtic light, beginning to break with the English romantic movement and certain accepted traditions.

Many painters have experienced Wales as a constructive influence. The sparse mystical landscape compelled Sutherland to return, and many new, younger painters still work and find their inspiration in Pembrokeshire.

> The painting ought to have a separate life, leaving, of course, the atmosphere of the place to remain as an important overtone which should give life to the bare bones. [48]

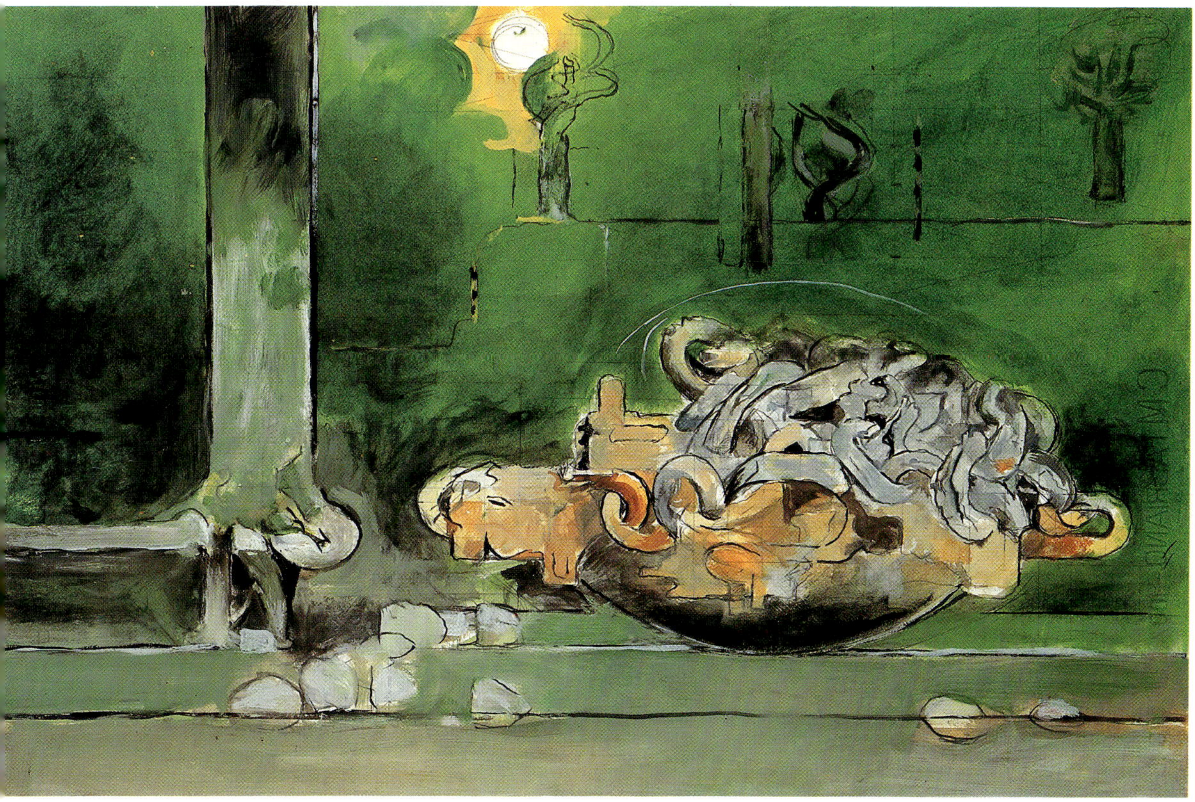

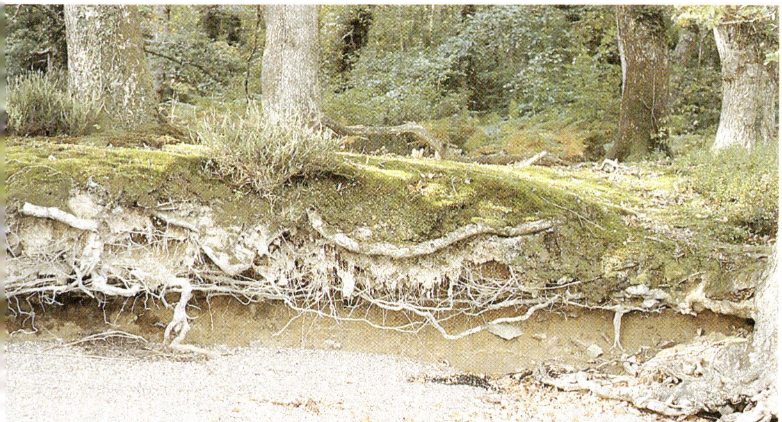

Above
105 *Forest with Chains*, 1973
Graham and Kathleen Sutherland Foundation, Picton Castle Trust

Left
106 Benton shore
Photograph Gilbert Adams FRPS

From these words of Sutherland's to me, we can understand how the *Standing Forms* (1949-52) were inspired in France whilst at the same time having deep-rooted reference to the early acquaintance with Pembrokeshire, and how *Bird over Sand* (1975-6: Plate 118) was inspired by the rising runnels of the upper reaches and shores of the Eastern Cleddau in Pembrokeshire. The bright light and glamorous nature of southern France, the bosky darkness of woodland shores and earthy nature in Wales – not only did particular places influence certain subjects, but Sutherland also expressed the external atmosphere of those places, and often the subconscious influence of events and people. Although Sutherland was too much of an individualist stylistically, and too inventive, to be *profoundly* distracted by contemporary life, yet every now and again we see glimpses of its effect upon him in, for example, the precarious combat of animals, or the agony of Christ. Essentially these personal responses are made apparent as, for example, in the *Thorn* subjects and *Standing Forms.*

During those late sixties and seventies, there were three equanimous sources of inspiration – France, Kent and Pembrokeshire – but the one which dominates all his later painting is Pembrokeshire. Atmospheres became interrelated and juxtaposed and finally submitted to the grand orchestrated design. Personally, I think it is nostalgia for the past that has made many people find the early nineteen-thirties Sutherland phase his most exciting – the new, primitive, stirring beginnings of recognition. If one considers only *Entrance to Lane* (Plate 25), *Green Tree Form: Interior of Woods* (Plate 23), *Form in a Wood* and *Gorse on Sea Wall*, they represent the Sutherland in ascendancy – the formative, dynamic, unique and individual painter. Those nineteen-thirties had in many spheres, not only in the arts, a heady romanticism. As a result of the war and his own highly complex spirit, he never recaptured quite the lyrical splendour of those years. Like every adult, he had to mature, and with him his works matured. Yet, after all, lyricism and poetry are only in the eyes of the beholder.

At the beginning of the seventies, the structure of his painting became more formalized than it had been in the late sixties. No longer did he submit to indecision, to a diffident linear control. His grand dramatic designs were like stage sets, animals and birds, beast and human, swooping across the stage to mime their wordless message.

When reintroduced to Pembrokeshire, Sutherland felt that, having amassed a store of images from this country and taken so much from her, he ought in return to give something back. Talking this over with his friends The Hon. Hanning and Lady Marion Philipps, he discovered that a part of the magnificent buildings of Picton Castle – the old laundry – could be converted into a gallery in which to house and show the large collection of works (all inspired in Wales) belonging to himself and his wife. The idea is particularly appealing in that works of art seen in the artist's studio or in the setting which inspired them acquire an extra dimension and human interest. Better communications have made the decentralization of works of art less necessary, but the more, therefore, to be encouraged. The journey to them is a happy adventure, just as it is to travel to the tomb of Tutankhamen and experience the arid atmosphere of the desert sands where lived those ancient kings, or to tread over wild plants whilst searching for the stones of some Doric temple. The

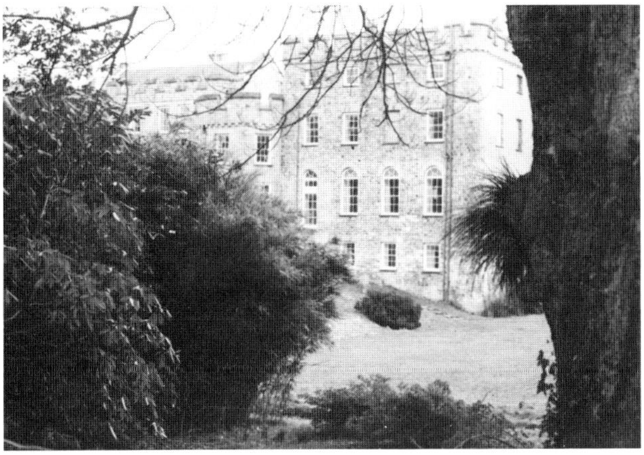

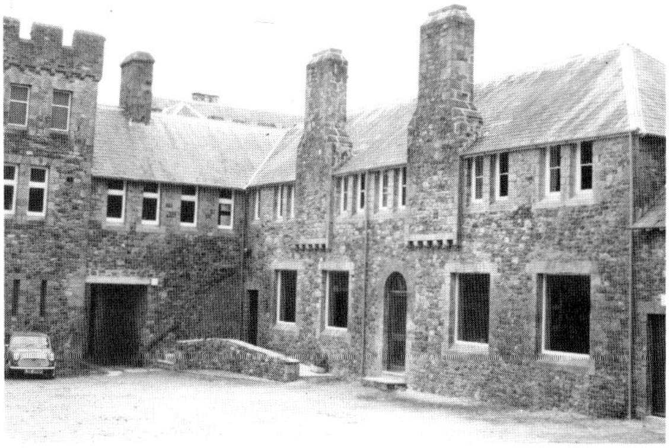

atmosphere, the light, the smell, the haunting presence of the creator are more important sensualities than the stark, silent, echoing rooms of galleries and museums. I am not by any means denouncing museums and galleries; it is only that an adventure is always stimulating, and almost invariably arouses an emotional response.

Picton Castle grounds, once surrounded by a deer park of some three hundred acres interspersed with oak trees and woodland until a hurricane gale destroyed over five hundred trees, have now been replanted with oak, beech, Japanese larch, Douglas fir, Norway and Sitka spruce, tsuga and thuja, and the gardens are adorned with rhododendrons, a few of which flower as early as January, camellias, magnolias and azaleas.

Sutherland recalled the laundry looking like a complete shambles when he first saw it but, courageous of faith, he knew the interior could be replanned and built. He wanted it to have a feeling of a large, elegant drawing-room, but not too grand – a place where people could feel comfortable; and, as with his Menton house, he wanted to retain the pure cube and not use skirting boards.

Above left
107 Picton Castle
Photograph Gilbert Adams FRPS

Above
108 The Graham and Kathleen Sutherland Foundation Gallery, Picton Castle
Photograph Studio Jon, Haverfordwest

This was the original Gallery. An extension was completed at the end of May 1982, providing space for a number of additional works, some of which have not been on exhibition before.

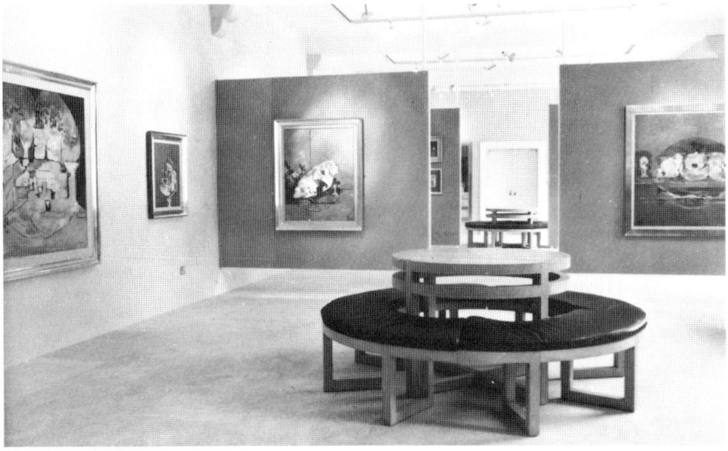

109 Interior of Graham and Kathleen Sutherland Foundation Gallery at Picton Castle
Photograph Studio Jon, Haverfordwest

Negotiations were begun for the financing of the place, and the efforts and contributions of the National Museum of Wales, the Wales Tourist Board, Dyfed County Council, South Pembrokeshire District Council, Preseli District Council and the Rayne Foundation, Pier Paolo and Marzia Ruggerini who gave the Sienese marble floor, the Monument Trust (who donated the glass cases and museum chairs) and Alistair McAlpine who paid for the cost of producing the catalogue, lent considerable weight to Sutherland's initiative. The gallery was opened in June 1976 by Lord Goodman. It is the ultimate example of how excellent and successful can be the decentralization of major cultural attractions, and has had visitors from all parts of the world.

Sutherland felt, as the construction of the gallery progressed, that the vast body of works which he and his wife had retained over the years – those inspired in Wales – was insufficient for the final form that the gallery would take. So he painted several works especially for the gallery – large oils which in format reciprocate the windows. The aubergine-coloured Pembrokeshire stone exterior is echoed within by soft pink natural floated plaster which has recently been modified, the marble floor provides a simple base on which round, carved tables and showcases exhibit a facsimile edition of Sutherland's *Welsh Sketchbook* and small watercolours. There are books, postcards and posters. The fundamental attraction is the filtration of abundant, natural light through the windows. A number of early Pembrokeshire landscapes, several of Sutherland's war subjects, lithographs, etchings and aquatints are juxtaposed on free-standing hessian frames.

Two of Sutherland's early acquaintances went one day to see the gallery and told him later in that rhythmic Celtic lilt, 'You see, I'm afraid Mr Sutherland, we didn't understand any of it, but when we took a walk around the gardens and down to the estuary we decided to return and have another look. Then we began to understand what your paintings were all about.'

With the gallery's successful contribution, both to Wales and to the British art scene, Sutherland's answer to a question of mine on his ideas for future painting was, 'I should like to get nearer to what I know I want but cannot always do. I've always wanted to be a good painter. As long as I can keep my brain working without diminishing the emotional impact there will always be a challenge.' [49] To him Pembrokeshire was exciting in all seasons. But he did not bring out the usual painterly qualities of spring or autumn, mist and fog, except in a spring subject like *La Primavera* (1975: Plate 110). He seemed to create subjects removed from any suggestion of a particular season, or of weather. We are made more sharply aware of early morning or late evening. The mist, damp and wind around the western shores are elements with which he had to contend since the development of an arthritic knee, but it did not suppress his appetite for discovering new material to store in his mind. Well into his seventies he still stalked through bracken and bramble, over the stony ground around St David's; to the north where the sharp hills of Ordovician igneous rock rise out of flat plains; and to the south, where the triangular rock forms, protecting similar shaped farmhouses, hit the horizon. When he said that it was in this triangle that he learnt to paint, it was as though in the seventies – his seventies – he was entering a second

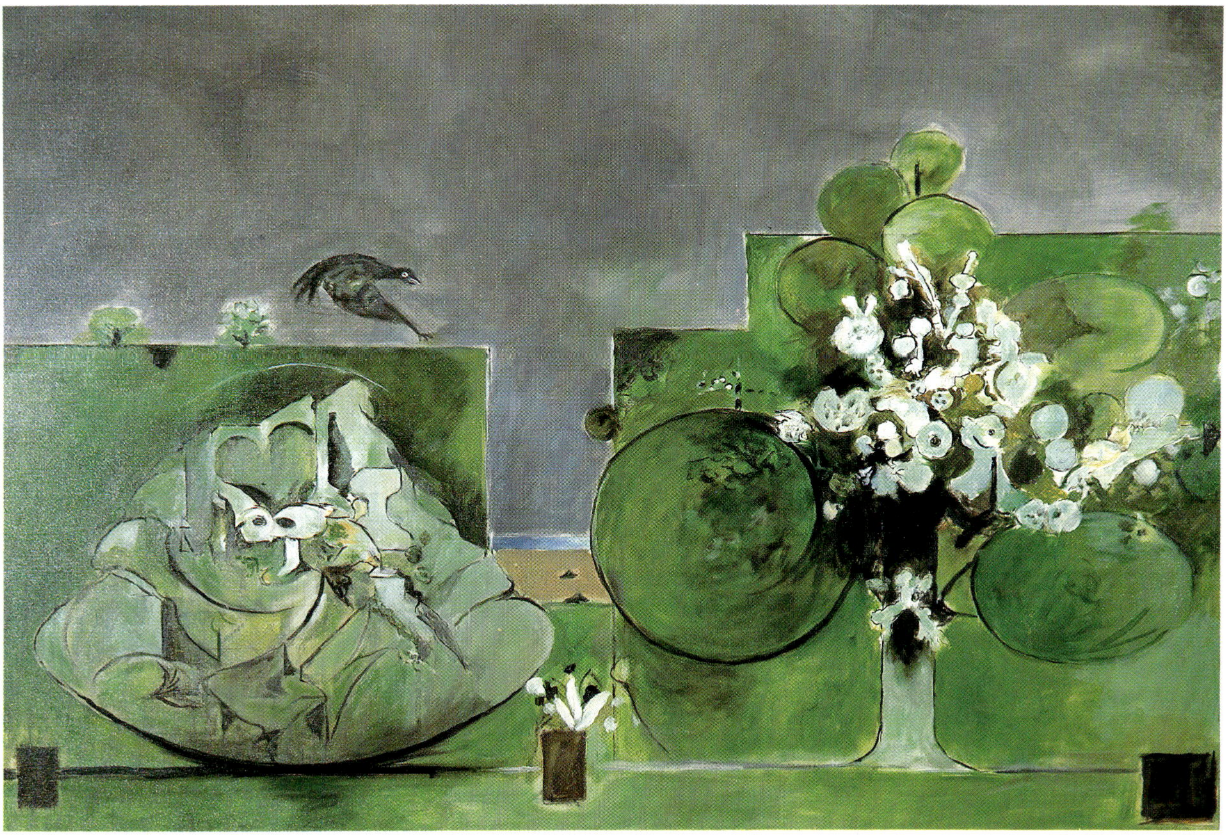

110 *La Primavera*, 1975
Private collection, Italy

childhood, walking these areas where large grey weathered stones, buttoned with clumps of foxgloves and studded with stonecrop, give way to spongy moss and circles of thrift, just as, when a boy, he had taken his long solitary walks and become 'involved with things beyond what I saw'. He used superb imagination and inventive spirit to balance the mould of the landscape. Yet, because of nature's configuration, we are left in no doubt as to the source of a painting such as *Porthclais with Setting Sun* (1979: Plate 111). He meandered round his favourite estuaries further south, his eyes constantly receptive to any small vision of colour and possibility of colour. In *Estuary with Birds* (1971-2: Plate 114), he took the liberty of magnifying scale – the sharp upward exaggerated triangles of red rock under an umbrella of oak. He flattened and elongated, heightened and squashed. He still made many notebook entries, often sighting some hidden object and isolating it in a sketch which gave it independent existence. The silence around this area of Pembrokeshire is compelling, and is matched by the strange shapes which nature's contortion and mutation have orchestrated. Another subject from which he gained repeated inspiration was the architectural rock formations pierced by

Right
111 *Porthclais with Setting Sun*, 1979
Private collection, Italy

Below
112 *Porthclais*, 1939-40

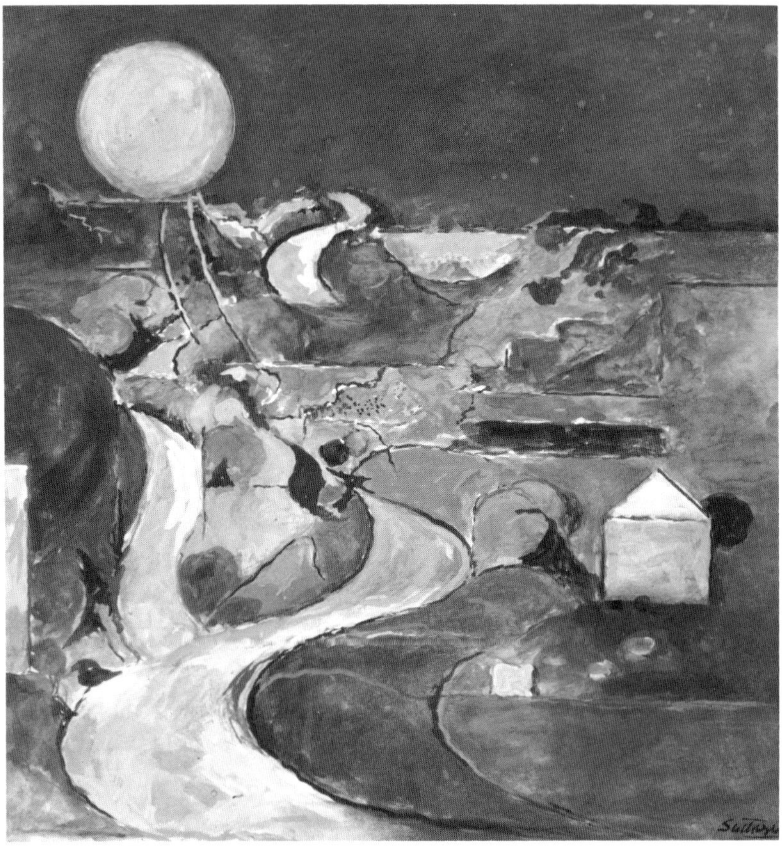

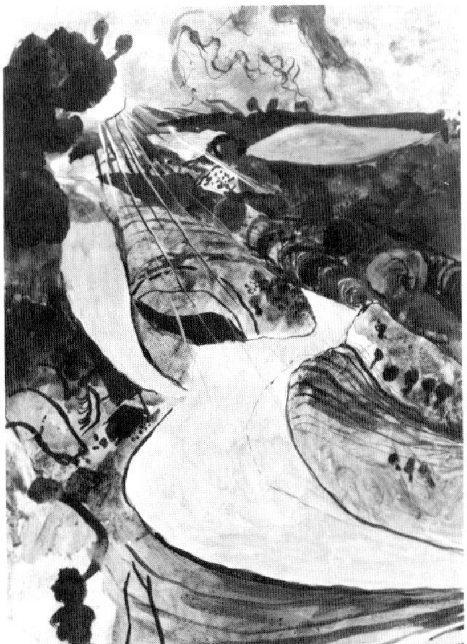

weather and sea erosion. He gives these rocks towering, ecclesiastical ovations in *Cathedral (Study of Rocks)* (1975: Plate 116). In these nature-contorted origins he found these rocks reached full cathedral strength with domes. As the sun sets, her rays translate the incisions (normally near black in their shadows) to a potent pink.

Sutherland's genius lay in his ability to paraphrase all that was about him and reconstruct monumental images, composing at the same time exciting patterns with poise and sympathy. During nearly fifty years of painting he used a palette which included chrome, ochre, yellow, cadmium, orange, violet and purple, ultramarine and cerulean – colours assimilated along the gorse-filled banks of Pembrokeshire. Violets and primroses strike out against a viridian backcloth. The deep wet purples and greys from the pebble shores were stored in his memory and reproduced during maturity.

As Sutherland never attempted to absorb the greater landscape, or did so only for atmospheric reference, we do, if we look, get from his work a feeling of 'where we are'. As a young man in the thirties, struggling to make a living as a painter – he told me he could have starved had he failed – he carefully observed the European art scene. He tried to break down the scenic element in landscape and represent it in other terms than those of abstract art which had been gaining recognition ever since Kandinski paved the way in 1910 for non-representational painting.

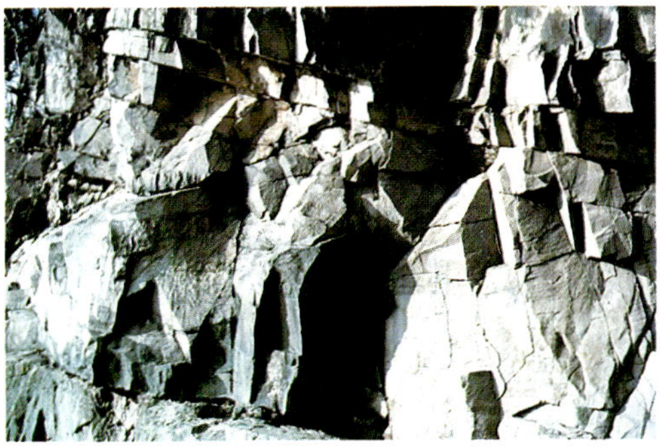

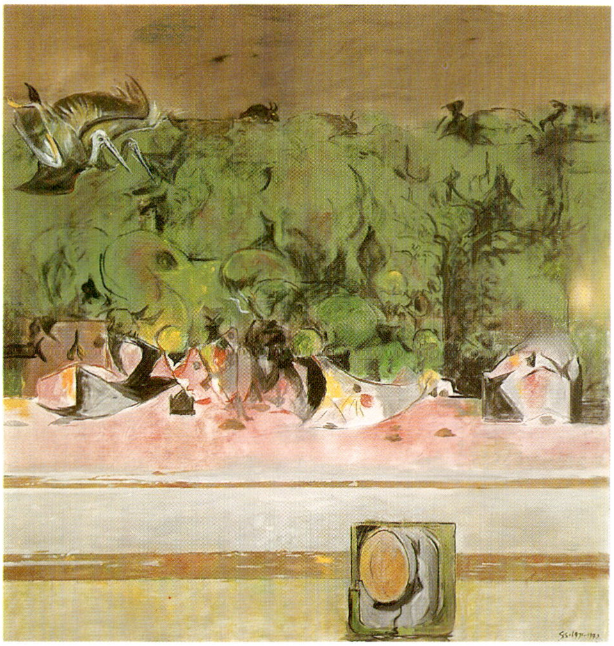

Above
113 Rock architecture
Photograph Gilbert Adams FRPS

Right
114 *Estuary with Birds*, 1972
Graham and Kathleen Sutherland Foundation, Picton Castle Trust

Below
115 *Estuary with Rocks*, 1937-8
Graham and Kathleen Sutherland Foundation, Picton Castle Trust

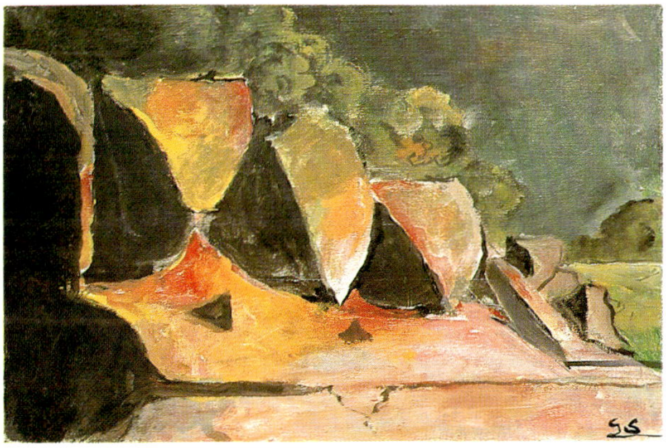

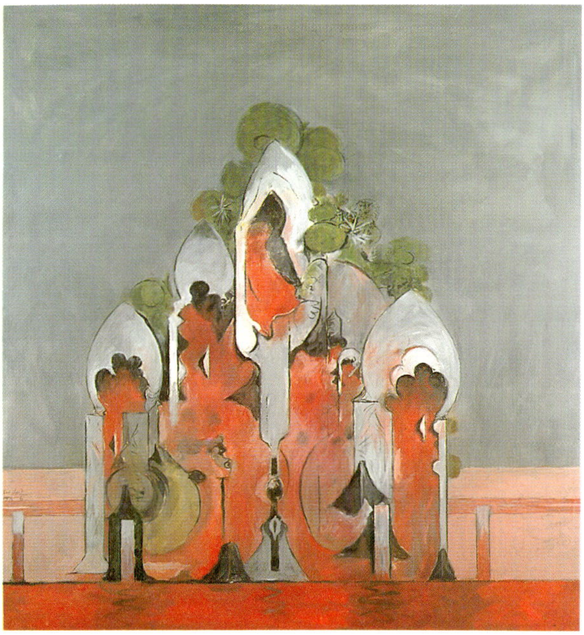

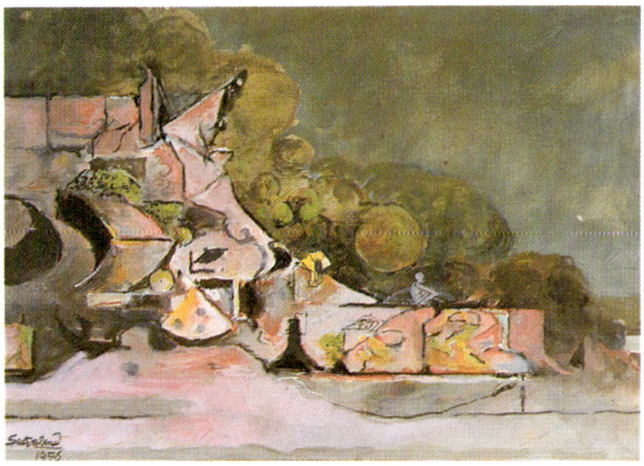

Above right
116 *Cathedral (Study of Rocks)*, 1975
Graham and Kathleen Sutherland Foundation, Picton Castle Trust

Below left
117 *Landscape*, 1976
Private collection, Italy

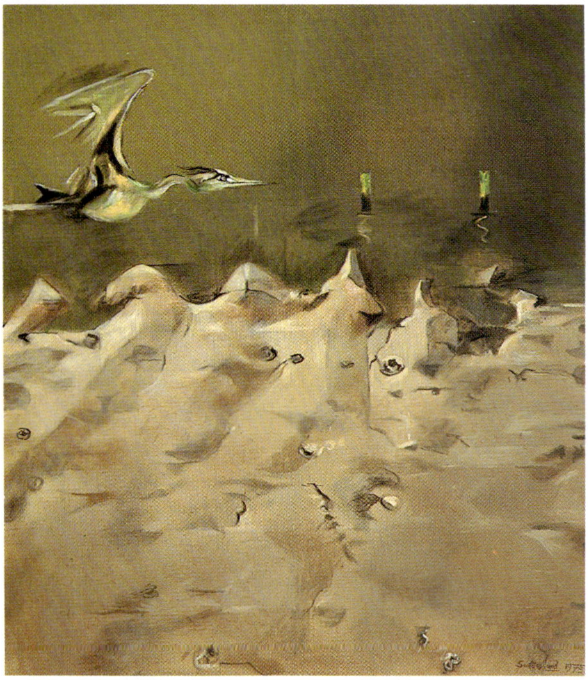

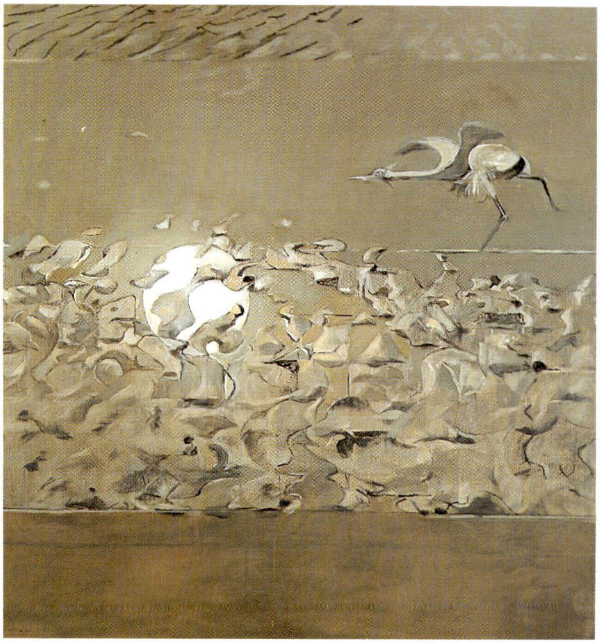

Above
118 *Bird over Sand*, 1975
Private collection, Italy

Above right
119 *Bird over Sand II*, 1976
Private collection, Italy

Opposite

Above left
120 *Study for the Conspirators*, 1977
Private collection, Italy

Above right
121 Graham Sutherland
Photograph Gilbert Adams FRPS

Centre left
122 *The Conspirators*, 1977
Private collection, Italy

Centre right
123 *The Thicket*, 1978
Private collection, Italy

Below right
124 *The Conspirators*, 1977
Private collection, Italy

Sutherland set about preserving his own idiom within certain limitations. Structure interested him more than the purely abstract. He was tremendously impressed and inspired by a number of his contemporaries, yet he maintained his own individual style. This may be the reason for his success and his great contribution to international art this century.

U-Shaped Form with Blue Sky (1976: Plate 102) is based on that discovery which Sutherland made near St David's in 1934, the forms which provided the very theme of his work, the balancing of the vertical, horizontal and oval. A year separated the two paintings *Bird over Sand* (1976: Plate 119) and *Sun Reflected in Sand* (1977), but the degree of refinement in the latter, where the runnels rise on the opposite foreshore, conveys not only Sutherland's tenacity in wishing to make a better representation, but also his will to return to a place time and again, both at the same time of day and different hours to catch different lights. Each time he was aware that something new could be added, abstracted, paraphrased. Often he improved on the original; sometimes the original is more ingenious and spontaneous and visually appealing. The three paintings, *Estuary with Rocks* (1937-8: Plate 115) which he described as his first straight landscape, *Cathedral (Study of Rocks)* (1975: Plate 116) and *Rocks on a Foreshore* (1976), were all inspired by a very small area of shore. They differ only in degree of arrangement, refinement and maturity. He maintained throughout the three works a similar dispersal of colour – the pink stone he capped by chrome lichen with dark areas of rock hollow in black or pink-black. The interest for us lies in the different approach to all three paintings, their developing stages, and the final form each painting takes. In reality, the original concepts of these paintings are similar, as the illustrations show. The Welsh paintings stem from the early small works

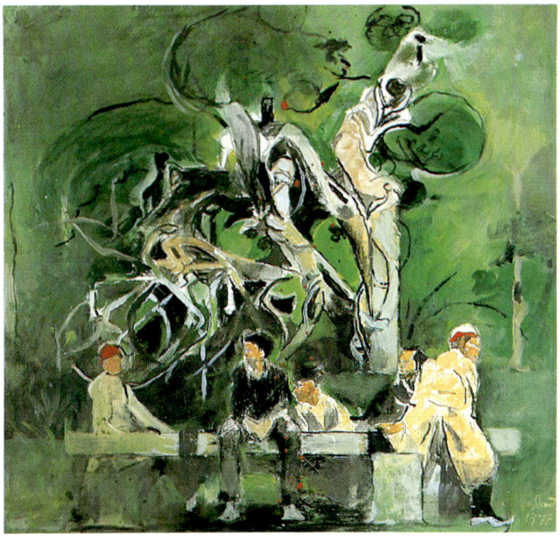

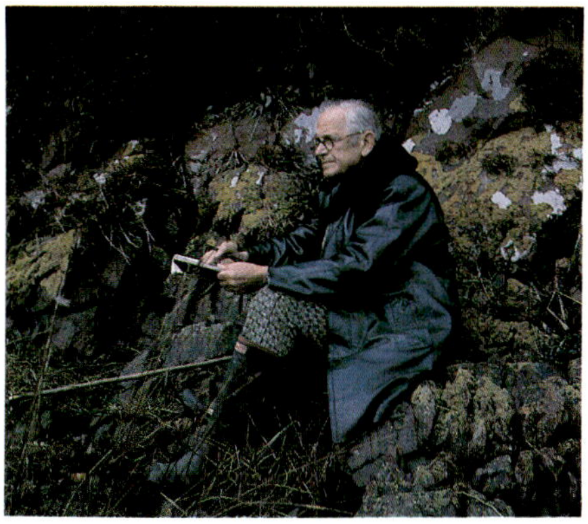

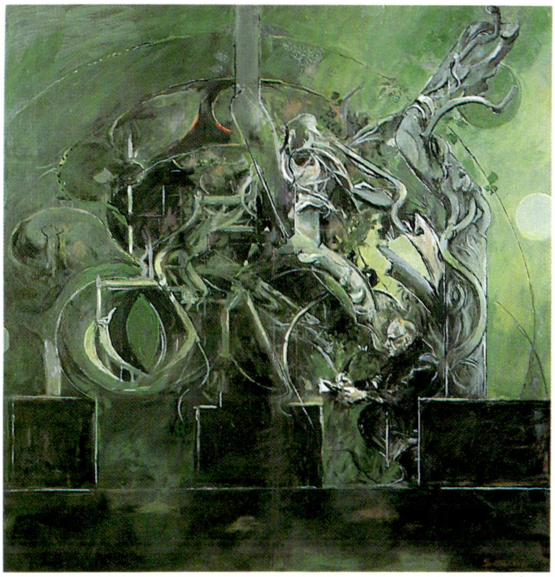

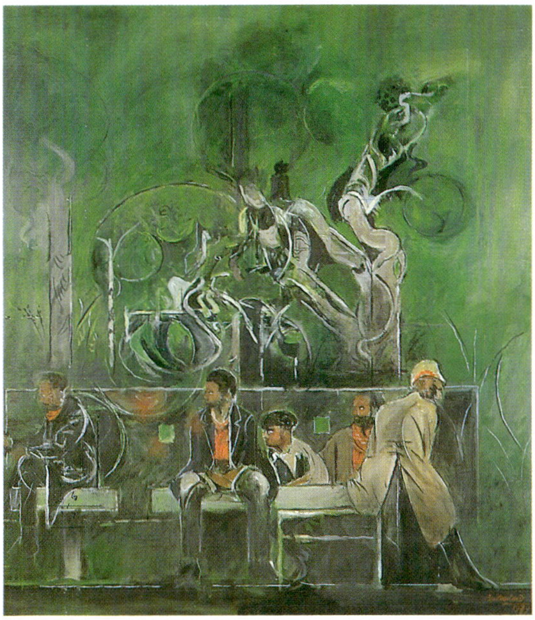

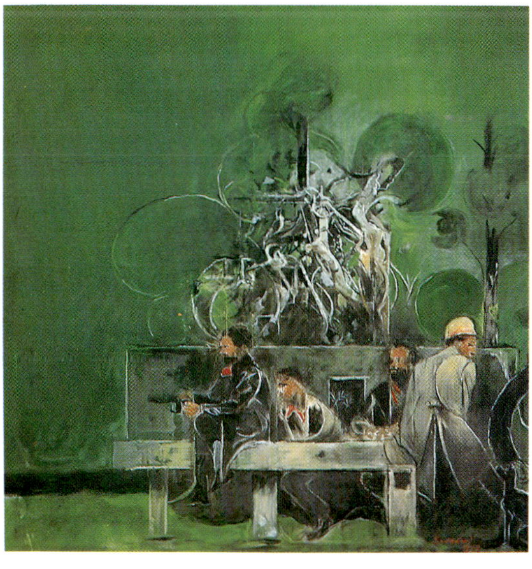

in mixed media. They are larger due to Sutherland's slightly failing eyesight towards the end. 'The structure of drawing, however,' Sutherland said, 'was of paramount importance. Tonalities were an obsession, the one thing giving the other strength. Colour was an emotional thing and a means of creating form and distance – very emotive.' [50]

In a conversation with me in the spring of 1977, Sutherland was anxious to tell me of his new painting. 'For some time I have been seriously considering ways of including figures in a landscape – along the lines of certain Titians or Rembrandt's *Belshazzar's Feast* – where figures could be seated around a table.' [51] This statement heralded a major new departure in the artist's life. The range of his work included his early pastoral etchings and lithographs, *The Bestiary (1* and *2),* aquatints of *The Bees*, designs for posters, the first and second Pembrokeshire phases, the war paintings, the religious work, the thorn subjects, the *Standing Forms*, the French subjects and the portraits. Now he intended to combine people and landscape. He actually felt that it could work, as if suddenly, towards the latter days of his life, he considered very powerfully the added dimension of human sympathy. People did belong to trees. The natural habitat was lived in not only by animals; humans also had their place in it. He became at last concerned with the fusion of 'nameable' objects (persons) with landscape. The painting was no longer to remain 'anonymous'.

One day in Pembrokeshire, while walking down to Sandy Haven, he saw three West Indians. He was conscious of an aura, an affinity with Rembrandt. *The Conspiracy of the Batavians* (1662) immediately came to mind. He had also seen recently the portrait of himself by the photographer Gilbert Adams, which he considered to be a masterly work of tone and colour, and thought he might include himself in a composition. The two influences of Rembrandt and Adams gave him courage to execute his own *Conspirators* (1977: Plate 122). The upward stabilizing effect of the tree balances the fluid movements of the figures. In the preparatory studies, he failed to adopt Rembrandt's powerful illuminating qualities but relied heavily on the flat arrangement of tone. The bosky darkness is, however, incisively lit near the central seated figure. In the gouache studies one feels that there is little co-ordination between the figures; they are 'staccato'. But in the final work we see a well-integrated arrangement.

The last Sutherland landscape, *Tree Forms* (1979), can only be described as a powerfully orchestrated design rooted in his seventy years of submission to art.

Chapter IX
CONCLUSION

For a brief period at the turn of the century new possibilities of rendering landscape were demonstrated by painters such as Cézanne and Picasso. Within a decade there were already many others beginning to use their own methods of individual interpretation in landscape painting. An entirely new wave of non-figurative work rolled through the art world. Once photography had become an accepted manner of facsimile reproduction, the painter was able to find new freedom of expression and alternative methods of selection and interpretation. Sutherland's style and innovation were therefore naturally accepted in the thirties. He somehow fitted into that small body of international painters and sculptors who could claim a style of their own. 'Composition, taken generally,' said Sir Joshua Reynolds, 'is the principal part of invention, and is by far the greatest difficulty the artist has to encounter. Every man that can paint at all can execute individual parts; but to keep those parts in a due subordination, as a relative to a whole, requires a comprehensive view of the art, that more strongly implies genius than perhaps any other quality.' In applying to Sutherland's work principles laid down by the great masters, one is forced to conclude that his galaxy of figurative naive forms were held together by a rare and brilliant balance of colour, with a thread of perceptive rhythmic and poetic line. According to Kenneth Clark, 'although Sutherland's anxiety that every touch should be completely sincere, sometimes gives his work a look of diffidence; he is in fact capable of great precision and manual dexterity: as is apparent when the object seen retains its original appearance.' [52]

A few years before he died Sutherland himself stated, 'I believe that somebody has to discover a way of making quite ordinary things which one perceives but does not look at, available in the form of a painting.' [53] It is fascinating to consider how Samuel Palmer, inspired by William Blake, saw in the ordinary English countryside an ethereal beauty which he was able to incorporate in glorious colour in his drawings; and how Sutherland, in turn inspired by Palmer, did the same with the Welsh countryside. But rather than continue, as Palmer did, with the pastoral scene, Sutherland created a personal vein, and throughout his life selected motifs culled from within the big landscape. Motifs, at first part of an image, then became separate symbols – everything became an extension of an idea, an extension of an extension, and finally an all-developing amalgam of extensions, with intense expressive use of colour; and the more he explored the greater became his involvement. When

Raymond Mortimer wrote that 'he projects his so personal and imaginative vision', he added, 'To live with his pictures entails, I have found, facing a continual challenge which brings with it a life-enhancing experience.' [54]

Sutherland was perhaps one of the greatest exponents of colour and the possibilities it could convey, at least in Britain. In 1952 Kenneth Clark suggested, 'Nor will he sacrifice his exceptional gifts of colour and design, which at present seem to be inseparable from the free transposition of appearances. He will continue to move a few steps ahead of his followers and admirers, because he still has within him a great reserve of formal inventions, waiting for the moment when some fresh encounter shall bring them into visible existence.' [55] This was true throughout Sutherland's artistic career. His great compositions provided him with deep academic concern, but the more inspirational works such as *Green Tree Form: Interior of Woods* (Plate 23), the *Vine Pergola* series, *The Conspirators*, were attempts to start a new phase. I have taken as the third example the last of the Welsh paintings because this would surely have become a new theme in Sutherland's work had he not died; it seemed that it was when he *began* to explore new subjects, as in Pembrokeshire in the late thirties and France in the late forties, that the motifs, restless in their initial excitement of 'being discovered' as it were, were also conveyed to the viewer as most exciting works.

The later years in Pembrokeshire would appear less a time of inspiration than a recharging of his emotional batteries whilst endeavouring to establish the gallery at Picton. The sophisticated experience of roaming the countryside in a Jaguar and taking a suite in a pleasant hotel, contrasted incongruously with the primitive living of the thirties and forties in Solva and St David's. The life style of an artist is in itself a study of movement. It is true that Sutherland came to enjoy the higher grades of social life. The change is noticeable more in the portraits than in any dramatic development of the landscapes. Few people in the graphic world could have retained their integrity at both ends of the social scale – the earthy cold of Wales and the social artificiality of the warm South of France. Sutherland managed it; he did so graciously, humbly and with considerable concern for fellow human beings and the Press.

He knew public interest was part of the artistic process, and the critic and writer can only be grateful for what he gave in terms of reference to his own work. To try to understand his work only creates for the writer the same series of contradictions and paradoxes as experienced by the creator. Sutherland had more than profound appreciation of this when he said:

> If one duty of painting is to explain the essence of things and emotions, may not it also be a duty, sometimes, not to explain – but to accept? Do we need an explanation of the flight of a bird, or a flash of lightning? Do we need to be told why a rose is shaped thus? Coleridge said that poetry gives most pleasure when generally and not perfectly understood. These lines of Blake are possibly obscure:

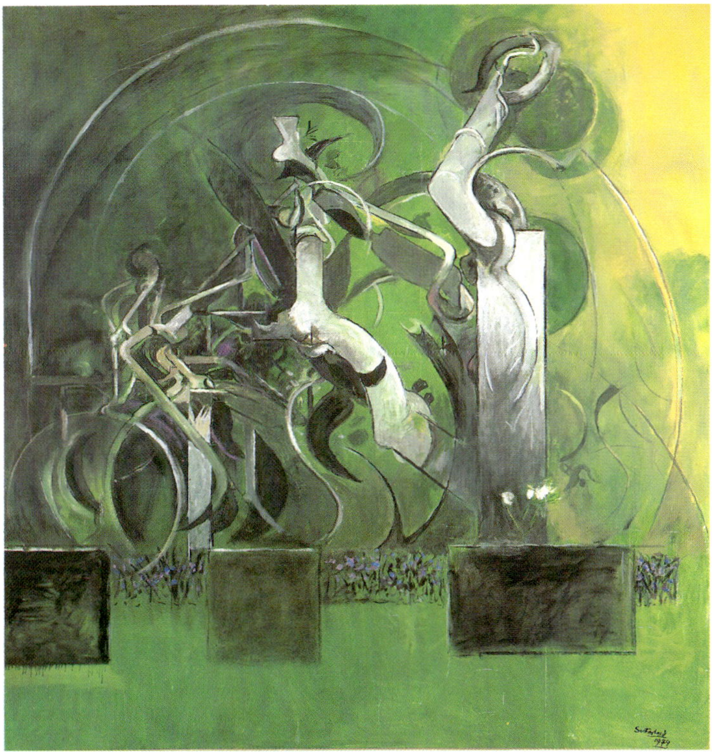

Left
125 *Path through Wood*, 1979
Crane Kalman Gallery, London

Below
126 *St Ishmael's*, 1976
Graham and Kathleen Sutherland Foundation Picton Castle Trust

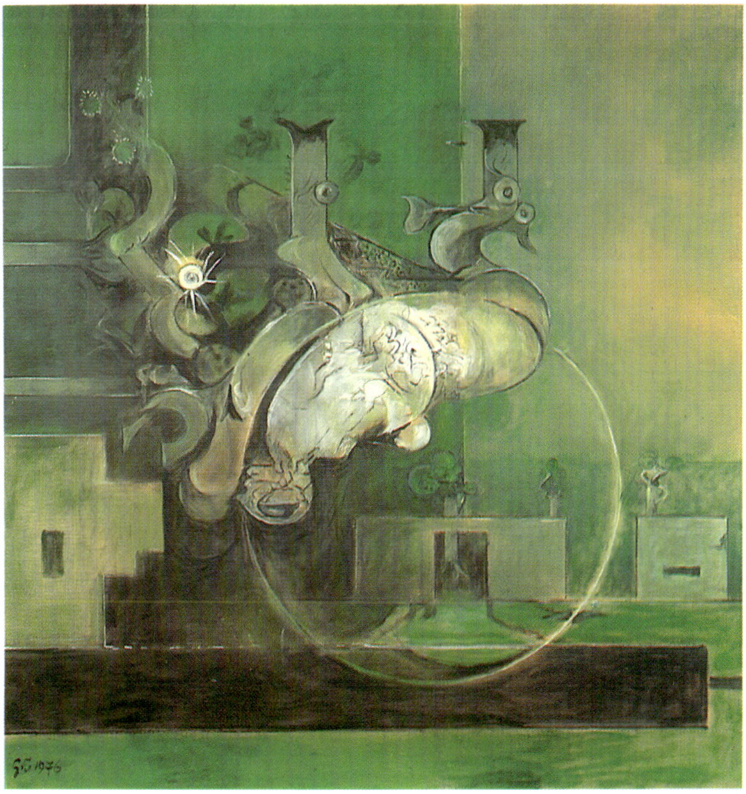

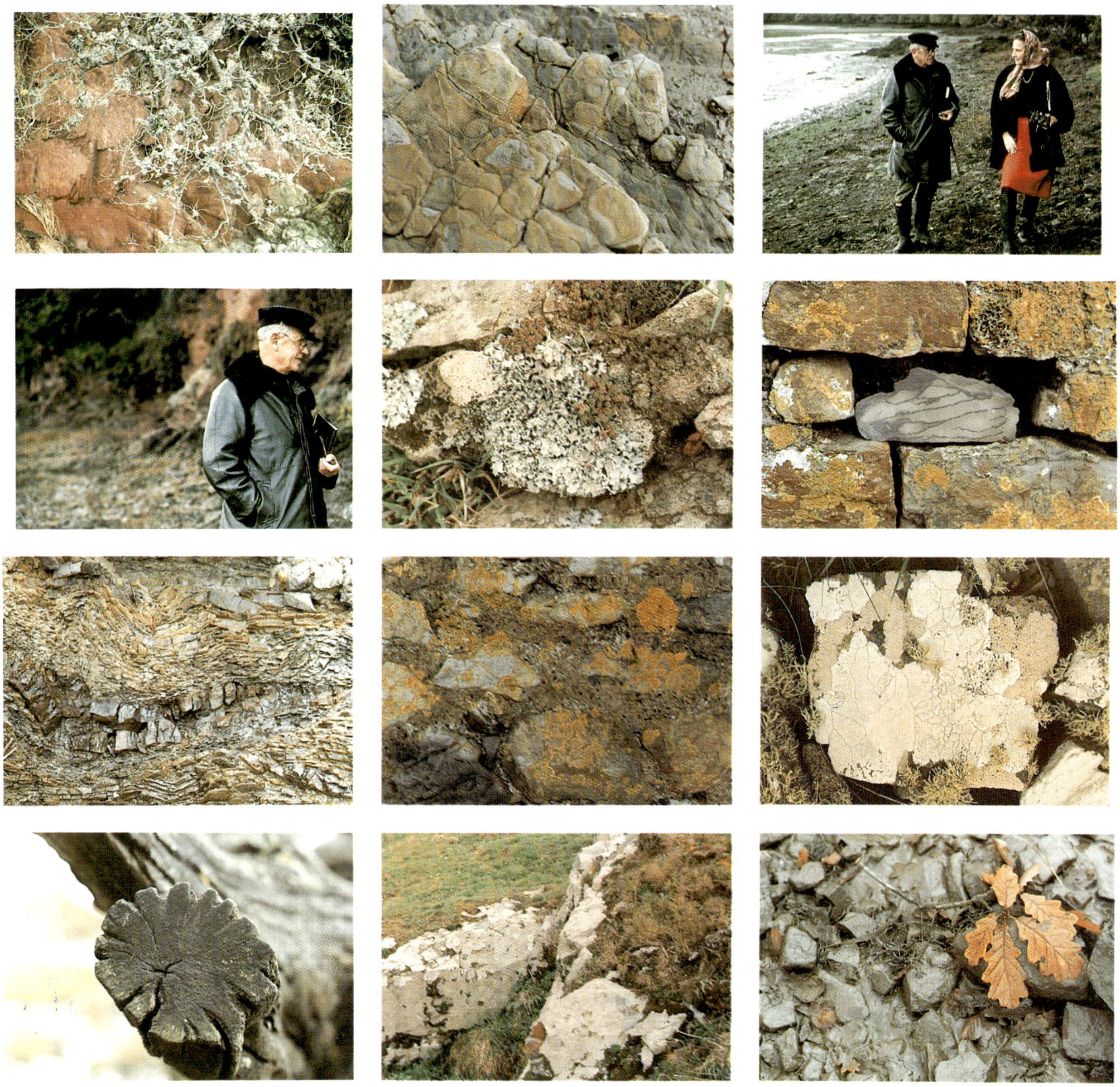

127 Graham Sutherland's inspiration continually derived from what he found within the grand landscape Photograph Gilbert Adams FRPS

My spectre round me night and day
Like a wild beast guards my way;
My emanation far within
Weeps incessantly for my sin

but it may be argued that their mysterious music is actually enhanced by that obscurity. So in painting it might be argued that its very obscurity preserves a magical and mysterious purpose. It could be said, on the other hand, that much contemporary work, which is thought to be obscure, may be merely suffering the time-lag in appreciation which has so often operated against painters in their lifetime. [56]

Sutherland, however, has been an exception; he won critical acclaim throughout his artistic career and richly deserved it. He was always responsive to clarification of his work and although it has often received adverse criticism, no one could say that the artist lacked sincerity and integrity combined with a true academic training. That he was stylish in appearance and a genius at simplifying the expression of art is a parameter which only the most apathetic of judges could justly challenge. He belonged to a tradition of artists who worked hard and in his lifetime he produced an enormous volume of work. Perhaps the greatest pleasure that one painter can derive from another is in seeing his notebooks. Sutherland's coloured sketchbooks were reproduced in facsimile in the Jacomet Workshops in Paris and made available to collectors through Marlborough Fine Art, London, in 1974. The colours which he claimed for his own throughout most of his working life were supplied by Messrs Robersons whose director, Mr Geoffrey Park, was a lifelong collaborator. These colours were flake white, Roberson green, Roberson yellow, yellow

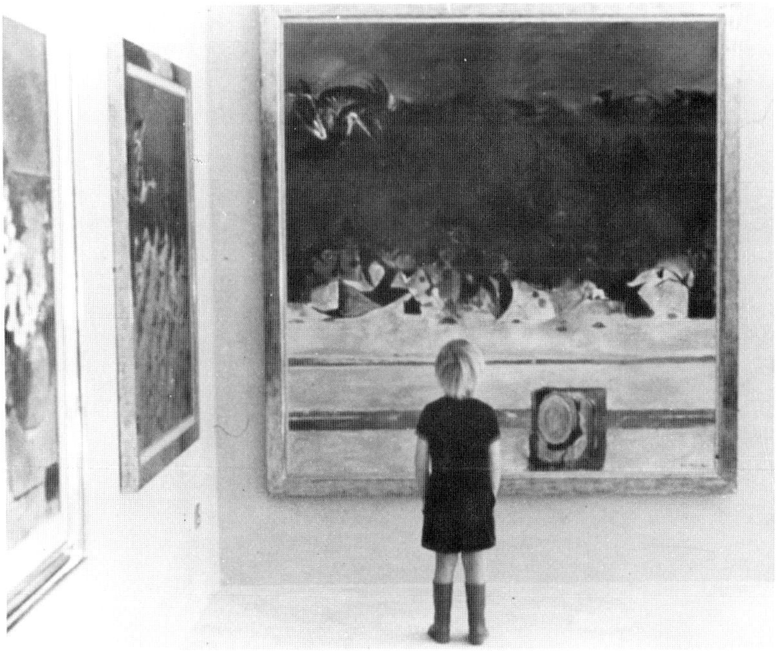

128 Small boy looking at *Estuary with Birds* at Graham and Kathleen Sutherland Gallery, Picton Castle
Photograph Gilbert Adams FRPS

ochre, pale cadmium, lemon yellow, cadmium red, alizarin crimson, violet alizarin, cerulean blue, olive green, raw umber, burnt umber, orange chrome – in watercolour he omitted flake white and orange chrome – a full-blooded and rigorous selection which gave his work that enormous vitality and colour which Raymond Mortimer so rightly says make it so exciting to live with. Although, as any artist might, he experimented with contemporary idioms, he fortunately veered away from them before becoming too involved. It was as though he had to experiment before rejecting, or perhaps it was a way of reassuring himself of his inventive philosophy.

If any two painters directly influenced Sutherland's painting, they were Picasso and Matisse. But Sutherland was himself inherently inventive. Already at Goldsmiths' his associates perceived that. His early recognition as a painter can undoubtedly be attributed to the unqualified friendship of his early patrons, chief amongst whom were Lord Clark and the late Sir Colin Anderson.

That he was an enigma and a genius there can be no doubt, and his place amongst the distinguished painters of our century is well established. Despite his international role, he never forgot his English ancestry or the magnitude of his debt to the landscape of Wales. In a letter to me he quoted something written by Thomas Hardy which I feel justifies the observations I have made about him: 'The exchange of international thought is the only salvation of the world.'

From the first moment I walked with Sutherland through his Pembrokeshire playground I have been inspired with the hitherto undiscovered character of the environment seen through his eyes and his intellect. Closer scrutiny of things emanates from the way he taught me to *look*.

He died on 17 February 1980.

Notes

1 Conversation with the author, 1977
2 Barber, Noel, *Conversations with Painters,* Collins, 1964, p. 49
3 Open letter to Colin Anderson, originally published as 'Welsh Sketch Book' in *Horizon*, April 1942; reprinted in the Picton Castle Trust catalogue, Graham and Kathleen Sutherland Foundation, London, 1976, pp. 11-15.
4 Picton Castle Trust catalogue, op. cit., p. 8.
5 Open letter to Colin Anderson, 'Welsh Sketch Book', op. cit., p. 14.
6 Undated letter believed to be 1951, British Council Archives.
7 Clark, Kenneth, Preface to the catalogue of works exhibited at the British pavilion of the XXVI Venice Biennale, 1952.
8 Letter to the author, 1977.
9 Frankland, Noble, *A Concise Catalogue of Paintings, Drawings and Sculpture of the Second World War*, Imperial War Museum, 1964, p. V.
10 Melville, Robert, *Profile* 29(12), British Council Feature Article Service, 1959.
11 Handwritten notes, believed to be for 'Thoughts on Painting' (*The Listener*, 6 Sep. 1951), British Council Archives.
12 'Thoughts on Painting', *The Listener*, 6 Sep. 1951, p. 378.
13 Clark, Kenneth, op. cit.
14 'Christ in Glory in the Tetramorph', a leaflet produced for the exhibition of studies and sketches by Graham Sutherland for the great tapestry in Coventry Cathedral, Herbert Art Gallery & Museum, Coventry, 1979.
15 Révai, Andrew (ed.), *Sutherland: Christ in Glory in the Tetramorph*, Pallas Gallery, A. Zwemmer Ltd, 1964, pp. 31-2.
16 Ibid., p. 83.
17 Ibid., p. 48.
18 'Christ in Glory in the Tetramorph', op. cit.
19 Barber, Noel, op. cit., p. 49.
20 Ibid.
21 Hendy, Philip, 'Graham Sutherland', *Britain Today,* no. 148, Aug. 1948, p. 1.
22 Ibid., p. 19.
23 Robertson, Bryan, BBC Television, 1980.
24 Hendy, Philip, op. cit., p. 1.
25 Barber, Noel, op. cit., p. 46.
26 Conversation with Bryan Robertson, *Kaleidoscope*, BBC Radio 4, 1978.
27 'Thoughts on Painting', op. cit., p. 377.
28 Handwritten notes on painting, undated but believed to be 1951.
29 Clark, Kenneth, op. cit.
30 Handwritten notes, undated but believed to be 1951.
31 Tassi, Roberto, *Graham Sutherland: Complete Graphic Work*, Thames & Hudson, 1978, unpaginated.
32 Clark, Kenneth, Introduction to the exhibition of paintings and drawings by Graham Sutherland at the Tate Gallery, 1953.
33 Handwritten notes, undated but believed to be 1951.
34 Conversation with the author, 1977.
35 Barber, Noel, op. cit., p. 51.
36 Ibid.
37 'Thoughts on Painting', op. cit.
38 Barber, Noel, op. cit., p. 52.
39 Ibid.
40 Ibid., p. 53.
41 Rothenstein, John, *Time's Thievish Progress*, Cassell, 1970, p. 136.
42 Hayes, John, *Portraits by Graham Sutherland*, National Portrait Gallery, 1977, p. 12.
43 Conversation with Gilbert Adams.
44 Barber, Noel, op. cit., p. 53.
45 Open letter to Colin Anderson, 'Welsh Sketch Book', op. cit., p. 15.
46 Picton Castle Trust catalogue, op. cit., p. 17.
47 Conversation with the author, 1977.
48 Letter to the author, 1977.
49 Conversation with the author, 1976.
50 Conversation with Bryan Robertson, *Kaleidoscope,* BBC Radio 4, 1978.
51 Conversation with the author, 1977.
52 Clark, Kenneth, Preface to the catalogue of works exhibited at the British pavilion of the XXVI Venice Biennale, 1952.
53 Conversation with Melvyn Bragg, *The South Bank Show*, ITV, 1979.
54 Catalogue to *Britian Today* exhibition, London, 1948.
55 Clark, Kenneth, op. cit.
56 'Thoughts on Painting', op. cit.

Biographical Notes

1903	Born in London, 24 August.
1919-20	Serves apprenticeship at the Midland Railway works in Derby.
1921-6	Studies at Goldsmiths' College School of Art in London.
1923	First etchings.
1926	Converted to Roman Catholic faith.
1927	Marries Kathleen Frances Barry, 29 December.
1928-32	Teaches engraving at Chelsea School of Art.
1931	Starts to paint in oils; also starts designing posters, fabrics, etc.
1932-9	Teaches composition and book illustration at Chelsea School of Art.
1934	First visit to Pembrokeshire.
1940	Book illustration and tapestry designing. Designs the setting and costumes for *The Wanderer*, a ballet by Frederick Ashton.
1940-5	Official War Artist.
1944	Commissioned to paint Crucifixion for St Matthew's Church, Northampton.
1947	First visit to the South of France and beginning of meridional subjects: *Vine Pergolas*, *Cactus*, *Cigale*, etc.
1949	First portrait, the painting of Somerset Maugham. Appointed a Trustee of the Tate Gallery, London.
1952	Visits Venice for exhibition of his works at the British pavilion of the XXVI Venice Biennale. Awarded prize by the Museu de Arte Moderna, São Paulo. Commissioned to design tapestry for Coventry Cathedral.
1954	Resigns as Trustee of the Tate Gallery. Paints portrait of Sir Winston Churchill.
1955	Buys house in Menton, France.
1957	Receives Foreign Minister's Prize, Tokyo.
1958	Works in Menton, Venice and Donaueschingen.
1960	Awarded the Order of Merit.
1962	Coventry tapestry completed. Receives degree of Doctor of Literature Honoris Causa from Oxford.
1963-4	Works on portrait of Konrad Adenauer.
1964	Designs window of English Church of Zürich.
1965	Prepares retrospective exhibition for Turin (and for Basel in 1966).
1968	BBC Television profile (in colour). Concludes work on *The Bestiary*, a suite of 25 coloured lithographs published by Marlborough Fine Art, London.
1970	Second BBC Television profile (in colour).
1972	Elected Honorary Fellow of the American Academy of Arts and Letters. IX International Art Biennale, Menton; awarded First Prize by the French President.
1973	Named Commandeur des Arts et des Lettres in France and Honorary Fellow of the Accademia di San Luca in Rome, Italy.
1974	Publication of *Graham Sutherland Sketchbook*, a facsimile edition of selected working drawings from his recent Welsh sketchbooks. Appointed Honorary President of the International Art Biennale, Menton. Awarded the Shakespeare Prize, Hamburg.
1976	Graham Sutherland Foundation (Picton Castle) inaugurated.
1977	Elected Honorary Member of Royal Scottish Academy.
1980	Dies in London, 17 February.

Public Collections

Australia	Melbourne	National Gallery of Victoria
	New South Wales	Government of New South Wales
Austria	Vienna	Albertina
Belgium	Brussels	Musée d'Art Contemporain
Brazil	São Paulo	São Paulo Museum
Canada	Montreal	Museum of Fine Arts
	New Brunswick	Beaverbrook Foundation, Fredericton
	Ottawa	National Gallery of Canada
	Toronto	Toronto Art Gallery
	Vancouver	Vancouver Art Gallery
France	Paris	Musée National d'Art Moderne
Germany	Berlin	Galerie des 20 Jahrhunderts
	Bochum	Stadtische Kunstgalerie
	Donaueschingen	Fürstenbergsche Gemäldesammlung
	Frankfurt	Stadtische Kunstinstitut
	Hamburg	Kunsthalle
Great Britain	Birmingham	Birmingham City Art Gallery
	Bradford	Bradford City Art Gallery
	Bristol	Bristol City Art Gallery
	Cambridge	Fitzwilliam Museum
	Cardiff	National Museum of Wales
	Doncaster	Doncaster Municipal Art Gallery
	Edinburgh	Museum of Modern Art
	Glasgow	Glasgow Art Gallery
	Leeds	Leeds City Art Gallery
	Leicester	Leicester City Museum & Art Gallery
	London	Arts Council of Great Britain
		British Council
		British Museum
		Contemporary Art Society
		Imperial War Museum
		National Portrait Gallery
		The Tate Gallery
		Victoria and Albert Museum
	Newcastle-upon-Tyne	Laing Art Gallery
	Oxford	Ashmolean Museum
	Pembrokeshire	Graham and Kathleen Sutherland Foundation Gallery, Picton Castle
	Preston	Preston Art Gallery, Lancashire
	Sheffield	Graves Art Gallery
	Southampton	Southampton Art Gallery
	Wakefield	Wakefield City Art Gallery
	West Riding	West Riding Education Committee, Yorkshire
Sweden	Gothenburg	Gothenburg Art Gallery
Switzerland	Basel	Kunstmuseum
United States of America	Buffalo	Albright Art Gallery
	California	Santa Barbara Museum of Art
	Chicago	Art Institute of Chicago
	Lincoln	University of Nebraska
	New York City	Museum of Modern Art
	Ohio	Toledo Museum of Art
	San Francisco	San Francisco Museum of Art
	Washington DC	Phillips Memorial Gallery

One-man Exhibitions

1925 Twenty-one Gallery, London
1928 Twenty-one Gallery, London
1938 Rosenberg & Helft Gallery, London
1940 Leicester Gallery, London
1941 City Art Gallery, Leeds
1946 Buchholz Gallery (Curt Valentin), New York
1947 Lefèvre Galleries, London
Roland Browse and Delbanco Gallery, London
1948 Hanover Gallery, London
Buchholz Gallery (Curt Valentin), New York
1951 Institute of Contemporary Arts, London
Hanover Gallery, London
1952 British Pavilion, XXVI Venice Biennale. Subsequently (1952-3) shown at the Musée National d'Art Moderne, Paris; Stedelijk Museum, Amsterdam; Kunsthaus, Zürich; Tate Gallery, London; organized by the British Council.
Redfern Gallery, London
Hanover Gallery, London
1953 Curt Valentin Gallery, New York
Institute of Contemporary Arts, Boston. Retrospective exhibition to mark the artist's fiftieth anniversary – it toured in USA and Canada.
Tate Gallery, London. Retrospective exhibition organized by the Arts Council.
Kunsthaus, Zürich
Stedelijk Museum, Amsterdam
1954 Akademie der Bildenden Künste, Vienna and Innsbruck; organized by the Arts Council and the Albertina.
1954-5 British Council touring exhibition to Berlin, Cologne, Stuttgart, Mannheim, and Hamburg
1955 Third Sao Paulo Biennale, Museu de Arte Moderna, Sao Paulo; organized by the British Council.
1956 Roland Browse and Delbanco Gallery, London
Lima, Peru
1957 Kunstkabinett, Frankfurt
Hoffman Galerie, Hamburg
1958 Redfern Gallery, London
1959 Arthur Jeffress Gallery, London
Redfern Gallery, London
Belfast Museum & Art Gallery, N. Ireland
Paul Rosenberg and Co., New York
1960 Roland Browse and Delbanco Gallery, London
1961 Galleria Galatea, Turin and Milan
1962 Marlborough Fine Art, London
1963 Galleria Fante di Spade
Galatea-Galleria d'Arte Contemporanea, Turin
Galleria il Centro, Naples
Welsh Committee of the Arts Council, and Llandaff Festival Committee, Prefendal House of Llandaff Cathedral
1964 Paul Rosenberg and Co., New York
Redfern Gallery, London. Sketches for Coventry Tapestry Collection to go to Herbert Art Gallery near Coventry
1965 Galleria Civica d'Arte Moderna, Turin
1966 Marlborough Fine Art, London
Kunsthalle, Basel
1967 Travelling exhibition to Haus der Kunst, Munich; Gemeentemuseum, The Hague; Haus am Waldsee, Berlin; Wallraf-Richartz Museum, Cologne.
1968 Marlborough Fine Art, London
1969 Kestner-Gesellschaft, Hanover
Galleria il Fauno, Turin
Palais de l'Europe, Menton
1969-70 Albrecht Dürer Gesellschaft Kunsthalle, Nuremberg
1972 Galleria il Fauno, Turin
Galleria Narciso, Turin
Galleria Bergamini, Milan
Marlborough Galerie, AG, Zürich
1973 Marlborough Fine Art, London
1974 Marlborough Fine Art, London
1976 Graham Sutherland Gallery, Picton Castle, Pembrokeshire
Redfern Gallery, London
1977 Marlborough Fine Art, London
National Portrait Gallery, London
1978 Marlborough Fine Art, London
Konrad Adenauer Foundation, Bonn
1979 Marlborough Fine Art, London
Palazzo Reale, Milan
1981 Galleria Bergamini, Milan
1982 Redfern Gallery, London
Tate Gallery, London (May-July)

Selected Mixed Exhibitions

1927 Paris, Musée des Arts Décoratifs; Exposition de la gravure moderne anglaise
1936 London, New Burlington Galleries; International Surrealist Exhibition
1937 Philadelphia, Franklin Institute; The New Manifesto
1939 London, Storrens Gallery
1939-40 New York, World Fair, and tour; Contemporary British Art
1941 New York, Museum of Modern Art; Britain at War
Ohio and tour, Toledo Museum of Art; Contemporary British Art
Leeds, London; Moore, Piper, Sutherland
1943-44 South America, tour; Contemporary British Art
1945 Paris; Contemporary British Art
1946 Paris, Lyons; International Exhibition of Contemporary Paintings
London, and tour; British Painters 1939-1945
1946-47 Brussels, Amsterdam, Copenhagen, Paris, Bern, Vienna, Prague, Warsaw and Rome;

Modern British Pictures

1947 New York, Brooklyn Museum; International Exhibition of Watercolours

Buffalo, Albright Art Gallery

Cairo; International Exhibition of Contemporary Art

1947-48 South Africa, Rhodesia, tour; Contemporary British Paintings and Drawings

Athens, Rome, Paris, Marseilles, Prague; Modern British Paintings

Sweden, tour; Contemporary British Art

1948 Canada, tour, subsequently Vienna; Contemporary British Drawings,

London, ICA; 40 Years of Modern Art 1907-1947

1948-49 Brussels, Dusseldorf, Hamburg, Amsterdam, Luxembourg; Contemporary Painting in Great Britain

1949 London, Victoria and Albert Museum

Paris, Salon de Mai

1950 New York, Museum of Modern Art; St Louis, City Art Museum; San Francisco, California Palace of the Legion of Honour; Masters of British Painting

New Burlington Galleries

ICA

1950 Pittsburgh International, Carnegie Institute

1950-52 Touring exhibition; Germany, Spain, New Zealand, Israel, Portugal, Canada, Luxembourg, Belgium, Poland, Norway, Italy, Yugoslavia, Austria, Sweden, Finland, Denmark, Greece, Malta, Gibraltar; British Watercolours and Drawings of the 20th century

1950-51 New Zealand, Christchurch and tour; Contemporary Painting

Germany, tour; Modern British Drawings

1951 Vancouver, and tour of USA; 21 Modern British Painters

London, New Burlington Gallery; First Anthology of British Painting 1925-50

1952 London, Tate Gallery; Seventeen Collectors,

Barcelona and Madrid; Modern British Drawings

Great Britain, touring exhibition; Three Young Collectors

Japan, Tokyo and tour; 1st International Art Exhibition

Cincinnati Art Museum; 2nd International Biennial of Contemporary Colour Lithography

Venice Biennale

Pittsburgh International, Carnegie Institute

1953 London, Arts Council Gallery; Drawings for Pictures

New York, Brooklyn Museum; International Exhibition of Watercolours

New Zealand, tour; 20th Century Watercolours and Drawings

Cardiff, Museum

Boston, ICA

1953-54 Sweden, tour; Ten Contemporary British Painters

Denmark, tour; European Art Exhibition

Belgrade, National Museum; English Watercolours

1954 Great Britain, tour; Recent British Paintings

Cincinnati Art Museum; 3rd International Biennial (see 1952)

Venice, Biennale; Recent Lithographs

USA, Washington DC, Newhaven, New York, Minneapolis

1955 Venezuela, Ateneo de Valencia; International Exhibition of Painting

Kassel, and subsequent exhibitions; Documenta I; Art of the 20th Century

London, Arthur Tooth Gallery

1956 Cincinnati Art Museum; 4th International Biennial (see 1952)

USA, Arizona, Newhaven, New York

1957-62 Kenya, Uganda, Tanganyika, Nyasaland, S Rhodesia, South Africa, Maritius, Nigeria, Ghana, Sierra Leone, Jamaica, Trinidad, Bahamas, Bermuda, British Honduras; touring exhibition

1957 London, Arthur Jeffress Gallery

Japan, Tokyo and tour; 4th International Art Exhibition

1958 Brussels, Palais International des Beaux-Arts; 50 Years of Modern Art

Pittsburgh International Exhibition, Carnegie Institute

1959 Kassel; Documenta II; Art since 1945

1959 Milan, Galleria dell'Ariete

1960 Moscow, Pushkin Museum; Leningrad, Hermitage; British Painting 1700-1960

1962 Netherlands, Eindhoven, Stedelijk van Abbesmuseum; Contemporary Paintings in London

Portugal, tour; 20th Century British Art

1962-63 San Francisco Museum of Art, Dallas Museum of Contemporary Arts, Santa Barbara Museum of Art; British Art Today

1963 London, Tate Gallery; British Painting in the Sixties

Naples, Galleria il Centro

Turin, Galleria del Arte Contemporanea

1964 London, Tate Gallery; Gulbenkian Exhib.

Kassel; Documenta III

1965 Netherlands, The Hague, Gemeentemuseum

1966 Netherlands, Amsterdam, Stedelijk Museum

1968 Northampton, University; Art in the Church

1969 Edinburgh, Scottish National Gallery; British Drawings 1939-49

1970 London, Marlborough Fine Art; Moore/Picasso/Sutherland

1972 France, Menton; 9th Biennale Internationale d'Art

1973 Canada, Toronto, Marlborough-Godard; Contemporary British Painters and Sculptors

1979 Ostend, Museum

Bibliography

Arcangeli, Francesco, *Sutherland*, Fratelli Fabbri, Milan, 1973; Harry N. Abrams, New York, 1975

Barber, Noel, *Conversations with Painters*, William Collins, London, 1964

Carrieri, R. and Soavi, G., *Dodici Acquarelli* (limited edition), Olivetti, Ivrea, 1971

Cooper, Douglas, *The Work of Graham Sutherland* (with full bibliography, biography, list of one-man and mixed exhibitions, etc), Lund Humphries, London, 1961

Cooper, Douglas, Russoli, F. and Viale, V., *Sutherland*, Galleria Civica d'Arte Moderna, Turin, 1965

Coulonges, H. and Révai, A., *Sutherland*, Chefs d'oeuvres de l'Art, Paris, 1968

Graham Sutherland Sketchbook (a facsimile reproduction), Marlborough Fine Art, London, 1974

Hayes, John, *Graham Sutherland*, Phaidon Press, London, 1980

Man, F.H., *Graham Sutherland, Das Grafische Werk 1922-70*, Galerie Ketterer, Munich, 1970

Melville, Robert, *Graham Sutherland*, Ambassador Editions, London, 1950

Révai, Andrew (ed.) *Sutherland: Christ in Glory in the Tetramorph* (based on conversations with the artist), Pallas Gallery, A. Zwemmer, London, 1964

Révai, Andrew, *Sutherland*, *'The Masters'* series (ed. John Rothenstein), no. 63, Purnell, London, 1966

Rothenstein, John, *Modern English Painters*, Macdonald and Jane's, London 1974

Sackville-West, Edward, *Graham Sutherland,* Penguin Books, 1943 (revised edition, 1953)

Sanesi, Roberto, *Graham Sutherland,* Milan, 1979

Soavi, G., *Storia con Sutherland*, All'Insegna de Pesce d'Oro, Milan, 1968

Soavi, G. and Janus, *The World of Graham Sutherland*, London and Turin, 1973

Tassi, Roberto, *Graham Sutherland: Complete Graphic Works,* Thames and Hudson, London, 1978

Tassi, Roberto, *Disegni di Guerra*, Electra Editrice, Milan, 1979; issued as *Sutherland: The Wartime Drawings*, trans. Julien Andrews, Sotheby Parke Bernet, 1980

Films on the Artist

Out of Chaos, a wartime documentary showing artists, including Sutherland, at work; produced by Two Cities, London, 1945

Graham Sutherland, produced in association with The Arts Council by John Read, 1954

Graham Sutherland, one of a series of half-hour documentaries produced by BBC Television Services, London, 1956

Graham Sutherland, BBC Television, London, produced by Margaret McCall, 1968

Graham Sutherland, RAI Rome Television, written and directed by Pier Paolo Ruggerini, 1969

Graham Sutherland, BBC Television, London, 1970

Sutherland in Wales, BBC Wales Television, written and produced by John Ormond, 1977

The South Bank Show, ITV Television, by Melvyn Bragg, 1979

Graham Sutherland, BBC Television tribute by Bryan Robertson, 1980

Articles written by the Artist

'A Trend in English Draughtsmanship', *Signature*, July 1936

'An English Stone Landmark', *The Painter's Object,* 1937

'Welsh Sketch Book', *Horizon*, April 1942, pp. 225-35; reprinted in the Picton Castle Trust catalogue, Graham and Kathleen Sutherland Foundation, London, 1976

Index

Page references to illustrations are in bold type. Dates appear in parentheses. Where illustration and text reference appear on the same page, this is repeated in parentheses.